The Majority Press

AFRICAN FUNDAMENTALISM:
A Literary and Cultural Anthology of Garvey's Harlem Renaissance

TONY MARTIN is Professor and Chairman of Black Studies at Wellesley College, Massachusetts. He did his M.A. and Ph.D. in history at Michigan State University and the B.Sc. in economics at the University of Hull, England. In 1965 he qualified as a barrister-at-law at Gray's Inn, London. He has taught at the University of Michigan-Flint, the Cipriani Labor College (Trinidad) and St. Mary's College (Trinidad). He has been visiting professor at the University of Minnesota, Brandeis University and Colorado College. He has authored and edited several books, including *Literary Garveyism: Garvey, Black Arts and the Harlem Renaissance, The Pan-African Connection* and *Race First: The Ideological and Organizational Struggles of Marcus Garvey and the Universal Negro Improvement Association.*

THE NEW MARCUS GARVEY LIBRARY

A Series of Original Works by TONY MARTIN

AFRICAN FUNDAMENTALISM

A Literary and Cultural Anthology of Garvey's Harlem Renaissance

Compiled and Edited
by

TONY MARTIN

The New Marcus Garvey Library, No. 5

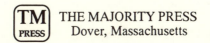
THE MAJORITY PRESS
Dover, Massachusetts

Library of Congress Cataloging in Publication Data

African fundamentalism: a literary and cultural anthology of Garvey's Harlem Renaissance / compiled and edited by Tony Martin.
      p.   cm.   —(The New Marcus Garvey library; no. 5)
    Most of the selections in this volume are excerpts from Negro world.
    Includes bibliographical references.
    ISBN 0-912469-09-9
      1. American literature—Afro- American authors. 2. American literature—Afro-American authors—History and criticism.
3. American literature—New York (N.Y.) 4. American literature—20th century. 5. Afro-American arts—New York (N.Y.)
6. Harlem Renaissance. 7. Garvey, Marcus, 1887- 1940.
8. Afro-American—Race identity. 9. Blacks—Literary collections.
10. Black nationalism. I. Martin, Tony, 1942-   . II. Negro world
(New York, N.Y.) III. Series.
    PS508.NeA34   1991
    810.9'896073—dc20   89-12755
                                          CIP

First published in 1991

10 9 8 7 6 5 4 3 2

The Majority Press
P.O. Box 538
Dover, Massachusetts 02030

Printed in the United States of America

Table of Contents

Preface

Marcus Garvey is well known for having organized and led the Universal Negro Improvement Association, the largest Pan-African organization of its kind ever. The U.N.I.A. flourished in the years immediately after World War I. This was the era of post-war militancy. The "New Negro" was frustrated by his vain sacrifices during the war, tired of being lynched and repressed, and alarmed at the subjugation of the African motherland. He wanted to reach out to his brothers and sisters in suffering throughout the African world. Garvey, more than anyone else, provided for the New Negro an avenue wherein he might vent his feelings and realize his ambitions.

As often happens in periods of revolutionary ferment, the New Negro movement spawned its literary counterpart. Commentators on the literary scene of the period have, however, focused their attention too narrowly on the so-called Harlem Renaissance which is said to have flourished from the mid-1920s to the mid-1930s. This deficiency is to some extent understandable, since the materials collected in this volume were for many years totally inaccessible and in recent years partially so.

Garvey is sometimes given credit for laying the basic political foundation which was reflected to varying degrees in the works of the Harlem Renaissance. The pervasive interest in Africa especially, has been ascribed to his influence. His importance to literary endeavor was in fact far greater than this. For in the years leading up to the mainstream Harlem Renaissance he created a "renaissance" of his own which was as astounding for its scope as it is for the lack of acknowledgment it has received.* So dependent in fact was the mainstream Harlem Renaissance on the Garvey Movement that it now appears to have borrowed the term "renaissance" itself from Garvey's literary editor William H. Ferris, who credited Garvey in 1922 with ushering in a "Negro renaissance." (See Chapter 1 of this volume.)

The U.N.I.A.'s weekly newspaper, the *Negro World,* provided the main vehicle for the Garveyite incursion into literature and the arts. With a circulation of 200,000 in the early 1920s, it was one of the world's largest

---

*The present author has attempted to remedy this lack in his *Literary Garveyism: Garvey, Black Arts and the Harlem Renaissance* (Dover, MA: The Majority Press, 1983).

Black newspapers and certainly the most widely distributed. The *Negro World* was simultaneously a highly political official organ and a major literary forum for the mass of New Negroes. Its editors, literary editors, and associate and assistant editors included some of the most illustrious names in literature and journalism. T. Thomas Fortune, the "dean" of Afro-American journalists, edited the paper from 1923 to his death in 1928. Prior to that he edited the *Negro World's* sister paper, the *Daily Negro Times*. John Edward Bruce, also one of Afro-America's most experienced and respected journalists, served as associate editor to his death in 1924. The editorial staff included Hubert H. Harrison, perhaps Harlem's most popular intellectual and a man who lectured widely on world literature. It included also William H. Ferris, graduate of Harvard and Yale and, like Fortune, Bruce and Harrison, an author himself. Eric D. Walrond, later a well-known short story writer of the Harlem Renaissance, served as associate editor for nearly two years. Amy Jacques Garvey, the second Mrs. Garvey, served as an associate editor and editor of the women's page. She authored and edited several books and pamphlets from the 1920s to the 1970s. Marcus Garvey himself presided over this assemblage of talent as managing editor.

This illustrious group of editors provided the lead for an amazing exercise in grassroots literary appreciation. They contributed poems, short stories, literary criticism, dramatic and musical criticism and much more. It was in the *Negro World* that Hubert H. Harrison pioneered, he said, the first regular book review column in an Afro-American publication. Apart from the paper's own editors, several of Afro-America's leading scholars published in the *Negro World*. Some of their names may seem surprising, given the widely held but inaccurate view of Garvey as hostile to all intellectuals. J. A. Rogers, Arthur A. Schomburg, Carter G. Woodson, Claude McKay and Zora Neale Hurston all published regularly at one time or another in the *Negro World*. Alain Locke contributed a long article on the colonial literature of France, which is reproduced here. Distinguished writers and political figures from the wider African world also appeared regularly. Dusé Mohamed Ali of Egypt was officially connected with the paper and wrote for it on a weekly basis in 1922. Kobina Sekyi, the Gold Coast (Ghana) lawyer and Pan-Africanist, contributed several poems. T. Albert Marryshow of Grenada, the "father of West Indian federation," appeared in the *Negro World* in the guise of poet.

Perhaps the paper's greatest service, however, was the outlet it afforded to a host of unknown hopefuls, especially in the field of poetry. No other publication came close to the *Negro World* in this regard. The *Negro World* did not only bring literature and art to the masses; it gave the masses a chance to express themselves artistically. The paper thus became *the* source, par excellence, of the genuine artistic voice of the New Negro. As important as traditional sources for the study of the Harlem Renaissance may be, it is not possible to obtain a complete picture of the Black literary and artistic world of the 1920s without recourse to the *Negro World* writings.

The present volume seeks to fill the void created by the erstwhile inaccessibility of the *Negro World*. The selections that follow reveal a whole new world of Black literature of the 1920s. It was a world dominated by Garvey's vision of the Black aesthetic—a world in which literature and the arts had an ennobling function, where art was both artistic and relevant. Here will be found the New Negro's views on white literary figures such as Rudyard Kipling and T. S. Stribling. There are appreciations of the 19th century Afro-American luminaries of pen and stage, such as Alexander Crummell and Ira Aldridge. The "establishment" literary figures of the 1920s are critiqued. W. E. B. DuBois and Benjamin Brawley especially are taken to task. The younger writers and artists of the Renaissance generation are showcased, praised, and criticized. Amy Jacques Garvey is wildly enthusiastic about Langston Hughes; Garvey and his editors alternatively praise and condemn Claude McKay; Zora Neale Hurston is given her first national and international exposure; and Augusta Savage comes to Harlem, works on a bust of Garvey, publishes poetry in the paper and marries the U.N.I.A.'s secretary general.

In these pages we relive the excitement that gripped Afro-America when the Martiniquan René Maran's novel, *Batouala,* first appeared in translation. *Batouala* won the Goncourt Prize, awarded in France, and was the international literary sensation of the season. In these pages too we see the young and relatively unknown J. A. Rogers burst upon the scene. It was in the *Negro World* that Rogers obtained his first sustained promotion from a major Black publication.

Here we revisit, from the perspective of the New Negro, the controversy that raged over jubilee music. We read an appreciation of Bert Williams, the blackface comedian who North America would not allow to be a serious actor. Eric D. Walrond waxes ecstatic over the legendary Florence Mills. The fledgling U.N.I.A. Dramatic Club strives to combine true art with subtle propaganda. Dusé Mohamed Ali pours scorn on the white-faced Dunbar Players of Washington, D.C. And most prolifically do we see the poets— famous poets, unknown bards, obscure aspirants to the favor of the muses, as they lend poetic raiment to the Garvey program. Here and there they pause for a nostalgic remembrance of home, for a paean of love. But mostly they are about the business of struggle.

The *Negro World* was a comprehensive literary forum. Not least of its contributions to posterity was its willingness to record the interesting but seldom documented sidelights of the literary scene. Did writers and editors of warring ideological camps sit down peaceably together on purely literary occasions? How did a group of young writers react to a visit to Arthur Schomburg's private library? Such questions may not be pivotal to anything, but the answers provided here help fill out the shadowy areas in our knowledge of the literary activity of the period.

The final section of this anthology contains a sampling of results from the U.N.I.A.'s literary competition of 1921. This device was not initiated, in the era of the 1920s, by the *Crisis* and *Opportunity* magazines, as has long been thought. The *Negro World* competition was earlier in the field by several years.

All but a very few of the selections in this volume are taken from the *Negro World*. These latter range from 1919 to 1928. The majority are from the period 1920 through 1924. They will help fill in a huge gap in the literary history of the New Negro era.

Wellesley, Massachusetts
March 1990

Part I

POLITICAL UNDERPINNINGS

1

Political Underpinnings

The literary outpourings of the Garvey Movement were buttressed by, and were largely a reflection of, Garvey's wider political program. This program in turn revolved around the ideas of race first, self-reliance and nationhood. Black folk should aggressively pursue their racial self-interest, should do for themselves rather than becoming dependent on the charity of others and should strive to govern themselves, especially in Africa. Literature and art in turn should seek to promote this racial political purpose. Art for its own sake was a luxury that a struggling people could not afford. These ideas amounted to what might be called a Garvey aesthetic. The selections in this section illustrate the political underpinnings of the Garvey aesthetic.

There can be no better way to begin this discussion than Garvey's own passionate essay on "African Fundamentalism." Here, in a controlled torrent of terse eloquence, Garvey distills the essence of his philosophy as it pertains to politics, literature, history and culture. "Race independence" must be the goal in every field. The race must create its own heroes, write and criticize its own literature, build its own strong nation. And history is on its side, for Africa civilized the world and Africa will be great again.

William H. Ferris, literary editor of Garvey's Negro World *newspaper, repeats Garvey's ideas in "The Negro Renaissance." It is interesting that he should have applied the term "Renaissance" to the U.N.I.A.'s work a few years before the better known, so-called Harlem Renaissance began.*

Hubert H. Harrison, another Negro World *editor, continues the plea for self-reliance and self-pride. In the process he makes what is in fact an early plea for Black Studies. Harrison's arguments here were heard many times over during the Black Studies revolution of the 1960s. His article anticipates also Carter G. Woodson's* Mis-education of the Negro *(1933), which also had its genesis among articles first published in the* Negro World.

A pseudonymed correspondent, "Hagar," follows up on Harrison's ideas by suggesting that the U.N.I.A. should itself inaugurate an after-school program in Black Studies.

Garvey provided a political program for the U.N.I.A., but did not stop there. He also personified the qualities that the good leader should possess. A. H. Maloney, sometime assistant chaplain general of the U.N.I.A., stresses the leader's role as an inspiration to the youth and posterity.

Race first and self-reliance could not co-exist easily with acceptance of white philanthropy, and so columnist Robert Lincoln Poston found himself in a quandary over $50,000 worth of foundation gifts to Carter G. Woodson's Association for the Study of Negro (now Afro-American) Life and History. He could not, in this instance, condemn Woodson, but nevertheless restated the ideal of self-reliance.

"If We Must Die" takes its title from Claude McKay's famous sonnet. Garveyites, as a major organizational manifestation of the New Negro spirit, naturally endorsed McKay's advice that the victims of mob violence should sell their lives as dearly as possible.

In "Negro Martyrs," Eric D. Walrond again extols the New Negro spirit of defiance, this time in relation to the South African, Prophet Enoch.

Politics for Garvey was indivisible, not only from literature, but also from religion. Richard A. Henry's prayer skillfully harnesses religion to the cause of racial uplift.

The section ends with two spirited defenses of Garvey's political program by Eric D. Walrond. Garvey has every right to move decisively against hangers-on within the movement, he argues. And as for the external threat— if the white powers that be are so against the U.N.I.A., then it must be doing something right.

African Fundamentalism

Marcus Garvey (1924)

The time has come for the Negro to forget and cast behind him his hero worship and adoration of other races, and to start out immediately to create and emulate heroes of his own. We must canonize our own saints, create our own martyrs, and elevate to positions of fame and honor black men and women who have made their distinct contributions to our racial history. Sojourner Truth is worthy of the place of sainthood alongside of Joan of Arc; Crispus Attucks and George William Gordon are entitled to the halo of martyrdom with no less glory than that of the martyrs of any other race. Toussaint L'Ouverture's brilliancy as a soldier and statesman outshone that of Cromwell, Napoleon and Washington; hence, he is entitled to the highest place as a hero among men. Africa has produced countless numbers of men and women, in war and in peace, whose lustre and bravery outshine that of any other people. Then why not see good and perfection in ourselves? We must inspire a literature and promulgate a doctrine of our own without any apologies to the powers that be. The right is ours and God's. Let contrary sentiment and cross opinions go to the winds. Opposition to race independence is the weapon of the enemy to defeat the hopes of an unfortunate people. We are entitled to our own opinions and not obligated to or bound by the opinions of others.

A Peep at the Past

If others laugh at you, return the laughter to them; if they mimic you, return the compliment with equal force. They have no more right to dishonor, disrespect and disregard your feeling and manhood than you have in dealing with them. Honor them when they honor you; disrespect and disregard them when they vilely treat you. Their arrogance is but skin deep and an assumption that has no foundation in morals or in law. They have sprung from the same family tree of obscurity as we have; their history is as rude in its primitiveness as ours; their ancestors ran wild and naked, lived in caves and in branches of trees, like monkeys, as ours; they made human sacrifices, ate the flesh of their own dead and the raw meat of the wild beast for centuries even as they accuse us of doing; their cannibalism was more prolonged than ours; when we were embracing the arts and sciences on the banks of the Nile their ancestors were still drinking human blood and eating out of the skulls of their conquered dead; when our civilization had reached the noon-day of progress they were still running naked and sleeping in holes and caves with rats, bats and other insects and animals. After we had already unfathomed the mystery of the stars and reduced the heavenly constellations to minute and regular calculus they were still backwoodsmen, living in ignorance and blatant darkness.

Why Be Discouraged?

The world today is indebted to us for the benefits of civilization. They stole our arts and sciences from Africa. Then why should we be ashamed of ourselves? Their *modern improvements* are but *duplicates* of a grander civilization that we reflected thousands of years ago, without the advantage of what is buried and still hidden, to be resurrected and reintroduced by the intelligence of our generation and our posterity. Why should we be discouraged because somebody laughs at us today? Who to tell what tomorrow will bring forth? Did they not laugh at Moses, Christ and Mohammed? Was there not a Carthage, Greece and Rome? We see and have changes every day, so pray, work, be steadfast and be not dismayed.

Nothing Must Kill the Empire Urge

As the Jew is held together by his *religion,* the white races by the assumption and the unwritten law of *superiority,* and the Mongolian by the precious tie of *blood,* so likewise the Negro must be united in one *grand racial hierarchy.* Our *union must know no clime, boundary* or *nationality.* Like the great Church of Rome, Negroes the world over *must practice one faith,* that of Confidence in themselves, with One God! One Aim! One Destiny! Let no religious scruples, no political machination divide us, but let us hold together under all climes and in every country, making among ourselves a Racial Empire upon which "the sun shall never set."

Allegiance to Self First

Let no voice but your own speak to you from the depths. Let no influence but your own rouse you in time of peace and time of war. Hear all, but attend only to that which concerns you. Your allegiance shall be to your God, then to your family, race and country. Remember always that the Jew in his political and economic urge is always first a Jew; the white man is first a white man under all circumstances, and you can do no less than being first and always a Negro, and then all else will take care of itself. Let no one inoculate you with evil doctrines to suit their own conveniences. There is no humanity before that which starts with yourself. "Charity begins at home." First to thyself be true, and "thou canst not then be false to any man."

We Are Arbiters of Our Own Destiny

God and Nature first made us what we are, and then out of our own creative genius we make ourselves what we want to be. Follow always that great law. Let the sky and God be our limit, and eternity our measurement. There is no height to which we cannot climb by using the active intelligence of our own minds. Mind creates, and as much as we desire in Nature we can have through the creation of our own minds. Being at present the scientifically weaker race, you shall treat others only as they treat you; but in your homes and everywhere possible you must teach the higher development of science to your children; and be sure to develop a race of scientists par excellence, for in science and religion lies our only hope to withstand the evil designs and modern materialism. Never forget your God. Remember, we live, work and pray for the establishing of a great and binding *racial hierarchy,* the founding of a *racial empire* whose only natural, spiritual and political limits shall be God and "Africa, at home and abroad."

The Negro Renaissance

William H. Ferris (1922)

Why do we term the miraculous rise and growth of the U.N.I.A. the Negro Renaissance rather than the Negro Rebirth? The Rebirth, the being born again, means the entering into a new spiritual experience. But the Renaissance means the revival of that which formerly existed.

The Renaissance or Revival or Learning which Petrarch started in the fourteenth century A.D. was not the introduction of something new in human history, but it was the rediscovery of the Greek world, the flowering again of Greek civilization in Medieval Europe.

So, too, when the U.N.I.A. taught the Negro not to despise himself because he was black, but to look up to the stars and feel his kinship in the Divine, when it taught the Negro that he was created in the Devine image the same as other men, when it taught the world to take seriously the Black

Man's desire for justice and his ambitions to achieve big things in the scientific, literary, industrial, commercial and political world, it was not introducing anything new to human history. But it was restoring to black men that confidence in themselves and prestige in the world which they enjoyed twenty-five, thirty and thirty-five centuries ago by the waters of the Nile, the Tigris and the Euphrates and on the plains and plateaus of Ethiopia.

Dr. Booker T. Washington came along and said, "Behold, I bring you good news of great joy and glad tidings. I have persuaded millionaires to plant and endow industrial schools in the Sunny South. Follow me and I will land you in the political and educational jobs." The Negro vigorously applauded. Dr. W. E. B. DuBois came along. He, too, said, "Behold, I bring you good news of great joy and glad tidings. I have persuaded editors, scholars and philanthropists, of brains, wealth, family and prestige to help you obtain your citizenship rights and justice in the courts." The Negro vigorously applauded.

And then comes a short, broad-shouldered black youth from Jamaica with keen, sagacious eyes and heavy jaws. And he said, "Behold, I bring you good news of great joy and glad tidings. Though you are created of the dust of the earth, God has also breathed the breath of a spiritual life into your nostrils and you have become living souls. You are ashamed because you are black. But I tell you God Almighty estimates a man by the worth of his soul and not the color of his skin. When the angel troubles the pool, you are waiting for some friend to lift and carry you into the healing waters. But I say unto you, as Christ said unto the man sick of the palsy, 'Rise, take up thy bed and walk.' Nerve yourself, make a supreme effort to rise and get into the pool yourself and you will command the respect and challenge the admiration of a hostile world. You can operate factories, found cities and build up enterprises the same as other men." And then the Negro not only vigorously applauded but threw up his hat, jumped on his feet and broke into deafening cheers.

Marcus Garvey, despite his perfervid rhetoric, brought to black men something worth while, namely: the belief that they were somebody and counted for something in the world. Next to belief in God, the greatest force that can inspire a man is belief in himself.

A century ago Novalis was asked whether philosophy could bake any bread. He replied; "No; but it can give us God's freedom and immortality." The bread problem is the basic problem of human life. But the stirring of the soul of a race is not to be despised.

The aliatory element, the element of luck and chance, has played an important part in the affairs of men. On a Sunday in the latter part of November, 1919, we stood on a pile of logs and watched hundreds of people jump up and down, throw up hats and handkerchiefs and cheer while the *Yarmouth*, the first steamship of the Black Star Line, backed from the wharf at West 135th street and slowly glided down the North River. It was sturdily built, but it was not a large, speedy, modern-equipped boat. But the news that black men had actually purchased a steamship, manned by a Negro captain and crew and sent her out into the briny deep electrified the Negro peoples of the world as no other event since the Emancipation Proclamation of Abraham Lincoln did. The fact that the boat actually made two trips to the West Indies, under Negro captain and crew and one under a white captain and Negro crew kept the flame of this idealism alive until the U.N.I.A. encircled the globe as a great fraternal organization. A commercial venture ended as an uplift of the spirit. It was sown a natural body, it was raised a spiritual body. And that was something of a miracle.

The successful carrying out of a vast industrial program takes years. And perhaps some day, sooner than we expect, the industrial aspect, the bread and butter aspect of the U.N.I.A. and its allied corporations, will be as roseate as the spiritual and fraternal aspects are now. It is one of the ironies of human life that one generation harvests what the preceding generation sows; that the generation which does the clearing of forests rarely sees the mills and factories and thriving marts of trade rise. But we hope that those who have done the pioneer work in the present instance, will live to see the fruits of their labor.

The Racial Roots of Culture

Hubert H. Harrison (1920)

Education is the name which we give to that process by which the ripened generation brings to bear upon the rising generation the stored-up knowledge and experience of the past and present generations to fit it for the business of life. If we are not to waste money and energy, our educational systems should shape our youth for what we intend them to become.

We Negroes, in a world in which we are the under-dog, must shape our youth for living in such a world. Shall we shape them mentally to accept the status of under-dog as their predestined lot? Or shall we shape them into men and women fit for a free world? To do the former needs nothing more than continuing as we are. To do the latter is to shape their souls for continued conflict with a theory and practice in which most of the white world that surrounds them are at one.

The educational system in the United States and the West Indies was shaped by white people for white youth, and from their point of view, it fits their purpose well. Into this system came the children of Negro parents when chattel slavery was ended—and their relation to the problems of life was obviously different. The white boy and girl draw exclusively from the stored-up knowledge and experience of the past and present generations of white people to fit them for the business of being dominant whites in a world full of colored folk. The examples of valor and virtue on which their minds are fed are exclusively white examples. What wonder, then, that each generation comes to maturity with the idea imbedded in its mind that only white men are valorous and fit to rule and only white women are virtuous and entitled to chivalry, respect and protection? What wonder that they think, almost instinctively, that the Negro's proper place, nationally and internationally, is that of an inferior? It is only what we should naturally expect.

But what seems to escape attention is the fact that the Negro boy and girl, getting the same (tho' worse) instruction, also get from it the same notion of the Negro's place and part in life which the white children get. Is it any wonder, then, that they so readily accept the status of inferiors; that they tend to disparage themselves, and think themselves worth while only to the extent to which they look and act and think like the whites? They know nothing of the stored-up knowledge and experience of the past and present generations of Negroes in their ancestral lands, and conclude there is no such store of knowledge and experience. They readily accept the assumption that Negroes have never been anything but slaves and that they never had a glorious past as other fallen peoples like the Greeks and Persians have. And this despite the mass of collected testimony in the works of Barth, Schweinfurth, Mary Kingsley, Lady Lugard, Morel, Ludolphus, Blyden, Ellis, Ratzel, Kidd, Es-Saadi, Casely Hayford and a host of others, Negro and white.

A large part of the blame for this deplorable condition must be put upon the Negro colleges like Howard, Fisk, Livingstone and Lincoln in the United States, and Codrington, Harrison and the Mico in the West Indies. These are the institutions in which our cultural ideals and educational systems are fashioned for the shaping of the minds of the future generations of Negroes. It cannot be expected that it shall begin with the common schools; for, in spite of logic, educational ideas and ideals spread from above downwards. If we are ever to enter into the confraternity of colored peoples it should seem the duty of our Negro colleges to drop their silly smatterings of "little Latin and less Greek" and establish modern courses in Hausa and Arabic, for these are the living languages of millions of our brethren in modern Africa. Courses in Negro history and the culture of West African peoples, at least, should be given in every college that claims to be an institution of learning for Negroes. Surely an institution of learning for Negroes should not fail to be also an institution of Negro learning.

Negroes Should Be Taught Pride of Race

"Hagar" (1920)

Editor of the *Negro World:*

Negroes the world over are beginning to feel the imperative need of a determined race consciousness and to realize that such consciousness can be solidly built only upon the foundation of knowledge. It is no easy matter for a Negro man or woman whose time is for the most part occupied with the problem of making a living to acquire education along racial lines; and the writer knows of no institution to which Negro children may be sent to learn the facts about themselves.

It is the writer's opinion that a school for Negro children with sessions that do not interfere with their attendance at the public or parochial school, that taught those facts about the Negro's status during the several civilizations which the other schools so carefully overlook, is a vital necessity if we would instill a pride of race in our coming generation. There is no more fertile field for this work of education than here in Harlem; and the work of such an institution could be supplemented by courses of lectures for adults and the organization of Negro culture clubs. Text books could be edited to meet the particular demands of such an institution and systems of instruction by correspondence would make it possible to reach people living in remote districts. The [Universal] Negro Improvement Association has been so remarkably active during the short span of its existence that it seems to be the logical body to undertake this work.

The writer would be grateful to have the editor's opinion of her idea, and, if possible, to hear what other readers, especially mothers, have to suggest along the lines.

New York, April 17

[Editor's note: The U.N.I.A. has had this idea under consideration for some time. Plans to put it in operation have been held in abeyance pending the convention in August.]

Leadership That Inspires

Arnold Hamilton Maloney (1922)

Some few years ago I was shown a letter written by one of the great leaders of the race to a young man who had essayed to make excursions into the realm of literature. This young man had hopes of becoming a writer of short-story and verse; and he was in active training with that end in view. He had received some encouragement from his teacher, and had been lionized by the humble folk of his town; but he was anxious to have his work passed upon by the reputed literary chieftain of the race. Full of hope, he had sent a few of the best of his amateur attempts to this leader with a personal letter asking him to review them and (if he found them good enough) to publish them in the organ of which this leader is the editor. In response this young man received the letter to which I have referred. This letter was like a wet blanket used to smother a fire; it was like a frigid wave of wind congealing the blood. I read the letter and I sighed; and when I had become sufficiently composed to speak, I gave expression to this thought: "God, spare us of this type of leadership, if Thou really desirest that we shall go forward." And, there and then, I decided that leadership which is deserving of respect, leadership which is effective, must be leadership which strikes a strong note of help and hope to youth. The leader should never discourage; he should always encourage. He should never repel; he should attract. He should never quench; he should elicit the possibilities of those who would by time be led. And ever since that time I have used that test as one of the gauges for measuring the genuineness of leadership.

There are always disagreeable surprises in store for those who would persist in discrediting the scions of the masses. I wonder why men who are historians should act in such flagrant violation of the lessons of history. When you think of orators like Price and Booker Washington, of statesmen like Diocletian and Cromwell, of reformers like Savonarola and Sojourner Truth, of scholars like Blyden and Bannaker, of poets like Burns and Dunbar— when you think of men by the thousands in every walk of life who, coming forth from amongst the masses, have shaken the earth by their power, their influence, and their natural greatness of mind and soul, how can you persist in questioning the inherent possibilities of the rank and file in the face of youth, ambition, and determination?

I have read of Jesus encouraging young men by his advice; I have seen letters of inspiration to budding inventors from Granville T. Wood; I have seen and heard sentiments of suggestion and helpfulness expressed to scores of youngsters by Booker Washington, Gilbert H. Jones, I. N. Rendall, Pezavia O'Connell, Kelly Miller, Prof. Crogman; and I have read and heard words of inspiration from the pen and the lips of John A. Gregg to the young manhood and womanhood of the race.

Leadership which, like a contract, ceases to function in the absence of "consideration," leadership that receives its sanction from the principle of quid pro quo, is leadership that we must repudiate. But leadership that we should encourage is leadership which has a keen and abiding interest in posterity and therefore endeavors to bring to the fore the latent possibilities of the group.

Wall Street Gives $50,000 For Study of Negro History

Robert L. Poston (1922)

The daily press announced last week that the Carnegie and Rockefeller Foundations have given $50,000 to Carter Woodson to be used for the study of Negro history. We are not among those who think that every gift coming from white people has a string to it and should be considered as dangerous, for there are many white people assisting Negroes from high motives. But in view of the fact that gifts coming from the above named foundations are always questionable, we wish to remind those who have to do with the spending of this money of some dangers that may lurk in the way. Most institutions endowed by these foundations—a notable example is Chicago University, a child of Rockefeller charity—having the reputation of impressing upon their subjects the capitalistic viewpoint. It cannot be denied that until recent years the charity of both Rockefeller and Carnegie, so far as colored people are concerned, was confined to those institutions not devoted to the higher development of the Negro, such as Tuskegee, Hampton, etc., and some of the libraries of Carnegie have been noted for what they do not contain. While it is hoped that the $50,000 given to Mr. Woodson for the study of Negro history is given without any harmful conditions attached to it, yet there is a possibility that such is not the case, and it is up to the people to see to it that these wealthy men with their money do not impose upon us a viewpoint detrimental to our best interest. Mr. Woodson, with whom we are acquainted, is a highly educated gentleman who gives us the impression of being a New Negro. But there is danger in spending money given you by other people, and Mr. Woodson's job is going to be to spend Rockefeller and Carnegie's money without accepting Rockefeller and Carnegie's viewpoint. We trust that Mr. Woodson will be successful in doing this; but in the event he is not, God help us all! For nothing could have a more harmful effect on the Negro than a Negro history dictated by white capitalists.

Some weeks ago, when Mr. Woodson's project was being discussed in a meeting at the 135th Street Public Library, a young man expressed the fear that there was too much of Rockefeller and Carnegie behind it. His fears were laughed at by the persons assembled, who were under the impression that the big forces behind this movement were colored and the major part of the support would come from this source. It now turns out from the newspaper reports of last week that this young man who had fears had some ground for them, while the rest of the audience was, as usual, carried away with sentiment.

But we may as well acknowledge one thing: As long as a people are poor and without, they will have a hard time taking an independent stand in anything. We feel obligated to those whose money we spend; and, consciously or unconsciously, we find ourselves directing our actions, if not to please them entirely, to offend as little as possible. The extent to which we must sink our individuality in conforming to such a course is apparent. Whether those who spend large sums of white people's money in writing a Negro history can do this without leaning too far toward the viewpoint of their benefactors remains to be seen. We are only pointing out the difficulty of such a source without committing ourselves to the proposition as to whether it can be done or not. We are aware of the position in which Mr. Woodson finds himself, and we would be reluctant to suggest to him that he take a course different from the one he is taking. The Negro race must have its history written. It takes money to do it. If the Negro will not furnish this money, shall Mr. Woodson refuse proffered help from other sources? We can accept but one answer to this question for the other answer would necessitate that we go down in our pockets and furnish the money ourselves, a thing we are too confounded stingy to do.

All of which brings us again to the sad realization of the fact that as a race we are in a devil of a fix all over the world—poor, dependent, yet desirous of having. Can't we at least be consistent with the rest of humanity? Why not try the only alternative of getting something, possessing our souls, being men?

In the case of Dr. Woodson and his history we have little to suggest. We have admitted that his course is hard. Only we might say: "Be as good to us as you possibly can, good doctor, and when you catch their heads turned, say a truth or so about the black man's part in America."

"If We Must Die"

Unsigned Editorial (1922)

Some time ago we emphasized the fact that one of the most wholesome, most sobering remedial agencies in the cure of lynching is the repayment of the lynchers in their own coin. When the mob knows that the group to whom their victims belong is sure to retaliate on the lynchers' group, [they may be restrained by] the knowledge that if one must die one will not die alone.

The most salutary example of "eye for an eye" was demonstrated by the Negroes of Washington, D.C., during the July riot of 1919. It is well known that the toll of death among the whites was so large, and so appalling, and overbalanced the death toll among Negroes to such an extent that the correct check-up was never given to the public. The men who paid these lynchers in their own coin, besides adding laurels to the courage and valor of their race, set an example in retaliation that will forever be an inspiration to members of the race when they face the situation, "If we must die."

This spirit of retaliation was exhibited by the martyred Sergeant Caldwell in Alabama several years ago who, seeing that he must die, either at the hands of a street car conductor and motorman, or be executed by the law of the State for defending himself against their assault, preferred to exact the lives of his assailants.

The same spirit, but with a different result from the Caldwell case, seized a frenzied mob of Negroes in Richmond, Va., Sunday when they pursued and put to death a white motorman of the Virginia Railway & Power Co. who, it is reported, assaulted a Negro during an altercation on a street car. It is almost the invariable custom of white street car conductors and motormen to unite in assault on Negroes who incur their displeasure. It was such a case that resulted in the Caldwell tragedy, and such cases that urge Negroes everywhere to consider how we should acquit ourselves.

It may be that public sentiment will run high, as in the Richmond case, at present, but intensity of public excitement is always followed by sober reflection when the check-up shows how disastrous results may have been avoided. One thing is certain, and that is that the cause is not likely to be repeated, especially when Negroes decree to exact a heavy toll.

Negro Martyrs

Eric D. Walrond (1922)

Terence McSwiney, the Irish patriot, left a blot on the escutcheon of civilization that is bound to haunt Lloyd George to his grave. The moral fibre of the man, as seen in his noble hunger strike at Cork, was the strongest force the Irish ever marshaled in their bloody struggle for independence. It was an index to the bulldog character of the Irish and it caused the English to reflect that people of such virility are not to be trifled with. Similarly Gabriele D'Annunzio, the Italian poet, attracted the attention of the world by his historic defense of Fiume. Gandhi, the Indian leader, is the man who is occupying the stage at the moment. That is, if we cull our information from the outgivings of the Associated Press. But there is a martyr, a black martyr, who the authorities at Capetown saw fit to incarcerate as a "dangerous rebel." Yes, and although he goes by the name of Enoch, Prophet Enoch, don't fool yourself, as does the *Times-Picayune* of New Orleans, La., into thinking that he is one of those white-collared ecclesiasts who go crawling into Dixie, but a bare-breasted, two-fisted personification of the awakened spirit of the Negro. Enoch, it seems, has been to America, and here caught the vision of an Africa Redeemed. Boiling with race pride, he went back to Africa, determined to organize the natives into strong, self-governing units. From coast to coast the doctrine of this violent lover of freedom created a furore, a realization of the slavery and thralldom in which the natives have been for centuries held. At once the blacks in fearless parades, told the white overlords of their determination to throw off the yoke of imperial domination.

Lloyd George, secure in his castle at Downing Street, wired his agents that this must not be. No, indeed, it is alarming, to say the least, and the next thing one heard was of the brutal arrest of Enoch and 100 of his disciples. They were given indefinite prison terms, but the spirit of the man lives on!

With all his cunning Lloyd George seems to have overlooked the fact that to spread a movement, persecute it!

Prayer For the U.N.I.A.

Richard A. Henry (1920)

Almighty and most merciful God Who by Thy Holy Apostles has taught us to make prayers and supplications, and to give thanks for all men, we humbly thank Thee for allowing us this great privilege to kneel in prayer before Thee once more. And we humbly ask Thee, Most Merciful Father, to open the hearts of every Negro man and woman, that they may learn to know that Africa is their home, and that the two hundred and forty millions of our brothers abroad are begging us to respond to our Moses. Ethiopia is calling for deliverance. Awake our minds, O Lord, to the knowledge of Thy Holy Scripture that last shall be first and first last; make us to understand that this race of ours was blessed with Thy divine wisdom, and was made of the same flesh and blood as any other race on the face of the earth, and that we have all rights to the same privilege of Thy everlasting mercy which Thou hast provided for Thy children. Inspire, continually, we pray Thee, this Universal Association of the race throughout the world; strengthen the leaders, dear Lord, especially those whose blood has been shed as a token of their heroic determination in the cause, so that they will be able to lead us victoriously out of the hands of our oppressors; and teach us to realize that we are children of the same God and have all rights to the same blessings of thy Omnipotent Being. Hear our prayers, we beseech Thee, O Lord, and grant us Thine divine blessings through Jesus, our only Mediator and Saviour. Amen.

Marcus Garvey—A Defense

Eric D. Walrond (1922)

The favorite parting shot of "dishonorably discharged" officers of the Universal Negro Improvement Association is to yelp and howl about the "dictatorship" of Mr. Marcus Garvey. "The Great I Am," "Imperialist," "Czar," etc., are epithets familiar to those editors and journalists who delight in wallowing in the mire of scandal and vituperation. Of the methods and administrative policies of Mr. Garvey they say a "mouthful." It is unfortunate that he is so iron-fisted and damning in his relations with his associates. For this reason the personnel of his organization is "inferior" in point of "culture" and "refinement" and "education." There is no comparison with it and other organizations with better trained men in them, with staffs which boast of college professors and competent experts.

All along the line criticism is directed against him because he demands of those about him 100 per cent loyalty above everything else. It is even gossiped that men of "brains" and "experience" have been passed up in preference to men who have shown a maximum of interest in Africa's redemption! Why not? This policy is the outgrowth—the direct psychological reaction to the tragedy, as the black world knows, of appointing men of "brains" and "experience" to positions of trust and responsibility. From the beginning it was Mr. Garvey's rule to pick out the ablest men he could find and place them in executive office. Experience had taught him that to succeed, to carry out his monster program, brains, and brains of the highest order, had to be pressed into service. With that in mind, he went about the formation of a cabinet, examining, selecting, rejecting. In those days it mattered not where a man had come from, what church he attended, what association he was a member of. Only one thing counted—his fitness. After a rigorous investigation of his character and qualifications he was brought in, appointed according to his ability, and left to do his bit in the mighty cause of Africa's freedom. But what did the majority of them do? Did they start to work with the idea of rendering service to the cause, of subordinating personal greed and power to the larger interests of the movement? No. To them affiliation with it meant a means to a very definite personal end. Money, and as much of it as they could lay their hands on, was their purpose. Apart from that they had no interest in Mr. Garvey and his "crazy organization." In time exposures, expulsions and prosecutions followed.

The man's eyes began to open. Were all Negroes—so-called "educated" Negroes—crooks and liars? With his comparative analytical mind he dismissed that as Anglo-Saxon. That was the white man's way of summing up the whole race. But he had learned his lesson—a pretty dear one, indeed—and he was going to profit by it. What did he do? The fastidious smart-Aleck who drops into his office and overwhelms him with his "cultured" ways and courtly manners and his protestations of love for the Motherland is seen in his true colors. If necessary, czar-like methods are adopted to exclude rogues and traitors from the organization. "Once bitten, twice shy." Can you blame him?

The Dice of Destiny

Eric D. Walrond (1922)

Once in a while we hear of a white employer truculently discharging a Negro who is in sympathy with the radical doctrines of Mr. Marcus Garvey. "Go to Garvey," screams the irate capitalist; "go and let him give you a job." The upshot of the matter is a minority of colored people who are of the opinion that Mr. Garvey's philosophy is untimely and premature and inimical to the prosperity of the race. But these people, unfortunately, are misguided. They ought to remember that whenever a white man opposes a movement started by black people, in the interest of black people, it is the best proof of that movement's virtue and timeliness. And when a white employer vents his spleen in such a high-handed manner, he unconsciously betrays fear of the awful potentialities of such a movement. Whitelike, he thinks of self-preservation, and the easiest way to gratify that is to "take it out of" his Negro help. But this ought to be a scorching lesson to the Negro. It ought to fortify him, to bring to his mind's eye the tragedy of what it is to be black, and upstanding. It ought to send him out in the world with the film torn from his eyes, seeing the red monster labeled race prejudice in all his grizzly colors. And then, when he comes to retrospect, to think of casting the dice of destiny, he is convinced that the organization that brings terror to the hearts of white men is the one for him!

PART II

LITERARY CRITICISM

2

General Principles

Though primarily a political newspaper, the Negro World *nevertheless outdistanced most contemporary literary journals in its literary output. Most of the paper's editors and regular columnists evinced a profound interest in literature, both Black and universal. The paper's editorial columns were frequently taken up with purely literary matters.*

Hubert H. Harrison's "On A Certain Condescension in White Publishers" has a timely ring about it which belies the fact that it was written many decades ago. The question of access to publishing houses is, of course, crucial, for without adequate opportunities for publishing a people's literature is hamstrung. Afro-America's writers, in whatever field, have almost always found it difficult to be published by major companies. And Afro-America has not developed major publishing houses of its own.

During the 19th and early 20th centuries, most Afro-American authors published their works privately, often by subscription. Such eminent authors as Carter G. Woodson and J. A. Rogers had to resort to self-publishing. Publishers have frequently been quite content to treat with scorn a market representing one-tenth or more of the population of these United States.

The only important exceptions to this general rule have been the periods of the Harlem Renaissance and the Civil Rights and the Black Power eras of the 1960s. Both of these periods, in retrospect, have turned out to be nothing but transient aberrations. Some of the "big names" of each period have found it impossible to be published once the fad has subsided and business has returned to the norm.

Harrison credited his Negro World *book review columns (begun in 1920) with being the first regular book review section of any Afro-American publication. He deals here with humor and insight with the problems attendant to being first in this field. The almighty profit motive, he contends, ought to induce a more enlightened attitude in white publishers. But, in the field of publishing, the profit motive has not always triumphed over prejudice.*

As massive as the Negro World's *literary output was, it still represented only a fraction of the material submitted by aspiring writers and poets. The editorial "Those Who Write Prose and Verse for the Negro World" reveals a very sympathetic newspaper attempting a balance between maximum exposure for its readers and the maintenance of reasonable standards.*

The Negro World *writers, following Garvey, almost always came down on the side of "propaganda," in the great debate of the 1920s on the place of propaganda in art. The anti-propagandists argued that art harnessed to the cause of racial uplift was bad art. The propagandists argued, with Garvey, that an art devoid of a noble social purpose was sterile and harmful.*

William H. Ferris developed his own variant of the propaganda position in the pages of the Negro World. *The most powerful propaganda art, he argued, was that which stated its case subtly, embodying it within a work of high technical proficiency. He develops this argument in "An African Novel." The great Black novel, he says, is yet to be written. When it is written, it will strike a powerful blow for the cause.*

As for the African continent—here the editorial "African Language and Literature Make for African Nationality" supports the view that African literature and nationalism will find their fullest expression through the medium of African languages. Frantz Fanon repeated this view four decades later.

The concluding article of this section, "On the Convention's Agenda," illustrates once more the U.N.I.A.'s abiding interest in things literary. The organization's international conventions more than once turned their attention to literary matters.

On a Certain Condescension in White Publishers

Hubert H. Harrison (1922)

It is an undoubted, if ignored, truth that in the arts of buying and selling the black brother is the equal of the whites. I mean not here to challenge that fine fiction to which we in America have dedicated our lives, but simply to insist that when the American farmer wants to get pennies for his pumpkins the color of the hands from which those pennies fall is of little concern to him. And we may safely presume that what is true of farmers is true also of most other men who have something to sell.

In my mind's eye there lurks a light similitude between the tiller of the agricultural soil and his more pretentious brother who tills and traffics in the product of the intellectual soil. These also "raise their crop," deciding at their own risks what weeds shall grow or what goodly harvests shall come up. But the point of chief importance in our comparison lies in the fact that publishers as well as farmers do finally bring or send their crops to market, where the bane or blessing rests with the hands from which must roll in either case the pennies that pay for pumpkins. Now, out of this necessity there springs a certain rough democracy of dealing; since we must sell, and all buyers' coins are equal, let us extend the courtesies of the market in equal measure to all prospective purchasers. It is this courtesy of trade which helps to reconcile the brother in black to the capitalist system of the brother in white; if all men are not equal, at least all moneys are. One dollar from Sam Jones will buy as much social service as one dollar from Lloyd George—and trade courtesy is a social service.

But life, alas, has some hard shocks for logic and the white publishers of America have given me many such. It is now two years since I inaugurated in this newspaper the first (and up to now the only) regular book-review section known to Negro newspaperdom. Since that time I have observed that the magazine called *The Crisis* has been attempting to follow my footsteps in the trail—with such success as was achievable by youth and inexperience.

When the book reviews were begun it was with this two-fold aim: to bring to the knowledge of the Negro reading public those books which were necessary if he would know what the white world was thinking and planning and doing in regard to the colored world; and to bring the white publisher and his wares to a market which needed those wares. Sometimes the books had been written by Negro authors with whose works Negro readers were thus made acquainted. I aimed to render a common service and to a certain extent I succeeded. But one would have thought that the white publishers would be eager to avail themselves of the novel opportunity thus offered to get some more pennies for their pumpkins. But it was not to be.

I recall my humorous amazement when, after writing to Boni & Liveright for a review copy of a book dealing with the anthropology of colored peoples, I received and read their reply. The supercilious magnificence of that reply was regal in its sweep. They wanted me to supply them with back numbers of this journal—and even then they simply subsided into silence. What could Negroes know of anthropology, whether as critics or simple readers? It reminded me so much of the outraged dowager's dignity of Mrs. Elsie Clews Parsons when a black man in West Africa wrote her some years ago for an exchange copy of *The Family.* She wrote to tell him in reply to his courteous request that the book was not of a sort to interest him and that, perhaps, he had been misled. It created laughter from Lagos to Sierra Leone because— the man who had written was John Mensa Sarbah, the illustrious author of the *Fanti Customary Laws,* who knew just about five times as much of social anthropology as Mrs. Parsons.

So I laughed at the top-lofty airs of Boni and Liveright at that time. The readers of this journal will recall that *The Story of Mankind,* by Hendrik Wellem Van Loon, was published by Boni and Liveright and was recently reviewed by me. All things change and white publishers may change also.

But Boni and Liveright were only an index. To this day I cannot get the New York representatives of Macmillan and company to take the Negro reading public seriously. It is more than three months since I wrote for a review copy of *A Social History of the American Negro,* by Benjamin Brawley—and up to now they have not even deigned to reply. Of course, one might raise the question of the intrinsic quality of the literary criticism done in this section. And that is fair enough, although I am stopped from taking the stand to testify. But other witnesses are not lacking. Eugene O'Neill, author of *The Emperor Jones,* has written to say that the review of that work done in this paper was one of the two or three best that had come from any source. The publishers of Hale's *Story of a Style,* Morel's *The Black Man's Burden,* Harris' *Africa Slave or Free* and Pratt's *Real South Africa,* have found, to their surprise, (and profit) that we can do workman-like work in book reviewing.

The publishers of Mr. Lothrop Stoddard's two books, *The Rising Tide of Color* and *The New World of Islam,* have had occasion to commend the thoroughness of our literary criticism of those two books; and Mr. Stoddard himself entered into friendly and faithful correspondence with us. Huebsch, Scribners, Doran and Dutton have had the product of their presses properly presented to our readers—to their mutual profit. And even the Macmillans have had *The Soul of John Brown,* by Stephen Graham, and *The Influence of Animism on Islam,* by Dr. Zwemer, reviewed by us. Yet the force of an ancient attitude is strong, and this and other publishing houses still seem unaware of the fact that many of the 12,000,000 Negroes in this country do buy and read not only books on the Negro but other literary and scientific works.

As the only "certificated" Negro book-reviewer in captivity I feel the onus of this backward view which white publishers take of the market which the Negro reading-public furnishes for their wares. It is not complimentary to us: it is short-sighted and unsound. After all, pennies are pennies, and books are published to be sold. We believe that the Negro reading public will buy books—when they know of their existence. One sees proof of this in the amazing stream of letters and money orders which flow in to Mr. Rogers at 513 Lenox Avenue for his books, *From Superman to Man* and *As Nature Leads.* This young Negro author's continued success is also proof of the great intellectual awakening which has been brought about by the forces of the last decade.

And now, a word to our own. I foresee that in the near future there will be many book reviewers (which is the name for literary critics in their working clothes) among us. Indeed, they are already treading on my heels in this paper. May one veteran (since my book reviewing began in the *New York Times* in 1906) offer a word of advice to the new recruits? In the first place, remember that in a book review you are writing for a public who want to know whether it is worth their while to read the book about which you are writing. They are primarily interested more in what the author set himself to do and how he does it than in your own private loves and hates. Not that these are without value, but they are strictly secondary. In the next place, respect yourself and your office so much that you will not complacently pass and praise drivel and rubbish. Grant that you don't know everything; you still must steer true to the lights of your knowledge. Give honest service: only so will your opinion come to have weight with your readers. Remember, too, that you cannot well review a work on African history, for instance, if that is the only work on the subject that you have read. Therefore, read widely and be well informed. Get the widest basis of knowledge for your judgment; then back your judgment to the limit. Here endeth the First Encyclical.

Those Who Write Prose and Verse For the *Negro World*

Unsigned Editorial (1923)

No reader of a newspaper can judge by what gets into its columns what is left out. An editor's mail bag is much like a mill into which all sorts of manuscripts come and are ground out, the grist being a very small percentage of the whole. And, we are persuaded, the editor grieves more over the large mass he must reject than he rejoices over the small mass he can use. This is so because the editor, although among the most sympathetic of creatures, and all embracing in his sympathies, must of necessity, be cold and unfeeling in accepting what is good and available and rejecting what is not.

The editor of *The Negro World* appreciates beyond expression the wide-awake interest of members of the Universal Negro Improvement Association, and others in all parts of the world, who take the trouble to send clippings from their local newspapers, articles and poems. It shows their interest in the race and the work of the Universal Negro Improvement Association, and it helps us all the more intelligently to edit *The Negro World*, which has come to be regarded as the greatest national and international newspaper the race has.

Those who send us prose articles should write only on one side of the paper. They should write legibly, typewritten copy being preferred, with open spacing. They should have one subject and stick to it. And they should not use more than six hundred words to say all they want to, three hundred being a good number to stop at. We can't undertake to return articles we do not use, and if we do not use them it is because of some objection to the subject, treatment or composition.

Those who send us verse, and there are many, are advised not to send us any unless they are familiar with the rules of versification. Most that is sent us is faulty because the authors are ignorant of the rules. Poetry is the highest form of expression, and no satisfactory impression will be got if the rules governing the expression are not understood and adhered to. We can correct a faulty sentence or paragraph of prose, but a faulty line or couplet of verse can only be corrected by rewriting it, and we cannot undertake to do that, and the author would not thank us for doing it.

But those who write prose or verse for *The Negro World* should not be discouraged; they should rather be encouraged to master the machinery of prose and verse making, and to keep on coming until they have done so. It is only by so doing can they hope to make the expression in words which works for impression on those they hope to reach and influence.

An African Novel

William H. Ferris (1920)

Although some of our talented writers have tried their hand at novel writing, they did not attain the same success in that field as they did in other fields. Dunbar's *Uncalled* is a fairly good novel, but it does not measure up to his poems. DuBois' *The Quest of the Silver Fleece* is a good novel but it does not measure up to *The Souls of Black Folk* and *Darkwater.* There are many passages of fine writing in it, but it lacks the touch of genius, lacks the spontaneity and naturalness which characterizes a great novel.

Mrs. Sarah Fleming's *Hope's Highway* is a clever story covering 110 pages. The plot is interesting. The characters stand out vividly and the story has life and movement. It deals with the strivings of an ambitious colored youth, who escapes from the chain gang, rescues his patroness from a fire, completes his education in Oxford, figures conspicuously in the World War and returns to the southland to educate his people.

Chesnutt's *The Conjure Woman, The Wife of His Youth* and *The House Behind the Cedars* gave him a deserved popularity. But most of the novels by Negro writers lack originality. They go over a ground which has been raked with a fine-tooth comb by white writers and write in the style and manner of white writers.

Mr. Henry Downing of New York City is writing *Songhay: An African Tale,* the scene of which is laid on the soil of Africa. It pictures the civilization of Timbucktu and the Songhay people during the Middle Ages. The tale hinges around "The Sacred Jar," which was given to Mohamed Askia and handed down by him to his descendants. It sustained the same relation to the Songhay people that the Ark of the Covenant did to the Children of Israel. The story tells of the plans of the Emperor of Morocco to obtain the Sacred Jar.

As Mr. Downing has lived many years in Africa and traveled widely in Africa, his story ought to have an African coloring and be a real African tale. His Liberian romance, *The American Cavalryman,* and his play, "The Arabian Lover," were praised by Matheson Lang, John Drinkwater, the late Herbert Tree and by British periodicals. One periodical said of "The Arabian Lover":—"The play is a by no means a slavish copy of a tale from the 'Thousand and One Nights,' but one of extremely original treatment—the author has evidently steeped himself in Oriental lore—and of dignified diction almost Shakespearean." This tribute shows that Mr. Downing is capable of giving us an African Tale which will be characterized by originality and individuality.

The novel has been a potent method of arousing the public conscience. Harriet Beecher Stowe's *Uncle Tom's Cabin* won more converts to the slave's cause than did the brilliant addresses of Sumner, Phillips and Douglass and the forceful editorials of Garrison. Novels which can powerfully picture the civilization of Africa during the Middle Ages, novels which can powerfully envisage the struggles of an aspiring Negro in a hostile Anglo-Saxon civilization will undoubtedly add to the prestige and standing of the Negro race. What Alexander Dumas did for France, what Sir Walter Scott did for Scotland, it is to be hoped that a Negro novelist will do for Africa and for the Negro in western lands.

But the question can be asked, Can a Negro scale the heights in novel writing? When we reflect that Alexander Dumas, the celebrated French novelist was one-fourth Negro and that his son, the playwright, and Poushkin, the famous Russian poet had a strong strain of Negro blood coursing through their veins, the answer is at hand. It would not surprise us to see within the next ten years a novel by a Negro picturing the Negro as he was in the past and is today which will grip the world by reason of its powerful plot, vivid characters, brilliant descriptions and masterful style.

African Language and Literature Make For African Nationality

Unsigned Editorial (1923)

It is a very generally accepted fact that a common habitat, language and religion make for a homogeneous people and a distinct nationality. An Italian philosopher laid this as law, and there can be no reasonable appeal from it. We have not seen the question discussed with a livelier sense of its application to the African people than in an article by a native African, signing himself "Ahinnana," published in our esteemed contemporary, the *Gold Coast Leader*, of October 20, and which we reproduce in another column of *The Negro World* today, under the caption, "African Nationality in Language and Literature."

Mr. Ahinnana, in discussing the "opinion of some, that the West African should neglect the cultivation of his language and adopt English for every day use, and also discard the use of his national customs even on suitable occasions," reaches the conclusion that "it has got to be remembered that the soul of a people is its language, and that once that is destroyed its inspiration is gone. There are certain modes of thought and depth of feeling which a Fanti, for example, can never express in any other way save in his own language." He very wisely concludes that "we shall be committing national suicide if, as a people, we lose any opportunity of preserving our language and developing a literature of our own." But a real clarion note is the following: "Don't you make a mistake—the soul of a people is its language, and to ape others is to be denationalized."

Mr. Ahinnana hopes that soon "there will be chairs in our universities for the proper study and cultivation of Fanti, Hausa and Yoruba as standard African languages." We consider this a very thoughtful and forward looking view of the question. The learned Americans and Europeans find it difficult to so master a language not their own as to catch the full spirit, feeling and meaning of it and reflect these in their conversation and in translations. Our great missionary associations could adopt generally the policy of teaching the people in their native language by first mastering it themselves and reducing it to a system, where this has not already been done, as well as teaching the people the industrial arts as the safest and surest way to conserve and develop their economic values and the productive resources of their country, this policy having already been adopted by some of our denominations working in the African field.

On the Convention's Agenda: Proposed History of Black Literature

Unsigned Editorial (1922)

One of the things that should be brought up at the August convention of the Universal Negro Improvement Association is the commissioning of a Negro scholar to write a comprehensive history of Negro literature. To those who cannot appreciate what this means, the suggestion may seem trite, even irrelevant; but nevertheless there is no denying the timeliness of it. Mr. Benjamin Brawley has written a very fine book on *The Negro in Art and Literature,* but it only scratches the surface of the subject. It tells in a very statistical way of the literary achievements of Phillis Wheatley, Paul Laurence Dunbar, Charles W. Chesnutt, W. E. B. DuBois, Wm. H. Ferris and others. On the other hand, James Weldon Johnson's *Book of American Negro Poetry* is open to a great deal of criticism in that it is not a very fair interpretation of the poets mentioned. Even Dunbar is not seen at his best, nor, as Mr. Arthur Schomburg informs us, does it include all the really worthwhile Negro poets between Phillis Wheatley and Paul Laurence Dunbar. The work in question must not be a mere jumble of names and dates and benefactors' titles, but a critical interpretation of the authors studied—the kind of interpretation George Brandes gives of Shakespeare. Indeed, the task as we see it is a monumental one, and explains in a way why most Negro graduates of leading American universities devote their lives to sociological and anthropological studies. The field is untouched. To the world the Negro is yet an enigma.

In the realm of Negro history alone there is a prodigious lot that is not known, and that, too, ought to come in for its share of attention. But this is the time for a shaft of light on the subject of Negro Literature. It is the psychological moment. At present the tide is in our favor and we ought to capitalize on it. Not only are the writings of white men about Negroes the subject of profound interest, but also the writings of Negroes themselves. It would, therefore, be a worthy task to trace its origin and development. We sincerely trust that some far-seeing delegate may bring the matter up at the convention.

3

On Batouala

Unlike most literary and scholarly publications, which review a book but once, the Negro World *placed no limit on its examination of works it considered important. René Maran's* Batouala: A True Black Novel *(1921) was an outstanding case in point. Maran, a Black Martiniquan, burst upon the international literary scene when* Batouala *was awarded the Goncourt Prize for the best French novel of 1921.*

Maran's novel was set in Ubangui Shari (now the Central African Republic). Maran himself had lived in Africa as an official in the French colonial service. He thus brought an unusual blend of perspectives to his novel. As a Black West Indian he could, presumably, empathize—to some extent at least—with the culture and anti-imperialist sentiments of the Africans. As a French colonial official, he could view with dispassion, perhaps even with a measure of disdain, the technologically backward aspects of his subjects' environments.

Perhaps because of Maran's own peculiar dual perspective, his work harbored an enigmatic quality. The commentators, even within the Negro World, *were not agreed as to whether it was a propaganda novel or not. Eric D. Walrond in "Batouala, Art and Propaganda," seems somewhat confused. William H. Ferris in "The Significance of René Maran" and "World's Ten Greatest Novels" sees Maran as representing the type of propaganda he prefers—subtle and understated, and embodied in a first-rate work of art. Yet Ferris, too, is not without confusion, for he bemoans the absence of an idealized Batouala, a circumstance which would doubtless have made it more difficult for Maran to maintain the subtlety of propaganda that Ferris claimed to see in the work.*

Alain Locke's "The Colonial Literature of France" was one of the longest pieces of literary criticism ever published in the Negro World. *Locke was a major mentor of the Harlem Renaissance and is best known for his anthology on* The New Negro *(1925). Several of the* Negro World's *writers were included in this work. Locke himself was a close friend of John Edward Bruce, a* Negro World *editor. Bruce's Negro Society for Historical Research sponsored his trip to Europe and Egypt in 1923, the same year that the present article appeared.*

Locke, unlike Walrond and Ferris, saw in Batouala *a case of art for its own sake. Yet he, too, felt the need to qualify his judgement. For he saw Maran as the great inaugurator of a move away from condescension and worse in French colonial literature—certainly a propaganda victory, if Locke's analysis was correct.*

Batouala, Art and Propaganda

Eric D. Walrond (1922)

Ernest Boyd in the *Literary Review* criticizes the judges who awarded the coveted "Prix Goncourt" to René Maran, the Martiniquan Negro, whose *Batouala* they adjudged the best French novel of the year. Tied to the conventions of literature, Boyd found too many African words in the book; it is replete with crotchets and quavers and demi semi-quavers. Ignoring the rules of rhetoric, the author plunges along at a desperate rate, forgetful of the landmarks of style, form, clarity. With all these things Mr. Boyd finds fault. Also, he sniffs at the introduction to the work, which is a carping, merciless indictment of the brutal colonial system of France. As far as Mr. Boyd can see, what on earth has all this to do with a work of art, a penetrating study of a savage chieftain? Incidentally, Mr. James Weldon Johnson throws a ray of light on the subject. Mr. Johnson tells us there is a tendency on the part of Negro poets to be propagandic. For this reason it is going to be very difficult for the American Negro poet to create a lasting work of art. He must first purge himself of the feelings and sufferings and emotions of an outraged being, and think and write along colorless sectionless lines. Hate, rancor, vituperation—all these things he must cleanse himself of. But is this possible? The Negro, for centuries to come, will never be able to divorce himself from the feeling that he has not had a square deal from the rest of mankind. His music is a piercing, yelping cry against his cruel enslavement. What little he has accomplished in the field of literature is confined to the life he knows best—the life of the underdog in revolt. So far he has ignored the most potent form of literary expression, the form that brought Maran the Goncourt award. When he does take it up, it is not going to be in any half-hearted, wishy manner, but straight from the shoulder, slashing, murdering, disemboweling! In the manner of H. L. Mencken!

The Significance of René Maran

William H. Ferris (1922)

Exposing the soul of the Congo, Batouala, the bitter Negro novel which has won the Goncourt prize for 1921 in Paris, gives a stark and lurid transcript of the passionate, unfettered life of the primitive Africans, and with compelling power presents a pulsing melodrama of a suppressed barbaric people.

These are the striking words which headline Mr. Herbert I. Seligman's [article] in the magazine section to the *New York World* for February 20. Like his critical analysis of Marcus Garvey in the same paper a few weeks ago, Mr. Seligman paints the commendable traits of the Negro in soft, subdued tints and his barbaric side in bright red colors. He puts the diminuendo on the Negro's good qualities and the crescendo on his bad qualities. (Perhaps he does so for dramatic effects.) But Mr. Seligman's article is not our theme, but only the text for departure.

René Maran and his famous novel, *Batouala,* is the theme for this week's editorial. As the novel is written in French and as we are not a French scholar we have never been fortunate enough to read it and cannot make a comparative study of it. We do not know whether it will rank with Dumas' *Three Musketeers,* Victor Hugo's *Les Misérables,* Scott's *Ivanhoe,* Bulwer Lytton's *Last Days of Pompeii,* Thackeray's *Vanity Fair,* Dickens' *Tale of Two Cities,* George Eliot's *Adam Bede,* Gen. Lew Wallace's *Ben-Hur,* Hawthorne's *Scarlet Letter* and Harriet Beecher Stowe's *Uncle Tom's Cabin* as among the great novels. Its significance for us resides in the fact that a Negro novelist startled the world by winning the coveted Goncourt prize for the best French novel of the year. Not only did daily newspapers give him big headlines, but magazines like the *Current Opinion* for March printed his photograph and devoted over two pages to the Negro author. By sheer force of genius René Maran succeeded, like Poushkin, Alexandre Dumas père and Samuel Coleridge Taylor, in transcending the limitations of race and color. As such his career ought to be an inspiration to men and women of color everywhere. It indicates that in the world of letters, art, music and science the coloring matter in the pigment cells is no handicap to a man if the light of genius shines through the soul.

The Innovation

What is remarkable in René Maran's novel, *Batouala,* winning the Goncourt prize is that the book won the approval of the French critics even though it arraigned French colonial rule in Africa and indicted Caucasian reign in the Dark Continent.

Now this in an innovation. Usually when a man of color writes a book, a magazine article or delivers an address it is not rated by the Caucasian world according to its philosophic, scientific, historical or literary value, but according as it does or does not represent the Caucasian's estimate of the Negro's place in the scale of creation.

We recall that one Negro historian was criticized a few years ago because he glorified the Negro and another Negro historian was commended by a New York paper because he did not discuss the delicate question of the civil and political status of the Negro. But such was not the case with René Maran. When Dr. Henri de Regnier took *Batouala* to a publisher and when Monsieur Manoel Galusto brought it to the attention of the Academie Goncourt they were not rating the novel in relation to its accordance or lack of accordance with French colonial policy but according to its literary value.

René Maran won the "much-coveted Goncourt prize" through producing a work of pure literature. Mr. T. R. Ybarra, writing in the *New York Times,* says that the description of a dance "reveals René Maran not only as one with a remarkable fund of original first-hand knowledge of the Negroes of whom he writes, but also a writer with a Zolaesque capacity for parading details of filth and degradation and brutality! His realism is unbounded; at times he goes to lengths before which even the most extreme of modern French writers might hesitate. On the other hand, he draws pictures of the African wilderness, creates an atmosphere of vast spaces and silence and mystery which recall W. H. Hudson at his best. And always, even when his Africans are dancing and reveling at their maddest, he succeeds in suggesting the unhappiness that besets them—the sword of Damocles which the white man holds suspended over their heads."

Maran will go down in literary history as a striking exponent of realism in literature, for he has an artist's touch in painting in lurid colors.

Batouala Not a Propaganda Novel

But although René Maran in his preface and in the words of Batouala and Batouala's father launches a forceful indictment of French colonial policy in Africa, *Batouala* is not a propaganda novel in the sense of presenting the Negro in a favorable light. It is a vivid picture, naked and unadorned, of the barbaric life and the degradation of semi-savages in the interior of Africa.

What Maran has given is not a picture of the African as he might become, but an envisagement of the African as he actually is in some portions of his native land. But we have no quarrel with Mr. Maran because he gave us a work of art instead of a sermon or essay in the guise of a novel. Novels, plays and poems with a conscious purpose usually fail of their desired effect. The novel and play should unfold itself naturally as a story. The poem should well up spontaneously from the soul depths of the inspired seer. There should be no straining for effect, no overanxiety to preach a sermon, point a moral and teach a lesson. Then the novel, play or poem will bring its message as a novel, play or poem.

Realism and Impressionalism in Art

A quarter of a century ago the novels of Emile Zola caused realism in literature to be a burning question. A quarter of a century ago cultured people crowded the Yale Art Building to hear La Farge lecture on realism and impressionalism in art. Then the question was asked, "Who is truer to nature—the writer who describes things as he actually sees them or the writer who idealizes, the painter who paints things as they actually are or the painter who idealizes?"

Realistic art is art, but idealized art is higher art. The greatness, grandeur and glory of Homer, Virgil, Dante, Milton, Goethe and Shakespeare reside in the fact that they not only saw the petty and sordid details of the actual, but that their large imaginations transcended the real and transfigured it in the divine light of the ideal. The magic spell of Homer's *Iliad* and *Odyssey* resides in the fact that they not only faithfully portray Greek life in the Homeric days, showing how men actually lived in those days, but because they idealized Grecian warriors and presented real heroes in Achilles, Patrocles, Diomedes, Ajax, Hector and Ulysses; a real beauty in Helen and real heroines in Andromache and Penelope, and sang of the glories of the Grecian skies, sea and land at the same time. The beauty and power of Tennyson's famous lines about "the flower in the crannied wall" reside in the fact that

Tennyson sees in "the flower in the crannied wall" something more than a mere flower.

This is the function of the imagination. It takes the material presented by the senses, takes perceptions and memory images, takes sights and sounds of nature and human life and combines and enlarges upon them so that it gives us a new creation. The imagination is a magic wand that touches plain homely things and causes them to take on new beauty and meaning.

Maran is a great artist, a great word painter, but he would be a greater artist if he saw the African not only as he actually is but as it is possible for him to become—the raw stuff and raw material out of which manhood is made.

Vision

We are told in the Scriptures, "Where there is no wisdom the people perish." Take Jesus of Nazareth, the Master Mind of the Bible. He saw poor, unlettered fishermen casting down their nets into the sea, and he saw the possibilities of their becoming fishers of men. He saw Matthew, the publican, sitting down and receiving taxes, and He saw that Matthew was capable of something nobler than remaining an extortionate tax collector. He saw the prodigal son living among the swine and eating their food, and saw that a higher and noble life was possible for him. He saw the lillies of field, not as mere waving lillies, but as arrayed in garments of beauty which surpassed the glittering raiment of Solomon. In that resided the magic power of Christianity in the early days. It taught that no matter how sunk a man was in vice and degradation he was still a child of God, created in the Divine image. There was still a divine spark within him. It was still possible for him to throw off the shackles of sin and walk in the newness of a redeemed life. And that is all there is in the Christian doctrine of regeneration and conversion.

And while we doff our hats to René Maran as a master psychologist and a master artist; while his achievement of breaking across the color line and winning the Goncourt prize will be immortalized in literary history, we regret that the brilliant young author did not see in some of those African children a future Mohammed Askia, Toussaint l'Ouverture, Paul Cuffee, Sir William Conrad Reeves, Frederick Douglass, Booker T. Washington, Paul Laurence Dunbar, Dusé Mohamed, Bishop A. J. Crowther, John Mensah Sarbah, Casely Hayford, K. Aggrey or Oreshatukeh Faduma.

Though the African at home and abroad may be sick of an intellectual palsy, it is still possible for him to rise, take up his bed and walk, still possible for him to not only master every detail of twentieth century civilization, but also to make a contribution of his own to civilization. Between the enervating effect of the heat of the tropics and the oppressive hand of the European, the

African is frequently crushed between the upper and the nether millstones. Thus far the African as a whole has felt the baleful rather than the beneficent effects of civilization. If Maran's novel should be the means of causing the European nations to adopt a more liberal colonial policy in Africa, at no distant day we may see the beginnings of another Ethiopia and another Timbuctoo.

World's Ten Greatest Novels
Why René Maran's *Batouala*
Won Goncourt Prize;
Novels For Propaganda

William H. Ferris (1922)

In the editorial on "Pushkin and Dumas," Mr. Eric Walrond, one of the members of the editorial staff of *The Negro World,* wrote: "At a time when so much is being said about Negro fiction it is well to note that fiction—that is, good fiction—must steer clear of propaganda. In his preface to *Batouala,* René Maran speaks of the utter objectivity of his book and also of a forthcoming work which he is at present engaged on and which will be entirely subjective. In other words, if he had tried to overwhelm the world with ideas on the brutality of French rule in equatorial Africa there would have been no *Batouala.* Still, if a Negro, paraphrasing Allen Wilson Porterfield, had written *Uncle Tom's Cabin* there is no telling where the race would be today."

To my mind this sums up the position that I maintained in my chapter on "The American Negro's Contribution to Literature" in *The African Abroad* nine years ago. This raises the question, "What is there wrong in propaganda fiction?"

The Ten Greatest Novels

Twelve years ago last spring a contest was launched by a Boston newspaper for the purpose of awarding prizes to those who selected the world's ten greatest novels. The committee of judges, consisting of noted college professors, authors and editors, decided upon the following as the world's ten greatest novels:

The Three Musketeers, by Alexandre Dumas; *Les Misérables,* by Victor Hugo; *Ivanhoe,* by Sir Walter Scott; *The Last Days of Pompeii,* by Lord Bulwer-Lytton; *Ben-Hur,* by General Lew Wallace; *Uncle Tom's Cabin,* by Harriet Beecher Stowe; *The Scarlet Letter,* by Nathaniel Hawthorne; *Adam Bede,* by George Elliot; *Vanity Fair,* by William Thackeray; *A Tale of Two Cities,* by Charles Dickens.

Passers-By, Homo Sum, Hypatia, Prussias, Quintus Claudius, The Gladiator, Barabbas and *Scottish Chiefs* impressed me as much as some of the selected ten. If a list were made out today possibly a novel of H. G. Wells or Hall Caine would get in the fortunate ten, and possibly not. In the totality of his work Balzac was wonderful. But there was no one particular novel of his that swept the English-speaking world.

A careful survey of the novels indicates that five of them—*The Three Musketeers, Ivanhoe, The Last Days of Pompeii, Ben-Hur* and *Uncle Tom's Cabin*—show that besides the adventures and love affairs of the greater and lesser heroes and heroines these novels are descriptive presentations of dramatic epochs of human history. The first tells of the glory of the court of Louis XIV of France and Cardinal Richelieu, with intrigues of states. The second pictures chivalry during the Middle Ages and breathes the spirit of that period. The third pictures the autumnal splendor of the Roman civilization. The fourth gives a wonderfully vivid picture of American civilization.

Of the remaining five novels, two—*Les Misérables* and *Vanity Fair*—brilliantly describe the Battle of Waterloo. Victor Hugo's is probably the world's greatest battle picture. Two—*Adam Bede* and *The Scarlet Letter*—not only give psychological analysis of human souls, but envisage the moral condition of the age of the heroes and heroines around whom the story centers.

Why René Maran's *Batouala* Won the Goncourt Prize

Now on a smaller scale the René Maran novel, *Batouala,* possesses the qualities which made *The Three Musketeers, Ivanhoe, The Last Days of Pompeii, Ben-Hur* and *Uncle Tom's Cabin* famous. The plot centers around a love romance. The favorite wife of Batouala, an African king, falls in love with a young and handsome Don Juan. But *Batouala* does more than unfold a love affair. It gives a realistic pen picture of primitive native life in a tropical jungle. The dance, the hunt and natural scenery show the touch of a realistic artist. Incidentally the oppression and injustice of Caucasian rule and French colonial policy are brought out.

And here is where *Batouala* differs from a propaganda novel per se, although it has a powerful propaganda effect. René Maran's ideas of the harshness and severity of French rule in equatorial Africa are not consciously forced upon the reader, but are revealed naturally in the course of the story. And here is where Maran's genius as a story teller shines superbly.

Novels for Propaganda

During the past year I have read a novel which will soon be published and a play which will some day be staged by Negro writers whose theme is the "eternal" race question. In the novel the plot centers around two colored girls, a colored man and a wealthy white artist. The white artist seduces a beautiful colored girl who posed for him. She, in revenge, slashes the picture and then commits suicide. The artist goes crazy, and the colored man she was once engaged to falls in love with and marries a noble colored girl. In the play the plot centers around the attempt of a Southern aristocrat to first seduce and then kidnap a beautiful and cultured colored girl, both of which attempts were frustrated.

Now, this novel and this play are powerful and dramatic in parts. They have wonderful possibilities. But this is where they fall short of *Batouala* and the great novels that I have mentioned. Evidently the phase of the race question that impressed the novelist and playwright most was the quest of some white men for pretty colored girls. But here is where the propaganda purpose partly defeats itself. After reading the first few chapters one could tell what the outcome would be. And the charm and fascination of a real story is that you don't know how it will end. And you read with breathless interest and are held spellbound because you don't know how it will end.

Then, again, the lure of sex which attracts some white men toward comely black, brown and yellow women is only one phase of the interrelation between blacks and whites in the Western Hemisphere, and a novel or play which hinges around this lure of sex only presents a fragmentary instead of a complete picture of the strivings of men and women of color in a hostile environment, and hence lacks the perspective and breadth of views of *The Three Musketeers, The Last Days of Pompeii, Ivanhoe, Ben-Hur* and *Uncle Tom's Cabin.*

Then, again, if Alexandre Dumas Père, Lord Bulwer-Lytton, Gen. Lew Wallace and Harriet Beecher Stowe were handling that love episode they would make it a side show instead of the main show of the story; make it a smaller incidental plot instead of the main theme.

There is nothing wrong in a propaganda novel or play per se. *Ben-Hur, Uncle Tom's Cabin* and *The Scarlet Letter* show how powerful propaganda can be woven into a story. But there is always this danger of a propaganda story or play—the novelist or playwright is liable to be swayed too much by his personal feelings and prejudices, to overemphasize the particular situation or problem that weighs upon his mind and oppresses his spirit, and hence he will present not the picture in its totality, but a fragment of the picture.

A safe rule to follow would be to weave the propaganda into the thread of the narrative instead of making it the fiber and texture out of which the story itself is woven.

The Complete Picture

We once met a talented young Negro writer, who had written a brilliant book on the Negro question in the form of a semi-novel, which white publishers were loath to publish.

It was designed to arouse sympathy for a Negro struggling for the higher life, but it was written from the standpoint of a partisan rather than a philosopher. The book did not even perfectly reflect the author's own experience. In his own experience white men as well as colored men had given him a helping hand and in his own experience colored men as well as white men had put stumbling blocks in his way. The result was that the book, which was, on the whole, scholarly, and, in parts, brilliant, was not exactly true to nature, not a complete picture of a Negro psychically reacting upon his environment.

The painter who will really interpret nature must not only paint the plains and the trees, but also the sky and the clouds, the hills and winding brooks. As he views a wonderful scene from a hilltop in Stockbridge, Mass., he may paint a splendid painting of the beautiful town of Stockbridge, but it will not be a perfect view of the Berkshire Hills unless the river and the plains beyond, which rise into the thickly wooded hills, are also included.

We find this completeness, this sense of fullness, in Homer, Shakespeare, *The Three Musketeers, The Last Days of Pompeii, Ben-Hur, Ivanhoe* and *Uncle Tom's Cabin.* And we need this completeness, this sense of fullness in the Negro novelist and Negro sociologist. What they often give is a powerful presentation of a section of the picture, a powerful reproduction of the segment of a circle, when the world calls for the presentation of the complete picture and the reproduction of the full circle.

The colored writers have a difficult task before them. The weight of race prejudice bears so heavily down upon them; the shoe of caste proscription pinches them so hard that it is almost impossible for them to get in a calm, judicial frame of mind and write dispassionately. A man tossed about and battered in the storm and stress of life and crucible of experience can not easily assume the philosophic point of view and write with the detachment of a disinterested spectator. He is in the combat. He feels the blows, the strain on muscles and sinews. He gets wearied; he pants and gasps for breath. And when we read the impassioned work of a colored novelist, playwright or scholar we must remember that we are not reading the works of a leisurely philosopher, smoking his pipe in peace and comfort, but of a man engaged in a struggle and race which taxes his mental, moral and physical energies to the utmost.

Still, just as the Heroic Age of Greece produced its Homer, just as the Middle Ages produced its Dante, just as medieval chivalry produced its Walter Scott and just as the anti-slavery movement produced its orator in Wendell Phillips and its writer in Harriet Beecher Stowe, who gave classic expression to the slaves' longing for freedom, so, I believe, the present tense, delicate and complicated race situation and race inter-relation today will produce a novelist who, with his pen, and the poet, who with his verse, will measure up to the demands of the occasion as Frederick Douglass, the orator, did with his voice fifty, sixty and seventy years ago.

The vision of God and the seeing of human life *sub specie aeternitatis* will assist in giving the Negro writer perspective and breadth of vision.

The Colonial Literature of France

Alain Locke (1923)

France is developing a new colonial literature for which no allowances and apologies need be made and to which no discounts or correctives need be applied—for she is developing—indeed she has already developed a new point of view in the portrayal of the African native and his life. Colonial fiction has been for generations now a synonym for provincialism and second-rate aesthetic values. Rarely has it even attempted to be fair and humane, scarcely ever has it achieved pure artistry or sterling humanism. And only in the novel of local color has the colonial scene come into the hands of the masters. There was both in England and France a promising flare when the cult of romantic exoticism turned toward the South Seas and the Tropics, but the paths of Pierre Loti and Conrad, unfortunately for the portrayal of American life, turned to farther, more exotic, ports and left Africa to the exploiting charlatans, the incompetent romancers, and the moralistic missionaries. And from these tainted or inartistic sources, what is known as "colonial literature" has sprung.

But in France not only is there developing a new colonial literature that is the portrayal in fiction of widely divergent human cultures. In other forms of art and art appreciation, aesthetic cosmopolitanism has been achieved, but fiction has always seemed to reflect the narrower, more stunted values, and to have absorbed the worst provincialisms and prejudices of the Caucasian and European bias. However emancipated the elite, the masses will never respond to the broader view until it expresses itself in the forms of the popular taste and the arts of the masses. Thus the importance, the peculiar social importance, of a broadening view in drama and fiction—the popular arts. When they begin to reflect cosmopolitan humanism, then to the wakeful eye the great day of humanity almost dawns. And whatever else may be said of it, René Maran's *Batouala* and its tremendous vogue are very largely responsible for this change, at least with respect to contemporary fiction. Before Maran, it was either landscape with the native incidentally thrown in as a conventionalized figure, or the life of the white colonial with the native life as an artistic foil. Even more so than in the American school of fiction was the native in colonial literature merely a dark note by which the false high-lights of the painting were keyed up; or as General Anglonvant aptly puts it—"In most of the novels, the Negro plays but a secondary part—appearing only to enhance the interest of the story by acting as a foil to the European characters described in the romance or drama." But a revolutionary change has occurred—there is a strong interest in the human portraiture of native life in and for itself, and without the bold realism of *Batouala* this never would have been. For, however rife this point of view may have been among artists and authors, without the creation of a new taste in the reading public it could never have come to public expression. But the public mind, with its predilection for fake and lurid chromos, by this brilliant, daring etching of Maran's has been, so to speak, resurfaced for a new impression, at once more artistic and true. With the stylistic capacities of a Flaubert or a de Maupassant, Maran seems almost to have chosen to be the Zola of colonial literature, and with cruel realism and cutting irony has sought to drive the lie and hypocrisy out of its traditional point of view. It was heroic work—and required to be done by the Negro himself—this revolutionary change from sentimentality to realism, from caricature to portraiture. And if I am not very mistaken, Maran's real thrust is more anti-romantic and anti-sentimentalist than anti-imperialist; it is the literary traducers whom he would annihilate. Let us have the unbiased truth and the same angle of vision for all; that is Maran's literary creed.

Gaston-Joseph's *Koffi* is written from quite another point of view—more humane, less objective—it is by its sponsor, General Anglonvant, ex-governor-general of the Colonies, characterized as an antidote for *Batouala*. It is an important book, in itself—as the winner of the Grand Prix de Litérature

Coloniale for 1923, and as reflecting the more enlightened official colonial attitude. Not any too well translated in the English version this romance in the original is a smooth, competent, restrained narrative, the work of Gaston-Joseph, a French colonial official whose fifteen years' of service in Senegal, on the Ivory Coast, in the Cameroons, Gaboon and the Middle Congo and whose authorship of a splendid monograph on *La Côte d'Ivoire* (1917) guarantee competence and sincerity. Koffi is the outstanding figure. All else, colonial officialdom, wife, natives, nature, are but so much background for this sober, full-length portrait of the man as a lad, a village runaway, at the coast in turn scullion-apprentice, house-boy, cook, trusted dragonman to M. Lere, colonial administrator, and finally as a climax to a seemingly successful career, through merit and his good offices, interpreter and chief of the Assonefanti. But at the height of his career comes sudden decline of fortune—caught midway in his efforts at tribal reform between reactionary factions of the medicine-men and the inroads of disease, Koffi succumbs to the environment—and passes, a discredited and deported exile, to a docile, resigned end in the Gaboons.

It is an unprofitable life, but not an unprofitable story. Many of the peculiarly difficult forces in the life of the native engaged in government service and living in the penumbra of the two civilizations are for the first time realistically and truthfully depicted. This psychological borderland of civilization has its special types and its peculiar problems, and Koffi is one of the best available ways of exploring it. But we cannot quite share the enthusiasm of General Anglonvant in hailing Koffi as "filling a void in our tropical colonial literature," for the book seems really to be of greater documentary than artistic interest and worth. Humane, conscientiously attempting to free itself from the attitude of condescension, with a painfully strained realism, it is throughout a laudable effort, and in part a success. Nowhere is the book more successful in breaking through its limitations than in the account of Koffi's love affair and eventual marriage with Afone, become in the interim of his absence the mistress of Mr. Martin, the white trader. It is a brilliant bit of writing, in which French literature excels by virtue of its combined candor and subtlety—the woman, torn between love and gain, facing the certainty of motherhood; the two men, each uncomfortably screened behind his tribal idols, jealousy and respectability, awaiting in concealed but genuine rivalry the riddle of paternity which only Nature could solve. And fate, that has eventually to be so cruel, awards Koffi a son, and it must be said a hereafter faithful spouse. Koffi's is a life of social but not of moral defeat; in this, I think, it is typical of his unfortunate but inevitable compeers—the buffer class between the black and white. What a conflict it is, especially for the half-educated mind, to strain between the forces of two powerful but incommensurable cultures, to be forced to live in terms of two compelling but incompatible systems of habit and thought. Koffi's defeat is not taken lightly by the author, however it may be by the superficial reader, nor by General Anglonvant when he says: "Where our duty and our will combine to try to lead the peoples confided to our guardianship toward higher social conditions, by creating a picked body of natives to act as leaders and cultivating their development, how many powerful secret forces oppose our actions! The description of the new king's life, a target for the attacks of the witch doctors, opposed by all the representatives of an ignorant past, is all the more striking because of the enforced restraint of a style which nevertheless evokes so many sights familiar to colonials."

Another remarkable book, also with a noteworthy preface, is *Samba Diouf's Adventure,* by the popular romancers Jean and Jerome Tharand. Among their popular successes the brothers Tharand seem to have turned aside to an unusually mature purpose, and, for all that their accustomed "purple patches" turn up occasionally, give us a very vivid and accurate and tasteful chronicle of the life of Samba Diouf and his great but unexpected adventure to the battlefields of Europe. This book makes one peculiarly regretful that as yet no artistic narrative of the very peculiar war experience of the American Negro in France has been written. Painful as the contrast might be, such a companion picture must eventually be painted, and for the double purpose of inspiring it and of revealing the French version of the Negro in arms I have asked permission to translate *La Rondonnée de Samba Diouf.* Already in its eleventh edition, the work has promise of very considerable vogue, and it deserves it, not merely as the romance of Samba Diouf, but because there in the background, not over obtrusive but still quite real, looms the epic of the 113th Black Battalion.

The book is dedicated to André Demaison in these charming words: "Few have penetrated the psychology of the West African native as yourself. From the Niger to the coast, from Senegal to Gambia, you have mastered subtle tongues and learned their curious folkways. In their villages, deep in the bush and forest, you have passed years and years, living their life; you have ridden at large with them, navigated their vast rivers; wandered from lake to lake in their long canoes or by motor launch, hearing their palavers day in and day out; and when they came to fight on our shores you followed fortune in one of their battalions. And all this vast treasury of the people and ways of Africa you have prodigally shared with us that we might write this story, woven out of the fragments of your talk, and to render it more true to life you have furnished a thousand details, now from the speech of the Ouloof, now from that of the Mandingoes, which are to you as familiar as your native Perigord.

"'Only—my friend, your blacks talk like academicians,'"—we had constantly to be saying to you—to which you have always answered—'Good heavens—what would you have me do? I give you their words as they speak them. If their speech is subtle and rich and full of fine shadings, that simply reveals the speech of the Ouloof, [who are obviously] not quite the brutes that a mediocre colonial literature has been pleased to paint them. These blacks could not speak as they do but for a background of civilization which, however simple it is, is nevertheless a civilization.'

"In his true dignity as a man of his people, may Samba Diouf bear favorable witness for his race."

This is the story of a simple Dakar fisherman, premier craftsman in his calling, who, on the verge of a successful courting, sets out through the jungle to bring back from the distant land of his mother the patrimony of cattle left him by his mother's brother. He reaches a village of the Mandingo just as they are being called upon for their quota of conscripts for the French colonial army, and at the end of a palmwine debauch recovers himself bound with thongs on the way to Mauso, an unwilling substitute for the scheming chieftain's son. Here he is enrolled and eventually embarked for France in a heterogeneous battalion of all the races of the French coast hinterland and Soudan. We are transported with them in rapid impressionistic word pictures, the best of which, with the possible exception of some brilliant sketches of the jungle, are those of the camp scenes of the black troops behind the lines. Their native contests, their hardships, their illnesses, their daily chatter are a triumph of descriptive art. And then occurs and incident which, regrettably, is exceptionally French. The men—hunters, traders, tillers of the soil, warriors—chafe under the "slave work" to which they have been assigned. They naively want to see the war and manfully want to bear it. Lamine Cissé, with the corporals of four companies, is commissioned to take their plaints to the adjutant. The adjutant listens—there is logic, there is sincerity, there is courage—he reports to the commandant—the commandant to the colonel, he in turn to the brigadier—and then happens what in the English or American army would have been a miracle—in three days the battalion is ordered to the firing line.

It is Samba Diouf's fortune to be gallantly wounded in the first assault attack, and then the story follows his fortunes—his hospital experiences, the naive letters from home, one with the disquieting shadow of gossip about the fidelity of his betrothed—his patient, good-natured convalescence, his decoration with the croix de guerre, and finally, after three years in all, his transhipment home by way of the country of his mother, where he expects at last to come into possession of the cattle he started out to fetch. There also fate awaits him—in cunning chicanery his uncle palms off on him the oldest and sterile animals of his herd; a hurricane in crossing a river carries off the greater part of the paltry flock; but another ordeal awaits. The feast of the homecoming is spoiled by the suspicious absence of Yanima and her father, and finally comes the disillusioning confirmation of old rumors as he encounters her next day with her nursing infant. And then, robbed of his occupation by his wounds, dependent solely on his government pension, disillusioned—there seems a likelihood of a total breakdown in his life—and the native African stoicism seizes happiness out of the ruins, as he goes to Yanima, he without patrimony, she without honor, but for each the more necessary to the other for all that. There is an Enoch Arden and almost idyllic charm to the story, for all that there is a true epic in the background; the night of his homecoming, his battalion and his compatriots go "over the top," and even a sophisticated reader reads the last lines through a moist, old-fashioned blur which is, after all, I suppose, the acid test of romance.

Notable as these books are, they lose something when contrasted with *Batouala,* with which indeed must be contrasted all colonial fiction of this decade. They are, the one condescendingly, the other sentimentally, more favorable—they will both be more liked and preferred by the average man. But they lack the great artistry, the daring objectivity, and more than that they leave the great dilemma of colonial imperialism concealed behind the cloaks of optimism and rhetoric. *Batouala* gains its universality of appeal and interest and its greater artistic validity from the very fact of its candor, its ruthlessness, and its humane but emotional human portraiture. Instead of reenforcing that decadent cult of the primitive which is the pastime of the sophisticated, René Maran insists upon treating the dilemma of the primitive life of Africa of today as it stands between the stagnant virtues of simplicity and the corrupting half-civilization of exploiting economic imperialism. The message—and there is one, for all that is not preached into the story, is this: "If you insist upon civilizing, civilize on the pattern of good virtues and not on the scheme of your vices. Do not discredit your civilization at its core; only as it is sound there, is it sound 'at home.'" There scarcely has been a more forceful indictment of the defects of expansive European civilization than the mute gestures, the sad reproach and the shrewd commentary of these simple folk of Ubangi-Shari. With this creed, René Maran enters the lists neither of the race partisans nor of the colonial apologists and propagandists, but those of the social surgeons, the indicting idealists, if you will—the prophetic reformers. While rendering due praise to others, we can take much satisfaction in the fact that the path to candid portraiture of the colonial system and of native life has been shown by one from whom it was least of all expected, but through whom it comes with the greatest acceptability—an educated Negro colonial official.

But we must not forget that the glory of all these writers, Maran's as well, is the common glory of the tradition of French culture and the great gift, as yet unaccepted, of the French genius to the western world. One will not say it is exclusively French, exceptional individuals elsewhere have had and still have it—but only of the French can we say that it is characteristic.

But of the three possible angles of literary approach, quite uniquely illustrated by these three novels, which shall prevail, which has the greatest artistic potentialities—the humanitarian, the sentimentally romantic, or the aesthetically objective? We predict the eventual triumph of the nonmoralistic and purely aesthetic approach—art for its own sake combined with that stark cult of veracity—the truth, whether it hurts or not, for the sake of eventual peace of human understanding.

We have further encouraging signs of the spread of this point of view in the approach to things African. *Ebony and Ivory* of Llewellyn Powys is an especially welcome work as one of the first English books that carry this point of view consistently. And quite recently, again in French, we have the charming travel sketches of a French woman traveler, artist and educator, Lucie Cousturier, whose work, while it is not fiction, exemplifies this new tendency by differing as widely from the average travel sketch as the new colonial novel differs from its predecessors. Her sketches alone show that she has been able to find the common human denominator, through the search for beauty. Her prose text, detailing her trip through Upper Nigeria from Kankan by an unfrequented route through Keronane to Macenta, shows that the eye that sees beauty sees without bias, and can look at human life as objectively and profitably as at nature herself. She applies to social values the same graceful touch. Of the short-sighted ethnographers and their pre-conceptions, she has this to say: "I am not over fond of ethnology. I would respect it more if it were merely a science, more or less exact, like the rest. But it is too often an art of calumniating peoples through invidious compari-sons—like so much [of] history. To set out the external customs and trappings of the life of a people for the life of the people itself—that is the still more serious fallacy and confusion of ethnography. It exhibits the chain and collar of the dog and says to us, 'Behold, the dog.'—Shows us the cell and dungeon for the prisoner, the string and binding wrappings, and insists, 'Here is the garland of fruits and flowers.'"

Throughout she is true to her intention to extricate human values from mere externalities of manners and customs. It is a charming book, born of a sympathetic, but more important still, an emancipated mind. Let us take as an example her purely artistic impressions of a fetish-dance at Zerecore. She found the fantastic pantomime of the Nioumons to have all the complexity and dexterity of a sophisticated ballet-pantomime, with charming conven-tionalizations, artistic refinement, grotesque, but decorative. "I was aware," she says, "at hearing the ensemble of the native orchestra of a complexity of rhythm perhaps more subtle than that of any other land, even African, which by default of special musical training I could not record, but which seemed almost to surpass notation . . . The phases of the pantomime, making allowances, were essentially those of our own best ballet conventions, which were achieved—a more difficult task, in spite of an excessively grotesque masking of the body which seemed quite to rob it of semblance to the human form." And a little further on more interesting still, these observations—"Far from having, as even the Greeks, the cult of nakedness, here we had the aesthetic passion and motive of pure abstractly decorative art.

"There was in the dance movements that same rigid and precise conventionalization as in the plastre art of the fetishes—it was an evocation of symbolism, profound, but ornamental, a creative artistic representation, not merely a crude imitation, more or less happy, of natural forms. I seem to recall having read in the narratives of travelers, apropos of African dances, that they were gestures and contortions. Such descriptions create a false impression and lead to false expectations. They suggested to me a primitive, almost bestial, character and I expected to see that. On the contrary, I found quite the reverse. Everything among these Negroes was artifice and discipline, and the deeper I advanced into the forest, the more rigorous and conventionalized I found their life and ways. Their art shows crude realism, and for that very reason the dancers I saw were men exclusively, never women." But, pardon—one should read the book itself.

How far such points of view will upset the stereotyped interpretations and preconceptions, one cannot say, but we can safely predict a great reappraisal when Africa is eventually seen, as it must be, not through the traders', nor the military surveyors', nor even through the missionaries', but with the artists' eye. Thus we look at our own culture, or we could not endure the sight of it. We know what the conception of Oriental culture was; curious, perverse, childish, sensual, until our eyes were artistically opened and we saw it to be disciplined, profound, aesthetic, ultra-sophisticated; and through the same medium, Africa will ultimately be estimated as a land of its own unique beauty and civilization.

4

On J. A. Rogers

J. A. Rogers shared with René Maran the distinction of being one of the two authors most often reviewed in the Negro World. *Shorter, more formal reviews and longer review articles frequently addressed the works of both men. Maran's* Batouala *and Rogers'* From Superman to Man *were both given away free with subscriptions to the paper.*

Hubert H. Harrison's "White People Versus Negroes" is reminiscent of his attack on white publishers. Here he uses Rogers' experience at self-publishing and self-marketing to score the Black middle class intellectuals. As a class he considers them effete, narrow-minded and stupid. In a biting sarcasm not too different from E. Franklin Frazier's Black Bourgeoisie, *he suggests that they do not have enough sense even to independently recognize an important work of Black writing. They would rather wait on the sidelines and jump on the bandwagon after white critics have expressed their approval.*

Some of them would even block the progress of new Black talent, from whom they perceive a threat. With the many Black intellectuals whom Rogers sent copies of From Superman to Man, *Harrison contrasts white liberals, who were helpful, and ordinary non-intellectual Black folk, many of them engaged in humble occupations. The latter were heroic in their support for Rogers.*

In "Hodge Kirnon Analyzes Work of Young West Indian Author, J. A. Rogers," Kirnon, a regular Negro World *columnist, sees Rogers as an "intellectual supplement to the spiritual side of Garveyism."*

White People Versus Negroes

Being the Story of J. A. Rogers' Great Book

Hubert H. Harrison (1922)

Some time in August, 1917, I picked up in a Negro book shop a book entitled *From Superman to Man,* by J. A. Rogers. I sat down to read it and did not rise from my seat until I had read it through. Then I paid for it and took it home, realizing that I had found a genuine treasure. Of the author I could learn nothing, as there was no publisher's name and address in the volume, which had been published by the author at his own expense. Two years later, while in Washington, I came across a second edition of the book, bearing this time the imprint of "The Goodspeed Press." I wrote them at once, got the author's address, and wrote to tell him how highly I thought of his book. Since then I have reviewed it in *The Negro World* and elsewhere. I still insist that it is the greatest book ever written in English on the Negro by a Negro, and I am glad to know that increasing thousands of black and white readers re-echo the high opinion of it which I had expressed.

During the period from 1917 to the present this book has made its way to success without one word of encouragement or praise from any of the more prominent Negro writers or editors except Mr. Ferris and myself, although free copies had been sent to Dr. DuBois, Kelly Miller, Benjamin Brawley, Monroe Trotter, Prof. Scarborough, Braithwaite, and many others, including the National Association for the Advancement of Colored People. Almost the only colored people who helped to spread its fame were the lesser known and humble classes, who still pilgrimage to 512 Lenox Avenue in quest of it. The best known Negroes have failed to notice it.

What the Whites Did

It was a colored woman who used to do day's work at the University of Chicago, who showed a copy to one of the university professors, Professor Baber, a Southern white woman. She read it and at once wrote Mr. Rogers to say that she considered it to be "the finest bit of literature she had read on the subject," and that she had placed it on the required reading list for her classes. In addition, she had it placed in the university library. Some time later she gave a reception at her home to her students (all white) and invited the author (a Negro) to come and speak to them on the subject of the book—the Negro in history and civilization. She bought fourteen copies and sent them to leading white educators at such leading universities as Minnesota and Michigan, and to librarians at the leading scientific libraries.

A colored Catholic got hold of the book by accident. It was then passed on to the Catholic Board for Mission Work Among Colored People. They sent a white priest to Chicago to look up the author; but this man failed to find Rogers, who was away from home working as a Pullman porter. So they sent a letter saying that: "The members of the board have read with much interest and pleasure your book, *From Superman to Man.* There are more objections against the colored race answered satisfactorily and convincingly in this book than in any book we have read upon the question. We intend using it as a textbook for the advancement of our students in the knowledge of the race question." The letter ended with an immediate order for twenty-five copies. The Catholic College in Greensburg, Pa., followed with an order for ten copies for use in their sociology class.

Since then they have asked Mr. Rogers to write for them a catechism on the race question for use in their schools, to be printed first in their magazine of 60,000 circulation. And about two weeks age they sent him a present of $200 for Christmas as a recognition of genius and encouragement of the same. Mr. Rogers, by the way, is not a Catholic. These two cases are just samples.

What the Big Negroes Didn't

In the meanwhile he had sent a copy of the book to every leading Negro college in the country, to Atlanta, Fisk, Wilberforce, Howard, Tuskegee, Shaw; to Dr. DuBois, Dr. Spingarn and Dr. Bentley, head of the N.A.A.C.P. in Chicago, and to the N.A.A.C.P. in New York, under the curious delusion that an Association for the Advancement of Colored People would like to hear of a book in which the cause of colored people was so well advanced. He also mailed them letters, but they were too ill-bred and unmannerly to vouchsafe him a reply. Copies of the book, accompanied by letters, were also sent to Kelly Miller, Braithwaite, Scarborough, Isaac Fisher, of Tuskegee; Brawley, of Morehouse College; Banks, of Mound Bayou, and many others. Kelly Miller and Isaac Fisher acknowledged receipt but made no comment. The lady-like Brawley opined that the book was "rather interesting" but that the author made a gross error in putting philosophy in the form of fiction, and hoped that if he ever wrote again he wouldn't commit the same grave error against the transcendental technics of the exalted art of saying nothing. The book, by the way, is no more a work of fiction than is Carlyle's *Sartor Resartus,* or the *Dialogues of Plato.* The truth is that Brawley, as usual, was too stupid to form any critical opinion worth a tinker's dam—as Brander Matthews, of Colombia, subtly hinted a short while ago.

The others didn't answer. But Vardaman of Mississippi, whom the book attacked, sent a courteous note of acknowledgement. The leading Negro journals like the *Chicago Defender,* the *Boston Guardian,* the *Crisis,* the *Christian Recorder,* all got copies but took no notice of it. The *Indianapolis Freeman* wrote an article on it—and the writer sent Rogers a bill for that! Three years later the *Defender* carried a notice of the book, and charged him $28. The *Journal of Negro History,* as well as the *Crisis* have also received copies of Rogers' second book, *As Nature Leads,* but they have taken no notice so far.

What the Little Negroes Did

"On the other hand," Mr. Rogers says, "Negroes to whom the book was not sent recognized it for themselves and sought me out with helpful greetings and generous praise. Among these were the Rev. George Frazier Miller, of St. Augustine Church, Brooklyn; Messrs. Authur Schomburg, Wm. H. Ferris, John E. Bruce and Hubert Harrison. None of them knew me personally except Ferris. Harrison wrote me a warm letter of congratulation in 1919 and reviewed the book in a magazine and later in the *Negro World.* He also suggested that I send a copy to the *Crisis,* 'but don't let them know that you are colored or they'll never notice you.' They are somewhat colorblind on genius. Harrison's belief was confirmed beforehand, as the book had been sent two years before, and no notice had been taken of it. . . . But two colored school teachers of Washington—Mrs. N. T. Myers and Mrs. R. G. Moore— sold hundreds of copies, refusing any remuneration and Mr. Nathaniel Guy sent a copy at his own expense to every judge and truant officer in the District of Columbia. The book is now in its third edition."

Can We Explain?

Such is the history of a masterpiece of literature. How can we explain the conduct of the colored big-wigs? Perhaps there are two explanations. The Negroes whom Christian slavery reduced to the social level of brutes still have today some of the traits of the slave. And one of these finds continuous expression in our "big Negroes" namely, "Don't help to push any other Negro into notice if you have won notice yourself. Notice for them detracts from your notice." So, we find that "big Negroes" prefer to advance ignoramuses since their own superiority will thereby be enhanced. To advance a "comer" might abate their own brilliance. God help us as a race, so long as this contemptible trait shall flourish among us!

But I don't think that this explains all of it. There is another reason which will shock many. The truth is that many of our "brightest" minds have not yet developed any intellect of their own. They can give you the most brilliant expositions of Shaw, Dunbar or Marin—provided he has been previously explained for them. But when they are asked to explain a new writer whom no one from whom they draw their opinions has yet seen or sampled, they are "stuck." I know young men like Mr. King and Mr. Sunday who can do it. But they are not prominent yet. No one knows them. DuBois and Owen, Brawley and Randolph, Johnson and Kelly Miller can't do it. It requires a quality of independent judgment that is certain of itself and sure of its ground. Herein "education" (which can be poured into a person) is no substitute for intellect, which is one's own. The men whom I have named are men of "education"—some of them men of culture. But Ernest Just, Alain LeRoy Locke, King and Kirnon are men of intellect. They can think for themselves in the face of a brand-new fact. The others can't. Yet it is these others that our black world mistakes for men of light and leading.

When Claude McKay erupted into notice these colored pseudo-intellectuals couldn't tell from reading his poems that he was worth noticing. But now that their superiors have spoken they take Claude out to lunch and lionize him "most much." As with McKay, so with Rogers. As soon as these copy-cats shall have learned from their teachers how great is *From Superman to Man,* they will slobber over him and give space to his book. In the meanwhile it is well that they should know how those of us who have eyes to see have taken their tiny measure. "Quiss custodiet ipsos custodes?" asks the old Vulgate, and we of today re-echo it in modern terms: "Who shall put brains in our brainy men?"

Hodge Kirnon Analyses Work of Young West Indian Author, J. A. Rogers

Hodge Kirnon (1922)

There is amongst us a young Negro writer, J. A. Rogers, who at present is living right here in Harlem, and who is working in a field of literary activity new and unique as far as Negroes are concerned. His work is worthy of the highest commendation and recognition. It has already won such from a few distinguished white and colored men of letters, already well known in the field of journalism. But the general reading public has yet to be well acquainted with the work of Mr. Rogers. Its worth, both intrinsic and extrinsic, will surely gain its merited recognition. That is only a question of time. If certain social and mental symptoms and ebullitions are to be considered indicative of certain definite psychological processes in the state of formation and function, then it seems quite evident that the writings of J. A. Rogers will not be long in reaching the reading masses of our people, for it is out of the passions and desires inherent in this psychic process and development that the urgent demand for such literature will eventually and inevitably grow.

Preconceived Views

It was in 1920 that I read Mr. Rogers' books, *From Superman to Man* and *As Nature Leads.* I immediately recognized the fact that this man was working in a field hardly touched by any Negro author. I held him high in my estimation as a pioneer worker. When Mr. Rogers came from Chicago to sojourn in New York I was sent an informal invitation by a friend to meet him. I complied without delay. Of course, I entertained certain preconceptions of Mr. Rogers. These were based upon his writings in which were displayed a sharp, forceful, keenly intellectual and scientific tone and spirit. I held the opinion for some reason or other that he was a Negro Huxley in conversation, with perhaps an incisive, biting sarcasm and irony so characteristic of Hubert Harrison. But I was greatly mistaken. I found Mr. Rogers a calm, quiet, easy-going, unassuming person—more willing to listen and to search for the grain of truth rather than to be controversial and bumptiously intellectually vain and upstarted. He showed erudition without the slightest disposition to out-talk or out-think any one. He deeply impressed me as a man eager for the truth and not as one who would engage his time and energy in searching for flaws and slight qualifications to fundamental and general truths. One of my first questions to Mr. Rogers after the formal introduction was: "Who are your favorite authors?"

"Shakespeare, Schopenhauer and Lester F. Ward in America," was the reply. I noted at once that he was interested in big and universal minds; in men who plumb the depths of the fundamental truths and principles of life which are applicable to all its various phases and manifestations, and who whilst in the pursuit of certain specific objectives have strewn the path with gems of rich thought.

DuBois as a Leader

At this time of turmoil and radicalism, which are always characteristic of any great intellectual awakening, we are quite apt to misplace and misunderstand our men of ability who are doing something for the race. We quite often fail to appreciate the work that they are best fitted to do, and because of this we not only measure them by false or wrong standards, but ignore or oversight their prime worth and effectiveness as contributors to our racial emancipation and development. Mr. DuBois, for instance, has been generally criticized for his lack of ability as a race leader. As a matter of fact, Mr. DuBois has not the necessary qualifications to be a great or popular leader of the Negro at this stage and time. He is by nature not fitted to move great masses by the kind of oratory that would stir radical and rebellious feelings. He cannot or will not indulge in bitter invectives and sweeping denouncements and generalizations which are so necessary at certain stages in the awakening of any people. In a word, he is not an agitator of a certain type. Even as an able writer, Dr. DuBois has his special place. His writings, especially in *Souls of Black Folk,* savor of the poetical. Intellectually, they evoke serious meditative and contemplative thoughts—not necessarily revolutionary ones. He is a good writer, but makes no new intellectual conquests. He does not lead us into the realm of things radical and scientific. Marcus Garvey is a man with a personality and ability to stir masses of men. He is primarily an organizer and propagandist. He has in a comparatively short time awakened and infused into the Negro a spirit of race pride and racial idealism that was almost beyond realization. He has done wonders towards educating the Negro into a deep sense of racial manhood and initiative.

But J. A. Rogers' sphere of activity is in another field. It is intellectual supplement to the spiritual side of Garveyism as well as a scientific exposition of the doctrine of radicalism. His writings show not only a comprehensive grasp of the subjects which he approaches, but a remarkable ability in pressing into service an abundance of historical and scientific data in the interest of perhaps the most important aspect of the whole Negro problem. His appeal and message are made direct to the intellect. He deals in matters of science, history and anthropology. Upon matters [concerning] which Garvey awakens feelings, Rogers supplies the requisite facts and knowledge. The wealth of information contained in *From 'Superman' to Man* and *As Nature Leads* is capable, if well assimilated, of rounding out to well adjusted proportions the newly awakened race consciousness of the Negro which, because of the lack of educational and scientific guidance, occasionally runs to extremes.

That Mr. Rogers has successfully applied the comparative method with great results in the various branches of knowledge which he has brought to bear on his subjects will be attested to by anyone who has read his books. This method is considered a distinctive nineteenth century product, and is held up in great admiration by such able white thinkers as John Fiske and Josiah Royce. Rogers has effectively utilized the white man's discoveries, sciences, methods and principles of inquiry and learning in general to the great advantage of the Negro relative to his status in general on the human race. In performing this task he has furnished his race with the knowledge that is necessary in its struggle towards the attainment of racial manhood and individuality, as well as for its freedom from mental slavery to the white man's cultural and esthetic ideals.

Racialism is a decided evolutionary process in the life of the Negro in the western worlds, whether it is so recognized by some or not. Perhaps that is why Dean Pickens called Garveyism a brutal reality. It is both natural and indispensable after the many long years of Caucasianization which the Negro has undergone. Racialisn is the specific radicalism of the Negro. Important as are other forms of radicalism such as economic radicalism, racial radicalism is of equal importance, for what would it profit the Negro if he should gain the whole economic work and suffer the loss of his racial soul? For those who see the hand of God at work in mysterious ways shaping the course of events, or those who see the reign of law at work everywhere at all times, a Garvey, a Rogers and others had to appear. The one is an organizer of men and a propagandist; the other a careful scientific writer who has organized the amassed facts and results of modern thought and scientific research along with the views and records of the greatest intellects that the world has seen, in support of an unqualified disproval of the almost universal belief amongst white people that the Negro is a naturally inferior being. But whilst doing this Mr. Rogers has both directly and indirectly removed the supercilious white man's self-assumed unique and distinctive position of superman to the level of other mortals and races.

From Superman to Man is the title of Mr. Rogers' first book. Its contents are a supposed conversation [between] a pullman porter and a U.S. Senator. The Senator brings forward every imaginable argument to support his view that the Negro is inherently an inferior being and can never under any circumstances reach to a level of culture and refinement that the white races have attained. Dixon, the porter, sweeps into oblivion every argument launched by the Senator. Where he lacks the necessary knowledge he brings the leading world thinkers to his side. Practically every department of learning is brought under contribution in this imaginary conversation. It is impossible to convey in words the pleasure, the "ecstasies of thought," as Shaw would say, that I have derived from this book. One must read it in order to understand and appreciate its worth.

As Nature Leads is the title of Mr. Rogers' second book. It purports to be "an informal discussion of the reason why Negro and Caucasian are mixing in spite of opposition." It is well nigh impossible to write anything in this article that would be pretentious of a review of this book. It is sufficient to say that it is an able and searching work. The ideas and thoughts contained in it are sure to put the reader's mind to a strong and vigorous intellectual exercise. It is not only what he actually proves that is interesting, but the many suggestive ideas thrown out throughout the entire volume that are bound to awaken a train of helpful and vitalizing thoughts. Even though Mr. Rogers deals with deep subjects, they are easy to comprehend, inasmuch as his method of presentation is conversational, a similar method to that of Plato and George Berkeley, the English metaphysician. The book now under discussion is constituted of a number of letters written by Hamilton, a widely read post office clerk to Trent, a university student, on miscegenation and other interesting topics. Letter No. 1 is devoted to a very illuminating discussion on the attitude of the native African toward a union with Caucasians. The observations are taken from some of the best recognized of African travelers. Then there are critical analyses of Lester F. Ward's principles concerning racial intermixture. To illustrate one point, Ward says: "The women of any social status which they regard as higher than their own." Without denying the truth of Ward's dictum, Rogers brings the following serious qualification to bear upon it: "The women of any social status, regardless of race, will freely accept the men of a social status which they regard as higher than their own." After proving this point, he goes on to examine the soundness of other laws of the philosopher and sociologist, Ward. One of these is: "That the women of any race will vehemently reject the men of a race which they regard as lower than their own." Mr. Rogers without a doubt has shown the limitations of this principle. Other interesting sections of the book are: "The Esthetics of Color," "Predominant Negro Characteristics," etc. From an advertisement in *The Negro World* some weeks ago I gleaned that the book *From Superman to Man* has been entirely sold out, but I learned recently that a new edition will be out in the near future. *As Nature Leads* can be had from the author at 513 Lenox Avenue.

It would indeed be hard to understand how any Negro addicted to the reading of good books or those who claim to have caught the new spirit could afford to miss reading and studying these books of J. A. Rogers, for in them race consciousness is made an intellectual and scientific issue and a rational foundation is laid for racialism.

5

On Poetry

The Negro World *published a massive amount of poetry, a representative sample of which appears later in this volume. These poems were supplemented by regular articles on poetry criticism and poetics. The five articles in this section cover a wide cross section of African-American poetical expression.*

John Edward Bruce (also known as "Bruce Grit") surveys African-American poetry to the 1920s in "The Negro in Poetry." Bruce was president and co-founder (together with bibliophile Arthur A. Schomburg) of the Negro Society for Historical Research (NSHR), organized in Yonkers, New York in 1911. The NSHR was Afro-America's second historical society. Bruce and Schomburg also helped, in one way or another, the members of Afro-America's first, the American Negro Historical Society of Philadelphia (1897) and its third, the Association for the Study of Negro (later "Afro-American") Life and History (1915).

Bruce's knowledge of Black history, ancient and modern, was profound. Some of this is brought to bear on the present article. Like Garvey in "African Fundamentalism," Bruce sees in Africa's past greatness a prophecy for its future regeneration. Like Garvey, he is convinced that "What man has done, man can do." Africans were once great and they will be great again. The European rose from barbarism and slavery to preeminence in the world of politics and letters. The African will have to do the same this time around.

Bruce demonstrates the underlying unity of Garveyite criticism in another area, too. Like Hubert H. Harrison in "White People Versus Negroes, Being the Story of J. A. Rogers' Great Book," he deplores the inability of Black folk to define their own literary and political heroes. Garvey addressed this point also in "African Fundamentalism"—the tendency of Black "leaders" to turn a blind eye to Black talent until white critics point the way.

The remaining articles deal with poets of the 1920s. Fenton Johnson's Champion Magazine *published Marcus Garvey's first United States article in 1917. Johnson's poetry seems to have influenced the* Negro World *poet, Leonard Brathwaite, a sample of whose work appears later in this volume.*

Garvey produced a large corpus of poetry, which this writer has collected in The Poetical Works of Marcus Garvey *(1983). His first offerings, written in the Atlanta Penitentiary, appeared in the* Negro World *in 1927. T. Thomas Fortune, the "dean of Afro-American journalists," was editing the* Negro World *at this time. Here Fortune, in "Mr. Garvey As A Poet," greets his employer's poetic efforts with enthusiasm. He interestingly links Garvey's poetry with his prose, which latter was in fact often unwittingly more poetic than his poetry.*

Ethel Trew Dunlap was the most prolific of the Negro World *poets. Marion S. Lakey, her* Negro World *fellow poet, illustrates another aspect of the Garvey aesthetic in his critique of her poetry. He admires her devotion to her race first, for she writes overwhelmingly of themes which simultaneously uplift the race and lessen her marketability in the world outside the U.N.I.A.*

R. L. Poston provides a new twist to the propaganda debate in his analysis of "Dunbar, Braithwaite, McKay." He clearly prefers McKay's propaganda verse to William S. Braithwaite's racially neutral offerings. But he fears that McKay could perhaps go the way of John Greenleaf Whittier—half forgotten by later generations who would have long won the struggles for which the poet wrote. Sixty years after Poston's article, McKay is not forgotten. Nor have the struggles of his generation been favored with a final victory.

The Negro In Poetry

John Edward Bruce (1923)

Cicero relates that the ugliest and most stupid slaves in Rome came from England, and he urges his friend Atticus not to purchase slaves from Britain because of their stupidity and inaptitude to learn music and other accomplishments.

With Caesar's opinion of the ancestors of the race which now dominates a goodly portion of the earth we are—most of us—somewhat familiar. He describes the Briton generally as a nation of very barbarous manners. "Most of the people of the interior," he says, "never sow corn, but live upon milk and flesh and are clothed with skins." In other words, he observes: "In their domestic and social habits the Britons are as degraded as the most savage nations and they are clothed with skins, wear the hair of their heads unshaven and long, but shave the rest of their bodies except the upper lip, and stain themselves a blue color with wood, which gives them a horrible aspect in battle." Yet these barbarous, degraded and repulsive looking people have given to the world some of the most eminent and erudite scholars and poets of which any nation can boast. Indeed there is no department of learning in which Englishmen have not excelled and, in many instances, been the pioneers in all advanced thought. In the drama, in the arts, in science and in poetry English scholarship has kept pace with the onward steady march of civilization, and the genius and profound knowledge of her great scholars have commanded the respect and the admiration of intellectual men the world over. Chaucer, Spenser, John Gower, Minot Caxton, Tom Moore, Tyndale, Thomas Cranmer, Henry Howard, Earl of Surrey, Robert Henryson, George Buchanan, Sir Phillip Sydney, Richard Hooker, Thomas Jackville, William Shakespeare, Francis Bacon, Ben Johnson, Lord Byron, Southey, Wordsworth, Locke, Coleridge and a host of others quite as brilliant and immortal have splendidly vindicated the Britons from the charge of barbarism and stupidity and have immortalized their names and their country's name and fame for all time to come.

Well, now, if people so degraded, so stupid, so horrible to look upon as were these early Britons could rise superior to their conditions and mount the heights of learning and scholarship, may we not assume that other races, notably the darker races, one of which, the African race, gave to the early Greeks and Romans the arts and sciences, letters, government and religion, may be born again by scholarship and rise on stepping-stones of its dead self to higher things?

It is my purpose at this time to tell you of some early Negro poets. I shall not class them with the great poets of Europe and America, whose names are household words, for we must remember that while Negroes have written and are still writing some really clever and creditable verse they have not had time to produce, according to modern standards, a really great poet. The signs of promise, however, are encouraging if the few selections I shall presently quote, culled from some of the brightest minds of the past and of the present generation, may be accepted as an augury of the future of the Negro poet.

You are to remember that I am dealing now with the American Negro poet.

It was said of Terence, the African poet, that his dramatic works were much admired by the Romans for their prudential maxims and moral sentences, and compared with his contemporaries he was much in advance of them in point of style. The African, Haitian, Arabian, Brazilian, Puerto Rican and Cuban poets of Negro stock do not suffer by comparison with those of any other race. No article or essay dealing with Negro poets would be complete without some reference to that dainty little African maiden, Miss Phillis Wheatley, who more than one hundred years ago achieved the great distinction and honor of being the first of her sex in this country to write and publish a book of poems. Equally interesting to some of my readers, perhaps, will be the statement that the first male in this country to mount Pegasus and ride to lofty heights was a Negro slave, Jupiter Hammon, the property of one Lloyd of Queens Village, L.I., in this State, who made his bow in the local paper at that place in December, 1760, in a broadside entitled "An Evening Thought." In 1778 he wrote an address in verse to Miss Wheatley of twenty-one verses, welcoming her to the fold and lauding her gifts in fulsome phrases. Most of my readers are familiar with the poems of Miss Phillis Wheatley, but I will quote a few stanzas from one of them, "The Providence of God," which discovers her remarkable talents, breadth of thought and elegance of diction:

The Providence of God

Arise, my soul! on wings enraptured rise,
To praise the Monarch of the earth and skies,
Whose goodness and beneficence appear
As round its center, moves the rolling year.
Or when the morning glows with rosy charms,
Or the sun slumbers in the ocean's arms,
Of light divine, be a rich portion lent
To guide my soul and favor my intent;
Celestial Muse, my arduous flight sustain,
And raise my mind to seraphic strain.

Another of this earlier group of Negro poets to attract the attention of men of letters was George Horton, the black slave poet of Chatham county who first came into public notice through the medium of the *Raleigh Register* in 1829, which published his "Hope of Liberty." Horton could neither read nor write, but dictated to his master, who wrote down his verses. His soul was full of the "divine fire."

At a meeting of the Anti-Slavery Society, Western Reserve (Ohio), in October, 1835, Theodore Weld recited this poem, a verse from which I will quote:

Alas! And am I born for this,
To wear this slavish chain?

Deprived of all created bliss,
Through hardship, toil and pain?
How long have I in bondage lain,
And languished to be free?
Alas, and must I still complain,
Deprived of Liberty?

For an untutored slave, ignorant of books and the rules of versification, this is not a bad showing of his remarkable gifts. Horton's first published volume of poems appeared in 1829. As I gather from the *Bibliographica Americana,* compiled by A. A. Schomburg, secretary of our Negro Society for Historical Research, a second edition of his poems was published at Philadelphia in 1827 [sic]. Another volume was issued at Hillsboro, N.C., by Dennis Heart, editor, *Hillsboro Recorder,* in 1845. Other volumes, chiefly reprints and verses, hitherto unpublished, appeared in 1854-55. So his heart yearned for freedom. These chains of slavery were galling to him. The insurrection of thought had precipitated open rebellion and his soul in agony cried out against the hated institution in a torrent of words that told what he felt, and how he felt over his condition as a slave. There is a note of despair and despondence in these lines which I now quote. They are really pathetic:

Am I sadly cast aside
On misfortune's rugged tide,
Will the world my plans deride
                    Forever?
Worst of all, must hope grow dim
And withhold her cheering beam,
Rather than let me dream
                    Forever?

I have said that the race has not yet had time in which to produce a great poet, and it can offer the same explanation for its failure to do so that Jefferson made to the Abbé Raynal, who had somewhere stated in criticism of America that it had not produced a single scholar of note. Mr. Jefferson's plea in extenuation for this shortcoming was the youth of the New Republic. But despite the youth of the Negro race in this country, it has made greater progress intellectually and industrially in the fifty-nine years of its freedom than was made by the colonists in the same period.

There are more educated men and women among 12,000,000 Negroes after fifty-nine years of freedom than there was among the white population in the entire thirteen colonies in the same period. The Negro race can today match the white race with a Negro man or woman who will hardly suffer by comparison with them in any department of learning or scholarship. I am almost ready to withdraw my statement that we have not yet produced a great poet. If this were a real, not a fictitious democracy in which the worth of a man in any legitimate field of endeavor was measured by his merit and ability and not his color or condition, socially, then J. Madison Bell, James David Corrothers, Daniel Webster Davis, Charlotte Forten, Frances Ellen Watkins Harper, J. Willies Menard, Islay Waldon, D. A. Payne, Alberry A. Whitman, George B. Vashon, W. J. Wilson of the earlier group of race poets were, advantage for advantage, as great poets as any group of white men or women of the same period who supported a commerce with the muses. The fact that these men and women belonged to a race which is generally regarded as inferior even to this day, obscured any inherent greatness that they possessed; and those who in our own day have achieved any distinction, owe it to the fact that some white author, more liberal than is usual, has put the seal of his approval upon their work and thus given them prestige and standing, which they could not otherwise have got. Thus Dunbar jumped into fame at almost a single bound. He came to his own, but his own received him not. William Dean Howell recognized his ability and with a stroke of his pen gave him international fame.

The psychology of this sort of recognition of Negro genius conceals more than it reveals. It is at once a reflection upon the ability or willingness of the race in the mass to recognize and appraise at their true value our own men and women who are striving in the higher reaches of thought to attain the goal of their ambition, and it is a tribute to the superior vision and keen judgement of the white man, in these circumstances. Thus he designates our poets, political leaders and moral advisers. We accept the designees and confirm the judgement and wisdom of white men by accepting these fortunate objects of their approval.

When Miss Phillis Wheatley [was] budding forth as the poetess of the Revolution, a galaxy of the most distinguished and celebrated white men, including John Hancock, the first signer of the Declaration of Independence, put the seal of their approval upon her book and her master took a solemn oath, duly signed and delivered, that she, with her own hand and out of her own African brain, composed and wrote the pieces bearing her name.

If any friends or any well known members of the race here in New York should singly or unitedly join in endorsing the work of some rising poet or story-writer here, it would perhaps appeal only to their immediate circle of acquaintances and friends, and the young author would probably have to hunt a job as elevator man in some public office, or enlist in the army. To me, this denotes an alarming condition, discovering all too plainly, our lack of confidence in each other in matters of this kind. I do not think I know of a white man, in whose judgement as to what is best for my race, I have absolute confidence. I can respect, but I cannot accept it as final, for I have not yet come to regard him as a superman. I think we are capable of deciding for ourselves who is who among us in the literary field and that we ought to encourage morally and substantially, just as our white friends do their own, our own undiscovered geniuses.

Negro poets, story-writers and authors are not going to be as popular with white readers generally as white authors. They are going to be popular only as they are made so by the endorsement of some noted author of the white race, who may be moved to endorse their books, to induce members of their own race to read them in order to find out what is back of the black man's mind.

Recently, a jury in New York City in the case of the United States versus Fredenheim, charged with violating the Espionage Act, could not come to an agreement because one of the jurors said that he could not believe a Negro. There are a great many people in the white race who feel as this man does about the Negro, and especially "us literary Negroes." They do not believe any more than some of us do of them, that we can teach them anything, or that we know anything that they do not know. Of course, they are mistaken, and they would only be convinced of it by a presidential proclamation, supplemented with the endorsement of the white authors' league and a few leading literary journals.

We are not, as a race, doing our honest duty toward our men and women who have hitched their wagons to a star and are trying to drive along the limitless pathway of the heavens. We do not properly support them with our means, nor encourage them with words of cheer. When we begin to do this we are going to produce some real great poets and authors of the later groups of our poets.

I may mention Paul Laurence Dunbar, George Reginald Margetson, Fenton Johnson, W. Stanley Braithwaite, James Weldon Johnson, Egbert Martin, Edward Smith Jones, H. Cordellia Ray, George Clinton Rowe, James M. Whitfield and a score of others of equal merit and ability, all of whom shone brilliantly and wrought wondrously in their day and generation. The Negro race is one of the oldest races and had a civilization thousands of years before Europe emerged from barbarism or America had a place in the social progression. Her scholars, philosophers and poets have already written their names on the pages of history and in the next twenty or thirty years there will be an awakening among Negroes throughout the world; a revival of letters such as distinguished the black race in another period when it was the acknowledged school-master of Greece and Rome.

This is not quite the Negro's day in literature. He is dead now but he is soon to arise with healing in his wings. Rejuvenated, disenthralled, re-deemed, he will stand forth in the full stature of a man and will ably fulfill the promise that Ethiopia shall suddenly stretch forth her hands unto God and then princes shall come out of Egypt. For out of Egypt have I called my son. We are coming and the Father of us all will bless and prosper the race that gave hospitality and protection to the Son of Righteousness, if it will only believe in itself and be itself.

A Negro Poet—Fenton Johnson

Anonymous (1920)

Twenty-five years ago the world was surprised when William Dean Howells announced the advent of a Negro poet, Paul Laurence Dunbar, saying in substance that he was the first Negro to feel the striving and woes of his race aesthetically and to express them lyrically. Since that time, many Negro poets of talent have lifted their heads above the horizon. James D. Corrothers, James D. Cotter, Jr., William Stanley Braithwaite, Margetson, Carmichael, Georgia Douglas Johnson, Lucian B. Watkins, Claude McKay, James Weldon Johnson and Fenton Johnson have produced some very good poetry. Indeed the work of James Weldon Johnson compares favorably with the best American poetry that has been produced in recent years.

Not the least of this group of talented poets is Fenton Johnson, of Chicago, who has given the world slender volumes of verse, which have received commendation from high sources. Of a thoughtful, meditive turn of mind, Fenton Johnson has a true poetic feeling and a light, graceful literary touch.

Recently he has turned his attention to more serious pursuits than cultivating the verses. First he edited the *Champion Magazine* and now he is editor of the *Favorite Magazine,* which is a blending of pithy editorials, sparkling poetry with interesting articles and stories.

In the rush for the almighty dollar and the pursuit of pleasure, in the stress of soul over vexatious social, political, economic and racial problems, we are prone to overlook the ministry of the fine arts. Literature, art and music have a two-fold value. They ennoble our ideas and like Mother Nature relieve the tensions of life and act as a wholesome recreation. Therefore, it might be well for us to encourage our painters, poets, sculptors and musicians. For it is true today, as it was two thousand years ago, that the life is more than meat and the body more than raiment.

Thursday evening, July 22, New Yorkers had an opportunity to hear Mr.

Johnson in the guise of a philosopher, when he spoke in the Metropolitian Baptist Church on "The Co-operation of the Races." Mr. Johnson visited the Universal Building twice last week, was shown around and expressed a pleasant surprise at seeing so many young colored men and women employed as clerks, stenographers, book keepers and accountants, etc. He said that he believed that economic independence and commercial strength were sure methods for the Negro to gain recognition.

Mr. Garvey as a Poet

T. Thomas Fortune (1927)

A great many people have been surprised and pleased at discovering that Honorable Marcus Garvey, President-General of the Universal Negro Improvement Association, is a poet of a high order; that is, that he possesses in large measure the divine power of expressing himself in the language of poetry, which a distinguished authority has declared to be the sublimest expression of the human soul after perfection. Only those who have suffered greatly or felt the ecstacies of joy in its highest and purest form, are capable of reaching the depths in poetic expression which affect and move great masses of people.

Lord Byron says, in effect, "Many are poets who have never penned a thought, and perhaps the best." The poets who have sung spontaneously, as it were, without suffering much, as Homer, David, Milton and Dante suffered, or loved deeply, as Petrarch, Shakespeare, Lord Byron and Edgar Allan Poe loved, only skim the surface of human sorrow and joy. They do not fathom the depths of human hope and aspiration. They please and charm but do not transport us.

Mr. Garvey has loved deeply and suffered deeply. In the few years he has lived he has experienced the extremes of human joy and agony. If he did not possess a poetic consciousness he would be mute, or express himself in common phrase, as the average person does; but, having the poetic consciousness, he not only writes poetry that moves the reader but he writes and speaks the prose which reaches and moves the masses. In the *Negro World* of September 17, we published a poem by Mr. Garvey, under the heading, "God in Man," in which the image of God in the image of man, as stated in the first chapter of Genesis, twenty-seventh verse, as follows: "So God created man in His own image, in the image of God created He him; male and female created He them," is very poetically brought out, as the following three concluding stanzas will disclose:

> Thou art the living force in part,
>   The Spirit of the Mighty I;
> The God of Heaven and your heart
>   Is Spirit that can never die.

> You're what you are in heart and mind,
>   Because you will it so to be;
> The man who tries himself to find,
>   Is light to all, and great is he.

> In each and every one is God,
>   In everything atomic life;
> There is no death beneath the sod,
>   This fact, not knowing, brings us strife.

But man has wandered far from the image and spirit of his creator and by the eating of flesh and crossing of breeds made something that does not resemble the original man.

On Miss Dunlap's Poems

Marion S. Lakey (1923)

Of all writers of poetry who have written for the cause of regaining the continent of Africa for the Negro people, Ethel Trew Dunlap is at once observed to be the most prominent. She is untiring in her efforts for the African cause, and is no less acute to the many other phases of the great problem of the Negro race in America and elsewhere.

Miss Dunlap may well be called a poetess-enthusiast of racial uplift when we consider the large amount of poetry she has written in the racial vein. Her art is distinctive and attractive. She is a staunch defender of her race, and some of the poems written in defense of her people are pregnant with noble interpretation and spiritual appeal. The poems written in this strain are generally mild in tone, though they are never lacking in the spirit of righteous indignation for any wrong done her people.

Miss Dunlap has shown herself to be heartily in accord with the U.N.I.A. movement, and her pen has been ever faithful in its cause. In her writings for the African cause she has always sought to create a more harmonious feeling between the white race and the Negro race, endeavoring to show that while the Negro yearns for independence and a government of his own, he is not necessarily embittered in his attitude toward the white race because of his efforts to attain these ends. Her poem, "If I Should Die Tonight," is an excellent example of Miss Dunlap's efforts to inculcate race pride, and at the same time to eliminate the spirit of race friction.

Her tender little poem, "Native Love," is especially charming in its simplicity. It follows:

Come to me, my little lamb,
Virgin black of land of Ham,
Like a lambkin gone astray,
From thy native fold away.
We are far from Afric shore
That our blood makes us adore.
In thine eye is Nubia's blaze,
Careless thine, like Egypt's ways.
Blessed Jesus made us black;
Some day He may take us back
Where the palms are sighing now
To caress our absent brow.
They have robbed us of the Nile,
But it flows back on thy smile.
Be my continent they stole
Though we never reach its goal;
In each other let us find
Tropic lands we left behind!

No less charming and touching than this is, "A Merciful Dream," which expresses the feminine longing for security, and the desire for the piety of country which, because of the Negro's peculiar position in America, it is well nigh impossible for the Negro to cherish in full for America. The "merciful dream" is the vision of Africa highly civilized and reclaimed and controlled by the Negro. The poem is a mild but keen satire directed at those who scoff the African redemption idea.

The poem opening with the line, "I am not black as Kedar's tents, and yet—" is fraught with impression of the mix-blooded Negro's fine spiritual reverence for the darker rather than the fairer side of his ancestry, a spirit which is now more than ever before binding all members of the race into a stronger, spiritual union. In the above-mentioned poem, Miss Dunlap fails to see beauty in "Aryan Visage Fair," and in the last line, though she is evidently of light complexion herself, she says, "I fancy that I see my image black."

Evidence of the fact that Miss Dunlap has made a serious study of ancient history relating to her people is found in the poems centering around Bible stories dealing to some extent with characters of the Ethiopian race, or the race that is today called the Negro. Among the poems suggested by Bible history are, "Sweet Zipporah" and "Simon of Cyrene." These poems woven from Bible history are rather mystical in atmosphere—which is exactly as they should be. Miss Dunlap throws an exceedingly chaste and romantic splendor about her "sable" characters.

"Joan of Arc" is an appreciation of the far-famed French heroine in which the poetess expresses a desire to do, like Joan of Arc, something worthy in the interest of her race.

Miss Dunlap seems to have but one notable handicap in writing her poetry. She seems to lack the power of carrying in her poems a large amount of intricately arranged rhyme without apparent difficulty. But this seeming handicap will count little if any against her in the popular view, since the majority of the people care little about the "meter" of a poem, and are chiefly concerned as to its material and treatment. But in order to gain recognition in the critical view the poet must be versatile in his forms and measures, as well as in his materials, and he must realize that poems written in intricate forms are usually the most striking and beautiful. However, the poems, "Congo Rome" and "Palm Shadows," show a decided break away from this minimum use of rhyme which I have mentioned, and demonstrate the poetess' possibilities of attaining to the highest in variation of metrical forms.

The reader's appreciation of Miss Dunlap's poems should not be lessened because of the above criticism, since the handicap mentioned is really slight from the broader viewpoint, and there is every reason to hope that she will become more versatile in her choice of forms and measures.

One comes to realize more and more as one reads Miss Dunlap's poems that it will be the women of the race who will lead the race to a higher and more genuinely cultured spiritual plane.

I will close my article by saying what is already known to every attentive reader of Miss Dunlap's poetry: Miss Dunlap is—yes—a poetess-laureate and a heroine to her race, in that she has dared to write for a cause that means everything to the future well-being of her race at a time when that cause is the object of the supercilious ridicule and contempt of many of her own people, thus, to a certain extent, sacrificing for the time her chance to win a larger but what could not be other than a less altruistic fame.

Dunbar, Braithwaite, McKay—
An Analysis

Robert L. Poston (1922)

Tuesday, June 27, was the fiftieth anniversary of the birth of Paul Laurence Dunbar, great poet. The poems of this great artist have been recited this week with renewed interest throughout the length and breadth of this country, and possibly in England, where he is favorably known and appreciated. There has been some effort of late to compare Claude McKay with Dunbar as a poet. This is unfortunate. For these men are of such different schools of poetry that a contrast would be more in order. Dunbar depicted the life of his people with the emphasis on "Love and Laughter." McKay is a militant poet who can hardly escape the consciousness of his unfortunate sur- roundings even when he describes a rose. After we have read Dunbar we have no other thought but that of the thrill it has given us, of the lovely disposition of a people capable of the sentiments he expresses and of the deep untrampled love in the heart of Dunbar himself, which permitted him to stand within a burning furnace and not lose his poise or equilibrium but impressing the world with his viewpoint, sometimes against the world's will. Hardly so with McKay. With a good number of his best poems our first impression is to question before we admire. For McKay believes in indict- ment—terrible indictment against a system which almost overwhelms him. Of course, the admiration comes, but only after we have analyzed the feelings which McKay's writings bring over us. Dunbar never could have written "If We Must Die," nor could McKay have written "Life" or "When Malindy Sings." But that does not make Dunbar or McKay any less great poets because they expressed different sentiments sometimes differently. The poetry of Dunbar will always live, because like Bobbie Burns he has set the history of his group to music. But as a poet to lay claim to everlasting fame McKay will have to run this danger: as I have stated McKay is quite often a propaganda poet.

This is true in spite of the effort of Max Eastman to make it appear that he writes with disinterestedness, with no particular axe to grind, and that the appeal of his poetry is universal. When we find McKay injecting certain viewpoints in poems where they are least expected to be found and where we are almost tempted to say they do not belong, we are compelled to take exception to Eastman's estimate. McKay writes some splendid poems without propaganda, but he is essentially at present a propaganda poet, and some of his poetry will stand the same danger of not attaining everlasting fame as some of the poems of John Greenleaf Whittier written during slavery. Changed conditions may bring about a changed interest in some of his poems. Yet it can not be denied that for the present they serve a splendid purpose. Dunbar is yet the greatest Negro poet produced, and his greatness, contrary to public opinion, does not rest altogether upon the poems he has written in Negro dialect. Dunbar's best poems were written in choice English as many of the prominent critics will attest, and one of the sad disappointments of his life was because of the fact that he was not taken seriously by publishers when he attempted these poems in King's English.

William Stanley Braithwaite and Claude McKay are often spoken of as the greatest living Negro poets. Braithwaite, because of his anthologies and his connection with a great white daily and because he does not in his poems indicate his racial extraction, is taken by many, who do not know him personally, to be a white man. McKay, though writing for a great white magazine, lets you know at once what race he belongs to. Of these two poets McKay holds the greater place in the hearts of the Negroes who have read both poets. But it cannot be expected that McKay would at this time replace Braithwaite in the affections of the white people. Because Braithwaite has become so Caucasianized in his writings, that he has lost his racial indentity entirely, if he ever had any, and the white people claim him as their own. Yet his "House of the Falling Leaves" has a universal appeal and is good poetry. Both Braithwaite and McKay have many years before them, and it is hoped that "Ere sleep comes down to soothe their weary eyes" they will have reached that stage of efficiency as poets rivalling, if not excelling, that of Paul Laurence Dunbar whose anniversary we celebrate this week.

6

On Dr. W. E. B. DuBois and Others

In the next seven selections, William H. Ferris, Mrs. Amy Jacques Garvey and Marcus Garvey himself apply the Garvey aesthetic to the works of some of the most prominent Black writers of the 1920s. The articles on DuBois were part of an ongoing feud between DuBois and the integrationist camp on the one hand, and Garvey and the Black nationalist camp on the other. Whereas the Garvey aesthetic, and the wider political creed of Garveyism from which it derived, stressed race first, self-reliance and nationhood and exhibited great interest in Africa, the integrationists saw nothing wrong in a reliance on white philanthropy and control, frowned upon racial separation in whatever form, emphasized their stake in the North American mainstream and saw Africa as at best peripheral to the Afro-American struggle. These ideological differences became personified in the bitter Garvey-DuBois conflict.

On a political level Ferris saw DuBois as a handpicked leader writing "from the standpoint of a disinterested white man" and hopelessly out of touch with the New Negro spirit of the Black masses.

From a purely literary standpoint, Ferris was full of praise for DuBois' inimitable style and his mastery of the short story form. So accomplished a short story writer was he, in fact, that he seemed to have no clear idea of where fiction began and fact ended. Ferris saw in some of DuBois' allegedly factual articles nothing but short stories based on "unmitigated prevarication."

DuBois' "Back to Africa" article was undoubtedly a case in point. Published in an influential white magazine while Garvey's mail fraud case was sub judice, *it combined facts, lies and innuendo into a damagingly prejudicial case against Garvey. Ferris was at understandable pains to document "Dr. DuBois' Ten Mistakes."*

One of the main characters in "Dr. DuBois' Dilemma," Bishop Alexander Walters of the A.M.E. Zion church, had chaired the first ever Pan-African Conference of 1900 in London. His widow, Mrs. Lelia Walters, whose disapproving letter to DuBois is quoted here, was an admirer of Garvey and a regular speaker at Liberty Hall, the U.N.I.A.'s meeting place.

The author of "Prof. Brawley and Other Negro Critics" returns to the now familiar theme of conservative handpicked spokesmen with no real allegiance to the Black masses in whose name they speak. He is almost as harsh on Benjamin Brawley as was Hubert H. Harrison. William Stanley Braithwaite, DuBois and James Weldon Johnson are also spurned as lacking in that basic orientation towards their own community that underpins the Garvey aesthetic.

By way of contrast, Amy Jacques Garvey positively exulted over Langston Hughes' famous essay on "The Negro Artist and the Racial Mountain." She did not know whether he was a paid-up member of the U.N.I.A., but as far as she was concerned he had to be at least a student of Garveyism. Who else would affirm so fearlessly, and in a white publication too, the right of Black artists to be "our individual dark-skinned selves?"

Marcus Garvey's article, though focused on Claude McKay's best selling novel, Home to Harlem, *is in fact a sweeping indictment of the mainstream writers of the Harlem Renaissance. Garvey sent this article to his paper from Paris, and it was printed on the front page in bold type, as were all his weekly editorials. The* Negro World *always carried a second editorial page which, as has been seen, carried regular editorials, both signed and unsigned, on literary subjects. These latter were written by William H. Ferris, Eric D. Walrond, Robert L. Poston, Hubert H. Harrison, John Edward Bruce and others.*

Garvey accuses DuBois, Walter White, Walrond (who by 1928 had long deserted the U.N.I.A.), James Weldon Johnson and, of course, McKay, of pandering at the behest of white publishers, to the worst stereotypes which the white public foisted onto the Black population. By this time at least two prominent members of Afro-America's literary mainstream, DuBois and Alain Locke, were able to corroborate the accuracy of Garvey's observation. DuBois, inconsistent as ever, nevertheless simultaneously published a novel, Dark Princess *(1928), which seemed to embody some of the negative characteristics that he had criticized in* Home to Harlem.

Garvey in any event went much further than DuBois or Locke could, in restating the essence of his aesthetic theory. "We want writers who will fight the Negro's cause," he said. It was inconceivable to Garvey that a great white writer would vilify his race for the titillation of a Black audience. Yet, the most lauded of Black writers seemed to have few scruples in the reverse situation.

The Century *article to which Garvey refers is the same one which Ferris criticized in "Dr. DuBois' Ten Mistakes."*

In the final article Ferris praises Walrond, his fellow Negro World *editor, on his appearance in a major publication. Walrond's subtle non-strident propaganda accorded well with Ferris' idea of the effective use of that device.*

Dr. DuBois' Ten Mistakes

William H. Ferris (1923)

"BACK TO AFRICA," by Dr. W. E. Burghardt DuBois, in the February issue of the *Century Magazine,* is one of the most brilliant bits of fiction and prose poetry that ever emanated from the facile pen of that gifted writer. Never did his genius as a short-story teller shine more resplendently. Prose and poetry, fact and fancy, fiction and history, and imagination and reality were so subtly blended and flowed so easily on the prose cadences of Dr. DuBois' inimitable style that the reader finds it difficult to tell when Dr. DuBois is envisaging reality and when imagining.

By getting some scraps of information here and there and by bringing his imagination into play, Dr. DuBois has created an imaginary Marcus Garvey and an imaginary Universal Negro Improvement Association which is both like and unlike the real person and the real organization. In his essay on Alexander Crummell, Dr. DuBois, by his poetic imagination and his magic style, made a real man look like an imaginary portrait. In his "Back to Africa" he made an imaginary portrait and an imaginary organization look like a real man and a real organization.

The same poetic description and philosophic musings which characterized *The Souls of Black Folk* and *Darkwater* may be observed in the article that we are now discussing. In his pen pictures of High Harlem at the beginning and ending of his article; in his philosophical reflections upon the Negro whirlpool and other smaller swirlings affecting the stream of American life, upon Garvey's movement representing something spiritual, upon the Negro's craving for manhood and in his showing that Garvey is a "type of dark man whom the white world is making daily—moulding, marring, tossing in the air"—Dr. DuBois writes in the vein that gave *Souls of Black Folk* and *Darkwater* their deserved fame.

Dr. DuBois an Impressionist and Not a Realist

And yet the reader somehow feels that with all the poetic descriptions, pensive musings and philosophical reflections there is yet something lacking, and that is a gripping hold upon reality. "Back to Africa," like *The Souls of Black Folk,* represents more the subjective impression which the Garvey movement made upon the sensitive mind of Dr. DuBois than an objective presentation of the movement as it really is. Dr. DuBois is more of an impressionistic rather than realistic painter. He gets a general impression and a few general outlines, and then his imagination completes the picture.

In the case of Marcus Garvey and the U.N.I.A., Garvey was thirty-three years old and the U.N.I.A. two and a half years old before Dr. DuBois began to consider them seriously. He heard that a Jamaican harangued the crowds from a soap box in Harlem, organized thirteen in a small room, started a weekly paper and talked about building factories and operating a steamship line, but he paid no attention to what he regarded as a transient ebullition of emotion.

Consequently, when in August, 1920, Garvey three times congested the streets of Harlem with a parade, packed Madison Square Garden to the very doors and held an international convention for thirty-one days in a Liberty Hall with twice the seating capacity of any Negro church in the world—filling it in the daytime, overcrowding it at night, and with thousands turned away from the Sunday evening services—the white people began to ask, "What does it all mean?" Quite naturally they would ask Dr. DuBois, a recognized Negro leader and writer, about it. He knew very little about it. For three months he wandered in the wilderness, picking up scraps of information from former officials and friends of present officials, getting nearly all of his information second hand. The result was the sketchy article in the *Crisis* in January, 1921.

Then Dr. DuBois began seriously to study Marcus Garvey and the movement he had launched. But the U.N.I.A. was too big and too complex and it had too many ramifications all over the world to be easily focused. The late Prof. Josiah Royce, Harvard's famous metaphysician, once said that it was very difficult to convince a man or change his views by merely arguing with him, for his point of view and his ideas are the resultant of his character, temperament, education, environment and the experiences that he has passed through. That is quite true.

It is very difficult to understand the psychic reactions of a man and his dominant motifs when you don't meet him or don't begin to study him until he is thirty-three. To really know him you must know his parents, his early teachers and associates and early environment. To really know him you must know him in his boyhood, his youth and early manhood; you must know the men who inspired him, the forces that fashioned and shaped him, the influences that operated upon him and the pleasant or rough experiences, the boosts or hard knocks that colored his ways of thinking. You can't simply see him as a man and then imagine what his previous experiences had been.

So is it with a movement. When Dr. DuBois first began really to study the U.N.I.A. it was like a mighty river rushing at high speed toward the ocean of destiny, bearing upon its bosom the hopes, strivings and aspirations of a struggling race. He did not know what tributaries fed the stream, what ideas went into the making and what men made their contributions to the movement. Consequently, with only scraps of information at his command, he had to draw considerably upon his imagination.

Thus Dr. DuBois intimates that the "Back to Africa" idea was the only dominant idea in the Garvey movement. But the two ideas—the colonization and empire idea—which formed the "Back to Africa" idea were only two of the eight ideas which went into the formation of the Universal Negro Improvement Association. The other six ideas were forming a confraternity of the black people of the world, protesting against caste prejudice and proscription which ignored the worth of a man and looked solely at his color, teaching black men to respect themselves and each other, building factories, launching a steamship line and developing Liberia industrially and commercially.

Dr. DuBois' Ten Mistakes

Dr. DuBois' *Century Magazine* article is so brilliant and perfect a literary creation that we hate to dissect it. It is like analyzing the beauty and fragrance of a rose and telling what chemical elements entered into its composition. But as Dr. DuBois is writing history, we must consider his article as history and not as a magnificent bit of prose poetry. These ten mistakes are not mistakes of interpretation, but of historical facts.

Mistake No. 1 Dr. DuBois, on page 539 of the *Century Magazine,* says of Garvey: "Beside him were 'potentates!'" *Answer:* In *reality* there was only one potentate, Gabriel M. Johnson of Monrovia.

Mistake No. 2. Dr. DuBois, on page 539, says: "Before him knelt a succession of several colored gentlemen. . . . Among the lucky recipients of titles was the former private secretary of Booker T. Washington." *Answer:* In *reality* Dr. Emmet J. Scott was in Washington, D.C., and did not attend the convention.

Mistake No. 3. On page 541 of the *Century Magazine* Dr. DuBois says,

"Then came the new economic demand for Negro peasant labor on the Panama Canal." *Answer:* But Colonel Goethals in his book, *How I Built the Panama Canal,* states that many West Indians were employed as engineers and mechanics, and many Italians as laborers.

Mistake No. 4. Dr. DuBois, on page 541 of the *Century Magazine,* says that "West Indians began to migrate in larger numbers to America during the World War." *Answer:* In *reality* West Indians began to migrate to America in 1895,* when the Brussels conference barred and boycotted West Indian and imported sugar and when the German beet sugar began to thrive. See article on Brussels in the *Encyclopedia Britannica.* It would be advisable for the learned scholar to also read Crabbe's *Guide to the British West Indies.*

Mistake No. 5. On page 543 of the *Century Magazine* Dr. DuBois refers to Marcus Garvey as "This black peasant of Jamaica." *Answer:* Marcus Garvey never worked as a farmer or agricultural laborer. When he quit school at the age of sixteen he worked four years as a printer, four years as a foreman of printing. Since then he has traveled and studied conditions in Europe and other parts of the world, edited newspapers and formed organizations.

Mistake No. 6. Dr. DuBois says of the *Yarmouth,* the first steamship of the Black Star Line, "She made three trips to the West Indies in three years." *Answer:* In reality she made three trips in nine months.

Mistake No. 7. On page 544 of the *Century Magazine* Dr. DuBois says, "Thus the bubble of Garveyism burst." *Answer:* There are still over 800 well-organized divisions functioning as they did before the delegates went to the League of Nations from the August convention of 1922.

Mistake No. 8. On page 545 of the *Century Magazine* Dr. DuBois says, "He did not quite dare call himself King Marcus I, but he sunned himself a while in the address of 'your Majesty.'" *Answer:* If Dr. DuBois would attend the meetings in Liberty Hall or read *The Negro World* carefully he would learn that Marcus Garvey's official title is "Your Excellency."

Mistake No. 9. On page 546 of the *Century Magazine* Dr. DuBois says of the U.N.I.A., "Its main and moving nucleus has been a knot of black Jamaican peasants resident in America." *Answer:* If Dr. DuBois had carefully observed the parades of 1920 he would have seen over a score of bright, resplendent banners with Barbados, Jamaica, Grenada, St. Kitts, Antigua, Cuba, Haiti, Porto Rico, Santo Domingo, Trinidad, Demerara, New York, New Jersey, Pennsylvania, Washington, Virginia, North Carolina, Georgia, Florida, etc., emblazoned upon them. These banners indicated that the groups of from ten to one hundred who marched behind them were born in the country, island or State designated on the banners, and that the Universal

---

*Ferris subsequently corrected the date of the Brussels conference to 1896.

Negro Improvement Association is recruited, not from the island of Jamaica, but from the black peoples of the world. Two-thirds of the two-score divisions, whose membership runs into the four figures, are located in the United States of America.

Mistake No. 10. Dr. DuBois, on page 548 of the *Century Magazine* says: "As compared with the homes, the business, the church, Garvey's basement represents nothing in accomplishment and only waste in attempt." *Answer:* On page 543 of the *Century Magazine* Dr. DuBois states that the *Yarmouth* made "three trips to the West Indies": that "Garvey sent the *Kanawha* down to do a small carrying trade between the West Indian islands," and that with the *Shadyside* "he carried excursionists up and down the Hudson during one summer." On page 544 he states that Garvey "has established a number of local grocery stores in Harlem and one or two shops, including a laundry and a printing press." We will state that the printing press includes a Goss supplement press, a steam table, a stereotyping machine, four linotype machines and smaller presses for job printing. Does the learned doctor regard these as accomplishments?

Conclusion

Dr. DuBois' article is written from the standpoint of a disinterested white man who studied the U.N.I.A. from long range and not from the standpoint of a racial leader who has kept his finger on the pulsebeat of the race that he is supposed to represent. When he characterizes the Black Star Line and the U.N.I.A. [as] "only waste in attempt," it indicates that he did not realize how Negrodom, how the black world was thrilled and electrified when it learned that a Jamaican and a New York organization had got out of the traditional ruts of church, lodge, agitation and small business into big business, trade and commerce, that the Negro's industrial and commercial horizon was about to be enlarged, that the new avenues of employment were about to be opened up to black men and black women, and that the Negro was about to leave his circling eddies and enter the stream of world commerce. It was the new spirit—the spirit of initiative and adventure—that Marcus Garvey and the U.N.I.A. represented—the Divine urge of progress—that was Garvey's contribution to the spiritual inheritance of the race.

*   *   *   *   *   *   *

The August convention of 1920, with delegates from nearly every State of the Union, from Cuba, Haiti, Santo Domingo, Porto Rico, the West Indies, Central America, South America, Liberia, Sierra Leone, the Gold Coast and South Africa, assembled to put over an industrial program as well as to perfect a fraternal organization and voice the black man's grievance at the wrongs and injustices to which he was subjected; [this] was something new in Negro history. The distinguished men of color who attended that convention, either as delegates or visitors, the crowds that congested Madison Square Garden the opening night and Liberty Hall for thirty consecutive nights, and the world publicity that that convention received, and the crowds and publicity given to the conventions of 1921 and 1922, indicates that the world recognized that the black man's soul was awakened and that a new dynamic force and impulse was operating in the black man's mind.

The world somehow recognized that the spirit of progress, of adventure and achievement on a colossal scale was stirring in his mind. Unfortunately some of the representatives of the U.N.I.A. allowed the aspects that the white press emphasized to sidetrack them from the main line that brought the immense hosts together.

A study of the psychology of religion and a comparative study of religion indicates that any religion which grips large masses of mankind gets its power not on account of its error but on account of the truth that it contains, on account of its powerful appeal to what is basic and fundamental in human nature. So it was with the U.N.I.A. It taught the Negro to think in international terms and gave him a vision of world politics and world commerce. It enlarged his mental horizon and the boundaries of his mind. It liberated his imagination and gave him new ideas. And this, according to Dr. Coué, is something worth while. It taught the Negro to think and feel that he was a man and could play a man's part in the affairs of men. For this reason it will live on as an uplifting psychic influence.

Five years is a brief moment in the life of an organization or corporation. If Dr. DuBois knows of any Negro corporation that at any time within the brief space of five years marshaled as many members as the U.N.I.A. has, invested as much money in industrial and commercial enterprises and gave as much employment to men and women of color, we would be grateful for the information.

Dr. DuBois' Dilemma

Unsigned Editorial (1923)

'Tis said that Homer sometimes nods and that the wisest and best of men sometimes make mistakes. Well, our good friend, Dr. DuBois, with the poet in his nature stronger than the scientist, following his usual custom of getting information second hand and sometimes third hand and fourth hand, erred somewhat in the New Year issue of the *Crisis* regarding two very distinguished men.

Dr. DuBois opens his editorial under the caption "Democrats" by saying: "Once we hoped an offer of our support would induce the Democratic party (a) to curb the Bourbon South; (b) to work for the human uplift of the black and lowly.

"We thought Wilson wanted to when he wrote to the late Bishop Walters, promising us 'Justice and not mere grudging justice.' After election he called the Bishop to him. 'Er—Bishop, what is this I hear about some letter I wrote you during the campaign? I don't seem to recollect its terms.'

" 'I have it right here—right here,' answered the Bishop, proudly.

" 'Yes-yes!' " hummed the great war President as he read it and carefully tucked it away in his pocket.

"The Bishop never saw the letter again."

We have always admitted that Dr. DuBois has the making of a great novelist and that sections of *Souls of Black Folk* and *Darkwater* indicate that he has a genius for telling a story. We do not know whether he could produce masterpieces if he would try his hand turning out long novels. But there is no greater short story writer in the country today than Dr. DuBois.

Now this story related about a conversation between a former President of the United States and a late colored Bishop, regarding a much-discussed and much-advertised letter, is admirable and superb as a story per se. It is short and sweet. It gives the imagination something to feed on. It moves as swiftly and as lightly to the climax as a tiger stalking a prey. It vividly contrasts the wary, wily, watchful and self-possessed former President and the good colored Bishop as frank and unsophisticated as a school boy, who, flattered by the President's interest, proudly produced the letter, on which the President, upon receiving and reading, transferred to his own pocket. A Victor Hugo, a Dumas or a Zola or a Balzac or any of the reigning French novelists could not have told the story more cleverly. We fancy that Dr. DuBois was proud of that little bit of writing.

Mrs. Lelia Walters' Letter

But Mrs. Lelia Walters, the widow of the distinguished Bishop, a lady of remarkable intelligence and nobility of character, steps upon the stage and introduces a new element in the drama. In a terse and trenchant letter to Dr. DuBois she characterizes his story as fiction, pure and simple, as something that was woven whole cloth out of someone's imagination and not as actual history. Translated in plain Anglo-Saxon, the episode that the learned editor relates was good as a story, but seems to be a lie, pure and simple, what some might term an unmitigated prevarication.

Mrs. Walters' letter to Dr. DuBois regarding the matter reads as follows:

Dr. W. E. B. DuBois,
Editor of *Crisis,*
New York City.

My Dear Dr. DuBois:
In the current issue of the *Crisis* there appears an article from your pen that purports to say that former President Wilson filched from the late Bishop Walters the letter which the colored people were pleased to term "That Famous Letter of Justice."

In reference to this publication I wish to say that no such incident ever occurred.

A few months ago an officer of the Anti-Lynching Crusaders rehearsed this same story to me, saying that she intended to use it as the basis of an article that would subsequently appear in the *Crisis.*

At this time I stated that there was not a scintilla of truth in the statement, and if it were published I could have no other recourse than to brand it as a wanton and malicious falsehood.

I am pained and surprised to know that the *Crisis,* without investigation or any attempt at verification—on mere unsupported rumor, would publish an article defaming the living and belittling the dead—a write-up which the Hon. Mr. Joseph P. Tumulty, who was secretary to former President Wilson at the time, characterizes as a deliberate fabrication.

Let us, Dr. DuBois, fight our battle with none other than the invincible weapon of truth.

If this letter is not convincing I would beg to suggest that you interrogate Mr. Wilson as to the truthfulness or falsity of your accusation.

Respectfully Yours,
MRS. LELIA WALTERS.
New York City, January 23, 1923.

Moral

Mrs. Walters, the wife of the Bishop, one of the two parties in the interview, characterizes the *Crisis'* story as "a wanton and malicious falsehood." Mr. Joseph P. Tumulty, former secretary to former President Wilson, the other of the two parties to the interview, characterizes the *Crisis'* story as "A deliberate fabrication." The wife of the late Bishop and the former secretary of the former President both emphatically deny the *Crisis'* story. What should Dr. DuBois do, who seems caught on the horns of a dilemma?

He must either go to a higher authority than the wife of the Bishop and the secretary of the former President and say that he received the story in person directly from the lips of Bishop Walters or former President Wilson, or else he must retract his story, saying that he meant it in good faith and did not intend to traduce the memory of Bishop Walters or injure the reputation of former President Wilson, but only mistook kitchen gossip and vague, floating rumors for the pure and unadulterated truth.

We can readily understand how a literary artist and a prose poet in his desire to produce dramatic effect could indulge in the luxury of rhetorical exaggeration. But it is always advisable for a scholar with a reputation to investigate and verify his statements from the parties or families involved instead of scattering broadcast to the four quarters of the globe vague, floating rumors which have not the basis of truth.

Prof. Brawley and Other Negro Critics

Unsigned Editorial (1922)

Prof. Benjamin Brawley is now included in the "Big Four." He, Braithwaite, Johnson and DuBois are regarded as the four Afro-American critics. Rev.

Anson Phelps Stokes, the philanthropist, mentioned the critical work of Prof. Brawley in a Hampton address. Mr. H. L. Panghorn in his "Uncle Tom Seventy Years After," an article which appeared in the Sunday *New York Herald* four weeks ago, speaks of the "valuable critical work of Brawley, Braithwaite, Washington, Moton, Johnson and especially DuBois."

It causes one to smile to read of the valuable "critical work" of Washington and Moton, who have shown organizing ability, but were men of limited training and education. This, however, en passant.

Prof. Brawley has written *A Short History of the American Negro, The Negro in Literature and Art* and *A Social History of the American Negro.* We have never had the opportunity to read these books, as none of our friends seem to possess one. But we glanced through them in a library last week.

From a fast glance through the three books we would infer that Prof. Brawley is a careful, painstaking scholar who aims to be fair and just. But he seems to lack originality and critical acumen.

One who desires a surface knowledge of Negro literature and Negro life will learn much from Prof. Brawley's three books. But the reader who desires psychological insight into various Negro movements will have to look elsewhere.

We regard Prof. Brawley's work as scholarly, but we do not see how it can be called critical unless it be that the Caucasians who select Negro leaders have selected him because he is conservative, will never break the traces and will never take the bit in his teeth and run away.

Regarding the other critics, we will say that Braithwaite is an appreciator rather than critic of poetry, and that James Weldon Johnson in his splendid anthology of Negro poetry does not seem to rank Margetson's "The Fledging Bard" among great Negro poems. He quotes from the poem and tells who Margetson is. But he does not quote from the finest passages and does not comment upon that poem as he does lesser poems. But then we must remember that Margetson is a bold, frank and fearless thinker. He possesses originality. And that is an animal that the Caucasian godfathers of the Negro are afraid of. To win their approval a Negro must think along certain prescribed and proscribed views.

Now for the fourth critic. Dr. DuBois is a scholar, a gentleman, a prose poet, who possesses an inimitable charm of style. He can be rightly regarded as a man of letters. But we do not quite see how he can be justly regarded as a great critic.

All of these four gentlemen are scholarly and cultured. But we are not absolutely sure whether they possess that philosophical analysis which entitles one to the rank of critic.

On Langston Hughes:
I Am a Negro—and Beautiful

Amy Jacques Garvey (1926)

Too much cannot be said in denouncing the class of "want-to-be-white" Negroes one finds everywhere. This race destroying group are dissatisfied with their mothers and with their creator—mother is too dark "to pass" and God made a mistake when he made black people. With this fallacy uppermost in their minds, they peel their skins off, and straighten their hair, in mad effort to look like their ideal type. To what end, one asks? To the end that they may be admitted to better jobs, moneyed circles, and in short, share the blessings of the prosperous white race. They are too lazy to help build a prosperous Negro race, but choose the easier route—crossing the racial border. It is the way of the weakling, and in their ignorance and stupidity they advise others to do likewise. As if 400,000,000 Negroes could change their skins overnight. And if they could, would they? Seeing that the bulk of Negroes are to be found on the great continent of Africa, and they, thank Heaven, are proud of their black skins and curly hair. The "would-be-white" few are fast disappearing in the Western world, as the entire race, through the preachments of Marcus Garvey, has found its soul, and is out to acquire for itself and its posterity all that makes other races honored and respected.

This urge for whiteness is not just a mental gesture. It is a slavish complex, the remnant of slavery, to look like "Massa," to speak like him, even to cuss and drink like him. In last week's issue of the *Nation* magazine, Langston Hughes, a poet, wrote a splendid article on the difficulties facing the Negro artist, in which he described the racial state of mind of a Philadelphia club woman, which is typical of the group under discussion. He states: "The old subsconscious 'white is best' runs through her mind. Years of study under white teachers, a lifetime of white books, pictures, and papers, and white manners, morals, and Puritan standards made her dislike the spirituals. And now she turns up her nose at jazz and all its manifestations—likewise almost everything else distinctly racial. She doesn't care for the Winold Reiss portraits of Negroes because they are 'too Negro.' She does not want a true picture of herself from anybody. She wants the artist to flatter her, to make the white world believe that all Negroes are as smug and as near white in soul as she wants to be."

We are delighted with the frank statement of Mr. Hughes in a white magazine; we do not know if he is a registered member of the Universal Negro Improvement Association; in any event his closing paragraph marks him as a keen student of Garveyism, and with stamina enough to express its ideals: "To my mind, it is the duty of the younger Negro artist, if he accepts any duties at all from outsiders, to change through the force of his art that old whispering 'I want to be white,' hidden in the aspirations of his people to 'Why should I want to be white? I am a Negro—and beautiful!'. . . We younger Negro artists who create now intend to express our individual dark-skinned selves without fear or shame. If white people are pleased we are glad. If they are not, it doesn't matter."

Bravo, Mr. Hughes! From now on under your leadership we expect our artists to express their real souls, and give us art that is colorful, full of ecstasy, dulcent and even tragic; for has it not been admitted by those who would undervalue us that the Negro is a born artist? Then let the canvas come to life with dark faces; let poetry charm the muses with the hopes and aspirations of our race; let the musicians drown our sorrows with the merry jazz; while a race is in the making, and steadily moving on to nationhood and to power.

Play up, boys, and let the world know "we are Negroes and beautiful."

"Home to Harlem," Claude McKay's Damaging Book Should Earn Wholesale Condemnation of Negroes

Marcus Garvey (1928)

Fellowmen of the Negro Race, Greeting:

It is my duty to bring to your attention this week a grave evil that afflicts us as a people at this time. Our race, within recent years, has developed a new group of writers who have been prostituting their intelligence under the direction of the white man, to bring out and show up the worst traits of our people. Several of these writers are American and West Indian Negroes. They have been writing books, novels, and poems, under the advice of white publishers, to portray to the world the looseness, laxity and immorality that are peculiar to our group, for the purpose of these publishers circulating the libel against us among the white people of the world, to further hold us up to ridicule and contempt and universal prejudice.

McKay's "Home to Harlem"

Several of these books have been published in America recently, the last of which is Claude McKay's "Home to Harlem," published by Harper Bros. of New York. This book of Claude McKay's is a damnable libel against the Negro. It is doing a great deal of harm in further creating prejudice among the white people against the Negro. I have now before me what purports to be a writeup or review of the book by "John O'London's Weekly." I am going to reproduce the entire review for the benefit of those who desire to see the impression such books create on the minds of white people. Claude McKay, the Jamaican Negro, is not singular in the authorship of such books. W. E. B. DuBois, of America; Walter White, Weldon Johnson, Eric Walrond, of British Guiana, and others, have written similar books, while we have had recently a large number of sappy poems from the rising poets.

White Publishers Use Negroes

The white people have these Negroes to write the kind of stuff that they desire to feed their public with so that that the Negro can still be regarded as a monkey or some imbecilic creature. Whenever authors of the Negro race write good literature for publication the white publishers refuse to publish it, but wherever the Negro is sufficiently known to attract attention he is advised to write in the way that the white man wants. That is just what has happened to Claude McKay. The time has come for us to boycott such Negro authors whom we may fairly designate as "literary prostitutes." We must make them understand that we are not going to stand for their insults indulged in to suit prejudiced white people who desire to hold the Negro up to contempt and ridicule. We must encourage our own black authors who have character, who are loyal to their race, who feel proud to be black, and in every way let them feel that we appreciate their efforts to advance our race through healthy and decent literature.

Writers to Fight Negro Cause

We want writers who will fight the Negro's cause, as H. G. Wells of the white race fights for the cause of the Anglo-Saxon group. Let us imagine Wells prostituting his intelligence and ability as an author to suit Negro publishers, as against the morals or interest of the Anglo-Saxon race. It is impossible.

Yet there are many Negro writers who have prostituted their intelligence to do the most damaging harm to the morals and reputations of the Black race. The following is the review of Claude McKay's book by the white paper, "John O'London's Weekly":

THINKING BLACK
A Negro's Extraordinary Novel About Negroes

If we may judge by the novels and plays which reach us in gay and un-European bindings, "high brow" America has "gone nigger." A few years ago there was Mr. Eugene O'Neill's "Emperor Jones" (it was, alas! a dismal failure on the London stage); more recently there have been Mr. Carl van Vechten's "Nigger Heaven"—which became almost a "best seller," even in England—the poems of Louis Varrey, Mr. J. W. Vandercooks' "Black Majesty," and many others of which the average English reader has never even heard. Now, in "Home to Harlem" (Harpers, 7s. 6d.), we have a remarkable novel about Negro life in America by a Negro author who has spared us neither vividness nor truth.

A Wanderer

Mr. Claude McKay has had a career highly colored with the romance that belong to all wanderers. He was born in Jamaica, of parents who had been abducted from their native Madagascar and auctioned as slaves. At the auction, we are told, they went on a "death-strike," vowing that if they were not sold to the same master they would kill themselves. Mr. McKay, who seems to have shown an early aptitude for learning, was offered the chance of an education in the United States by a friend and took it.

For two years he studied scientific farming in an American college, but the call of literature was not to be resisted, and so he left college to become a wanderer, a stoker, a Pullman-car attendant, a dock hand on the quays not only of New York but of London and Marseilles. It is in Europe, indeed, that he does his writing. "Home to Harlem," which is his first novel, has already gone into three editions in America within the space of two months.

A Social Document

"Home to Harlem" is not so much a novel as a social document about a race that few of us have tried to understand. Its hero is a slightly sentimental gentleman of color named Jake, who deserts from the American Expeditionary Force in France, not because he is a coward but because he is impatient to be "doing something." He comes to London to work at the docks at Limehouse, but after a time there comes the irresistible call of New York's colored colony: "It was two years since he had left Harlem. Fifth Avenue, Lenox Avenue, and One

Hundred and Thirty-fifth Street, with their chocolate-brown and wal-
nut-brown girls, were calling him: 'Oh, them legs!' Jake thought.
'Them tantalizing brown legs! . . . Barrons' Cabaret! . . . Leroy's
Cabaret! . . . Oh, boy!' "

And so Jake goes back to Harlem, with its cabaret, "speakeasies,"
its gin and flashing razors, its cinemas, in which only colored actors
and actresses are shown on the screen, its rouged dusky-brown girls
("rouge on brown, a warm, insidious chestnut"), its intermingled
poverty and luxury—a riot of color and gaiety (mixed with squalor),
at which the white man can only stand amazed. And as for the morals
of Harlem, we are shocked only when we begin to reflect that there
aren't any morals there at all.

Fantasia

Jake has his adventures. He falls in love with a Congo entertainer at a
cabaret, who disappears from his life as quickly as she comes into it.
He gets mixed up with a gin-drinking Negress and her old assortment
of friends; becomes embroiled in a strike; becomes (as did his creator)
a Pullman-car attendant; meets a Negro student who opens a new world
of culture to his gaze; falls ill almost to death; recovers, and at the end,
meets again the little Congo Rose who had set his heart aflame at the
beginning. These are some of the episodes that make up a book that,
in spite of the fact that it has the most slender of plots, holds our
attention till the last page. We read on, not so much because of Jake's
adventures as because of the shock and surprise of being in a new and
unfamiliar world; because of the extraordinary vividness with which
Mr. McKay describes an all-black Harlem cabaret:—

"It was a scene of blazing color. Soft, barbaric, burning, savage,
clashing, planless colors . . . all rioting together in wonderful harmony.
There is no human sight so rich as an assembly of Negroes ranging
from lacquer black through brown to cream, decked out in their
ceremonial finery. Negroes are like trees. They wear all colors naturally. And Felice, rouged to a ravishing maroon, and wearing a close-fit-
ting, chrome-orange frock and cork-brown slippers, just melted into
the scene."

We learn from Mr. McKay many hitherto unsuspected things about
Negro life, about their cooking, their food, about their attitude to white
men and to each other, about their work, and about their almost
incredible night life. The full-blooded Negro, for instance, has a
contempt for the half-caste that is almost as violent as the old Mary-
lander's for the Negro.

And again: "Jake was very American in spirit and shared a little of
that comfortable Yankee contempt for poor foreigners. And as an
American Negro he looked askew at foreign niggers. Africa was

jungle, and African bush niggers, cannibals. And West Indians were monkey-chasers."

The Real Tragedy

But the real tragedian of "Home to Harlem," in spite of his many misfortunes, is not Jake but Ray, the Negro student. As he himself confided to Jake:—

"The fact is, I don't know what I'll do with my little education. I wonder sometimes if I could get rid of it and go and lose myself in some savage culture in the jungles of Africa. I am a misfit—as the doctors who dole out newspaper advice to the well-fit might say—a misfit with my little education and constant dreaming, when I should be getting the nightmare habit to hog in a whole lot of dough like everybody else in this country. Would you like to be educated to be like me?"

Here, one feels, is unspeakable tragedy.

Proud Blood of the Negro

In the autobiography Claude McKay tries to make out that his parents were from Madagascar, and that they were so proud as to have gone on a death strike against being enslaved. I do not believe this. I don't believe McKay can trace his ancestry back to Madagascar. It is most likely that he came from the Congo. Negroes who are descendants from proud ancestors generally retain some of their proud blood. No proud man of any race ever debases his race. It is always those of low ancestry who are always willing to play the monkey for the satisfaction of others. But it is a trait of those libellers against the black race to always suggest when they come in contact with white people that they represent the best blood of the Negro.

DuBois' Royal House

If I am not mistaken, a friend told me that DuBois stated and suggested that he has claim to the ancestry of a Royal House in East Africa. It is rather amusing to hear these libelers of the race talking about their royal ancestry when they represent the lowest type of ancestry. Negroes of royal ancestry always want to be proud of their race; they do not think any race better than their own. Yet DuBois called a black man an ugly man simply because he was black. Those of you who remember his article in the "Century Magazine" in 1920 [sic] will remember that he positively stated that to be black was to be ugly. The black royal blood of East Africa believes in the honor and integrity of the black race. DuBois to the contrary believes that the standard of beauty is to be found in the white man.

Something Funny

It is funny that these writers are always suggesting that they are from royal black blood and yet they are prostituting their intelligence and ability as authors and writers against their race for the satisfaction of white people.

We are calling a halt on these libelous writers so that we may develop authors and poets worthy of our race and who will fight for the cause of the race.

Eric D. Walrond, of the Negro World, Writes "On Being Black" in The New Republic

The Short Story as Propaganda

William H. Ferris (1922)

A feature article, "On Being Black," by Eric D. Walrond, Associate Editor of *The Negro World,* appeared in the *New Republic* on Wednesday, November 1. The *New Republic* is a progressive magazine, a representative of advance thought in science, philosophy, politics, economics, literature, art and music, consequently it is very popular with the intellectuals.

Two or three colored men, among them Dr. W. E. DuBois, have already secured a hearing in its columns, and now Mr. Walrond adds his name to the list of colored writers of class.

Mr. Walrond does not contribute an article after the customary manner of dealing with the race question as a sociological, political or racial problem, but he tells three short stories showing the psychic reactions of an intelligent colored man who has been discriminated against. In the first story the hero goes in to buy a pair of spectacles and the proprietor thinks he is a chauffeur because he is colored. In the second instance he answers an ad for a stenographer. He receives a favorable reply to his letter. When he presents himself and the lady in charge sees that he is a colored man, he is informed that the position requires a man of banking experience. He is then referred to a colored friend in Harlem. And it happens that the colored proprietor was a former pupil of the hero. In the third instance the hero desires a stateroom for his wife, traveling to the West Indies. Although the staterooms were advertised for $150, he must pay $178 for a stateroom for his wife. She, being colored, must have a stateroom by herself, as a white lady wouldn't desire to share the stateroom with her.

The narration and dialogue are interesting and the descriptions vivid. The stories read easily and naturally, and at the close the reader is set thinking.

The novel and the short story have been very effective means of moulding public sentiment. Harriet Beecher Stowe's *Uncle Tom's Cabin* was more effective in moulding a sympathetic feeling towards the slave than the scholarship of Sumner, the logic of Harrison and the eloquence of Phillips, Douglass, Beecher, Parker and Starr King.

Within recent years the story has been more effective in acquainting the Caucasian world as to how black folks think than philosophical dissertations or impassioned eloquence.

About seventeen years ago Mr. Wilson, a former State assistant attorney of Chicago, wrote an article for the *Atlantic Monthly* upon "The Joys of Being a Negro." Then Chesnutt's *The House Behind the Cedars* and *The Marrow of Tradition;* DuBois' *The Souls of Black Folk* and *Darkwater* and James Weldon Johnson's *The Autobiography of an ex-Colored Man* through the medium of the story and reflections upon the black man's status have created a certain measure of interest in, and sympathy for, the aspirations and strivings of men and women of color. The world was wearied with philosophy, eloquence, argument and dissertations about the right or the wrong of America's treatment of the Negro. And then *The Souls of Black Folk* came along, revealing the agonized soul of a suffering Negro. And the country sat up and took notice.

The novel and the short story will be the medium through which the black man's cause will get a public hearing in the future. Twenty-five years ago monthly magazines like the *North American* and the *Forum,* and weekly magazines like the *Outlook* and the *Independent,* which made a feature of philosophical and scholarly articles, and were serious in tone from start to finish, had the right of way. But then the automobile, the golf club and the moving pictures came along. Men and women, even those who were educated, spent more of their leisure time in the open air and more in pleasure, recreation and relaxation. Hence they craved for light and pleasant reading, for reading that would not tire the mind and necessitate too much thought and take up too much time. Then the small book usurped the place of the big book and weekly and monthly magazines which made features of stories, pictures, poems, athletics and theatricals, usurped the place of the *North American Review,* the *Forum,* the *Outlook* and the *Independent.* The latter two journals are still widely read, but they now have competitors who reach a wide circle of readers. We are glad then that Mr. Walrond has joined the circle of story tellers. He is keen and wide awake, has the gift of expression, and we expect great things from him in the future.

7

On the Messenger

Latter day writers on the Harlem Renaissance have usually placed the Messenger *somewhere just behind the* Crisis *and* Opportunity *magazines as leading outlets for Black literary endeavor in the 1920s. In fact, none of these magazines equaled the* Negro World *in magnitude of literary output. And their editors were in no way superior to those of the Garvey organ. In fact, the* Negro World *editorial, "A Suggestion to the* Messenger," *seems to betray a touch of condescension towards the literary efforts of its rival. Nor, as has been seen, did William H. Ferris think too much of some of the articles of the* Crisis *editor, W. E. B. DuBois.*

Regular Negro World *contributor, Hodge Kirnon, in "Some Impressions of the* Messenger *Magazine," accurately pinpointed a serious flaw in the* Messenger's *effectiveness, at least in its earlier years. This was its narrowly sectarian focus. This in turn caused it to ignore or scurrilously ridicule many Black writers deserving of serious criticism. The* Negro World *of course also had its point of view. But its editors were on occasion surprisingly balanced in their treatment of non-Garveyite and even hostile writers.*

Hodge Kirnon alludes to the "Marcus Garvey Must Go" campaign spearheaded by the Messenger *editors (A. Philip Randolph and Chandler Owen) and supported by DuBois and other integrationists.*

A Suggestion to the *Messenger*

Unsigned Editorial (1922)

Mr. Floyd J. Calvin, a promising young colored writer, contributes an interesting book review in the October issue of the *Messenger Magazine.* His theme is *The Book of American Negro Poetry, Chosen and Edited with an Essay on the Negro's Creative Genius,* by James Weldon Johnson.

In the course of his review Mr. Calvin says: "But of more potential importance is the narrative of Phillis Wheatley. The author quite feasibly suggests she was first to hail General Washington as 'First in peace.' This shows careful research."

This is quite true, as Mr. Johnson on page 24 of his preface says: "It appears certain that Phillis was the first person to apply to George Washington the phrase, 'First in peace.'"

But it is also true that Mr. A. A. Schomburg of Brooklyn is the scholar to whom credit should be given for first discovering this fact. On page 13 of *Phillis Wheatley, Poems and Letters,* edited by Chas. Fred Heartman with an appreciation by Arthur A. Schomburg, in the summer of 1915, Mr. Schomburg, after quoting from her poem to George Washington in the *American Monthly Museum* for April, 1776:

"Thee, first in peace and honor we demand
The grace and glory of thy martial band,
Famed for thy valor for thy virtues more,
Hear! Every tongue thy guardian aid implore"

—says "It points clearly to the fact that she was the first to call him 'First in peace.'"

As Mr. Calvin was not living in New York City when this appreciation was published, and as he had little association with the savants who gather around Liberty Hall and discuss questions ranging from the freedom of Africa to Bergson's pragmatism and Einstein's relativity, his attention was probably not called to these facts since he has been in the city.

Some Impressions of
the *Messenger* Magazine

Hodge Kirnon (1923)

Though I recall having seen a few copies of the *Messenger* prior to 1919, I usually date my real acquaintance with it in the deeper and truer psychological sense from March, 1919. From that time up to the present the *Messenger* has become one of my regular periodicals, which is always read with much interest. From the outset I was always impressed with the *Messenger*. Its selection of subject-matter, its style and vigor, its method of presentation and general journalistic tone have always pleased me; but above all these considerations, its impression was most effective because of its decided radical, fearless and uncompromising manly temper. It seemed to have scorned the contemptuous, apologetic and servile spirit which was so characteristic of the old Negro journalism. To me it was reminiscent of the days when the *Voice,* a weekly paper edited by Hubert Harrison, spoke for the Negro who had radical inclinations. It stirred my revolutionary impulses in much the same way as when they were first fired by speakers like Emma Goldman and journals like the *Masses* and *Mother Earth.* More and more I was strengthened in the conviction that the *Messenger* was destined to make some contributions to the race along lines of radical thought.

Another point stood out quite clearly, however: the *Messenger* was not in reality a "journal of scientific radicalism." It was a radical propaganda journal for the diffusion of a specific radicalism in economic thought. It was somewhat orthodox in its judgement of men and events; that is, they were nearly always measured and judged in accordance to their relationship with a given standardized scheme of thought in much the same manner that orthodox Christians judge other religions. Of course, this method may be of service for propaganda purposes, but no one will lay claim to it as being scientific.

Immeasurable service has been rendered by the *Messenger* in its emphasis on the economic aspects of the race question; and more especially in their more indirect relations. The real import of the economic interpretation of the race problem in its many and varying forms which has now become common thought is to be largely credited to the *Messenger* for its popularization of that point of view. It also coined and familiarized such terms as "New Negro" and "Me-too-boss-hat-in-hand-Negro." By sharply contrasting their different connotations they were tremendously instrumental towards the growth and enhancement of the new spirit.

The *Messenger* Inconsistent

An inconsistent and perplexing feature of the *Messenger* is that while it claims devotion to radicalism and the New Negro, it actually utilizes more space to critical and cynical comments and strictures of the Negro characters of what it calls the old crowd; yet, strange to say, it is not at all keen in its detection and recognition of men of worth and budding achievement of the new spirit and school of thought. Aside from a bare passing mention of comparatively recent date the *Messenger* failed to recognize J. A. Rogers until Harrison, Ferris (the writer) and others wrote concerning his work. Ferris' work, *The African Abroad,* has never even been mentioned in its pages. Though it is doubtful as to whether the two volumes have ever been read throughout by anyone save the author, yet they contain a great deal of valuable matter on history, education, anthropology and philosophy. Above all, the *Messenger* has yet to speak of Hubert Harrison and his notable work in behalf of radicalism and general modern thought among Negroes and white alike. Harrison was the first Negro to introduce liberal and radical ideas in the various departments of learning among Negroes in New York. There is no doubt of the fact that the editors of the *Messenger* have derived much of educational worth from him. He is a man whose wide and accurate information and critical ability have astonished men of learning of both races. J. A. Rogers considers him the most effective Negro thinker of modern thought, yet up to this date he is yet to be recognized by the editors of the *Messenger.*

The *Messenger* has always shown a proneness toward fancy writing as well as indulgence in intellectual bombast. Passing over the Moens incident, which is an instance of the latter, I cite the following taken from the September, 1921, issue as another illustration of this charge. "We have in store for our readers some veritable treats this winter (1921). We shall enter discussion in two most interesting fields—domestic relations and medicine. What we shall have to say of marriage, divorce, prostitution and love will be scintillating; whereas our discussion of the fetich, of the germ, the drug, vaccination, super-surgery, along with our exposure of the fallacy of most of the M.D. practice and an explanation of etiology will keep the physicians scratching their heads." However, though over a year has passed, the promised articles are yet forthcoming.

Garveyism

The editors of the *Messenger* started some time ago an aggressive campaign against Garvey and Garveyism. Their slogan was "Garveyism must be destroyed!" Since then there have appeared in the *Messenger* several articles dealing with Garvey and the Garveyism movement. It is to be regretted that these articles have stamped a most deteriorating effect upon the *Messenger*. Its hitherto much-lauded journalistic dignity and high standard have been seriously marred by these articles. They breathe hate, malice and ill-will. The best that can be said of them is that they are good examples of cheap, tenth-rate abusive journalism. The commonplace abuse and vituperation which run through them have vitiated the whole career of the *Messenger*. Randolph's article, "Reply to Marcus Garvey," is a fair specimen.

Opposition to Garvey and his teachings could be pursued in a dignified journalistic tone without any fear of being classed as a straddler or compromiser. Dr. DuBois' articles on Garvey are worthy proofs of this. Owen advocates the deportation of Garvey. Not only is this opposed to Socialist principles, but it is also petty and unmanly. His article, "Should Marcus Garvey Be Deported?" is a piece of journalistic trash that is entirely unworthy of him. It now appears as if the anti-Garvey propaganda is being extended to an anti-West Indian propaganda. This is indicative of nothing but an intellectual and moral collapse of the editors of the *Messenger*.

At present there is no doubt of the fact that the *Messenger* is steadily retrogressing. Instead of waging a blind and indiscriminate war against Garvey, it should take due cognizance of the fact of race consciousness and the general moral effects of Garveyism which could be directed into channels quite helpful to the race in its spiritual and economic strivings. It is impossible in this age for any Negro to rise to leadership who ignores or undervalues race consciousness. The editors of the *Messenger* should also adjust themselves once more to internationalistic principles. In the November, 1922, issue they informed us that while everybody is interested in great persons, they were interested in the twelve smallest persons in America. Perhaps this accounts for the non-recognition of Harrison and others. The best that can be said at present for the *Messenger* is "while there is life there is hope."

8

On White Writers

The literary interests of the Negro World *writers were not confined to Black authors. They were very conversant with the content and trends of European, North American and other world literature, both past and present. Their writings were interspersed with references to white authors. And when white writers wrote on racial themes, they became appropriate subjects for extended* Negro World *criticism.*

John Edward Bruce's "Quoting Negro Authors and Poets," Eric D. Walrond's "The Morality of White Folks" and "The Word Nigger" and the unsigned editorial, "Back to the Mayflower!" all have a similar theme. They comment on the ethnocentric, arrogant and contemptuous elements observable in some white literary practice as it pertains to Black folk. Some of the authors criticized here—H. L. Mencken, Carl Sandburg, Heywood Broun and Lothrop Stoddard, were among the best known writers of the period. "Back to the Mayflower!" turns Lothrop Stoddard's alleged Ku Klux Klan involvement into an argument against integrationism and for Garvey's African program.

Rudyard Kipling, the Anglo-Indian poet, has been called the "poet laureate of British imperialism." As such, one would expect nothing but hostility to him from the Negro World. *H. G. Mudgal, a* Negro World *columnist (and later editor), had an additional reason to be hostile. He was himself originally from India. Another* Negro World *editor, T. Thomas Fortune, parodied Kipling's "White Man's Burden" in a poem entitled "Black Man's Burden" which appears later in this volume.*

T. S. Stribling's Birthright *was discussed or referred to several times in the* Negro World *(see Chapter 10). Here his two articles based on a trip through the West Indies elicited differing responses. In "Stribling On the Women of Trinidad" Walrond found a tribute, however unintended, to Black womanhood.*

Tom Watson may have been expected to receive treatment similar to that meted out to Rudyard Kipling. But such was not the case. The "Tom Watson" editorial is charming, seemingly surprisingly balanced and almost, but not quite, tongue-in-cheek. Its disingenuous reference to this "poor cracker" from "the sand hills of Georgia" illustrates an interesting characteristic of Afro-American journalism of the period. Even moderate papers (the New York Age, *for example) were quite free in their use of disparaging epithets for the poor and/or racist whites of the South and elsewhere.*

Quoting Negro Authors and Poets

Bruce Grit [John E. Bruce] (1922)

I do not recall but a single instance in American history where a white public speaker has had the decency to quote from a Negro poet or author and comment on the merit of the poem or book before a white audience. The man was Theodore Weld, the place the Ohio Reserve, the occasion an anti-slavery meeting in 1837. The poet quoted was a slave named James Horton.

James Redpath, author, dedicated his famous book, *Echoes from Harper's Ferry* to General Geffrard, who was at one time president of the Republic of Haiti. There may be others. If you know them, name them, and we will print them.

The Morality of White Folks

Eric D. Walrond (1922)

One of the joys of literary sailoring is to picture the moral depravity of the black. The travel literature of Africa and the West Indies, and paradoxical as it may seem, of our own Dixie, is full of this sort of thing. A Boston adventurer, let us say, goes to Turkey, or Martinique, or to a Spanish-American seaport. The first thing that attracts his attention is the awful lack of economic life, the free and unrestricted gratification of the sex instinct and the universal lowering of moral standards. He judges the native not by a local standard of things, but a far-fetched idealistic one. The art, morals, science, religion and literature of the country is examined without regard to the country's history, geography or anything else. Even if one were to proceed on the basis of absolute equality in the human family an unprejudiced investigator may prove that all is not hopeless with the darker race, and vice versa. "Civilization in the United States" is a mirror of the many Black Holes of Calcutta in Lincoln's great democracy. It is an enterprising book, but in looking over its list of contents we find essays on humor and advertising and engineering and a multitude of other things, but not a word on morality! For us black folk an inquiry into the morality of white folk would doubtless reveal a lot of data, mostly biologic, that would be of exceeding interest. But no such attempt will ever be made, not even by Mr. Mencken, and if we want it done we must do it ourselves.

But let us take a single day's news as an index. The day that the *New York World* heralded the indictment of Mr. Marcus Garvey it carried also a story of the indictment of Mr. Tex Rickard, the fight promoter, on a charge of illicit relations with two fifteen-year-old white girls. It also carried "sensational developments" in connection with a recent murder scandal at Hollywood, involving Miss Mabel Normand. Alongside of Mr. Fatty Arbuckle's recent depredations this puts the movie colony, we feel, in the category of any of the barrios of Chile or Peru. Then, a few weeks ago, the readers of the *Daily News* or the *American* were tickled, to slide into the jargon of the avenue, with the views of Mr. Garland, the notorious Socialist who flagrantly acknowledged a wife, mistress and a life of "free loving." One more case and we are through. There was a certain broker in New Jersey. After being married for a few years this man became tired of his wife and, with a young college girl, maintained a "love nest" somewhere in the outskirts of a so-called respectable millionaire colony. All these things are familiar to readers of the daily press, and don't forget that the press—the white press—is not immune from corruption and moral depravity!

The Word "Nigger"

Eric D. Walrond (1922)

Five years ago it was a common thing to speak of an Italian as a "Wop," a Jew as a "Sheeney," a Pole as a "Kike." Today the Negro, to a vast portion of the American public, is yet a "Nigger." The word is a stigma of inferiority and its users know it. Ever since its origin it was used to label the Negro as a member of an inferior race. The Russians and Poles and Lithuanians who came to America and were called "names" strenuously objected to it and the result is, being white, they have managed to grow far beyond the reaches of objectionable cognomens. But "Nigger" lingers, and here comes Prof. Heywood Broun of the *New York World* condoning the use of it. Prof. Broun, who is the dean of the school of spontaneity in literature, sides with Carl Sandburg, apostle of the free verse movement in poetry, who thinks that it is not a bad word at all and the Negro ought not to blush and mumble at its use. Says Prof. Broun:

"Carl Sandburg expressed himself about something yesterday which we had been turning over in our mind. He thinks that one of the necessary steps in the progress of the American Negro is for him to accept the word 'Nigger' and make it his own. To be sure, the word had its origin in contempt, but acceptance itself would serve to rob 'Nigger' of all sting. Some such process has gone on in connection with 'Yankee' and no Confederate soldier minded being called a 'Reb' after he himself had begun to use it.

"From the standpoint of language there is much to be said for 'Nigger.' 'Colored man' is hopelessly ornate and 'Negro' is tainted with ethnology. More than that, it is a literary word. 'Nigger' is a live word. There is a ring to it like that of a true coin upon a pavement. Nor are all the connotations of the word shameful to the Negro race. Something of the terrific contribution of physical energy which the Negro has made to America is inherent in the word 'Nigger.' To our mind it brings up a vision of a man wrestling with great burdens and conquering them. Blood and sweat and tears have all combined to make 'Nigger' stark and simple. Among namby-pamby words it looms like a great rock. It is basic, but not base.

"And, after all, it has been the function of the Negro in America to furnish a back for other men to stand upon. His labors have contributed vastly to our wealth. Few men of his race have won great distinctions in the arts, and yet it is from him that almost everything worth while in American literature and American music has been derived. Others have had the privilege of turning the somersaults, but their start has been from the stalwart shoulders of the man with both feet upon the earth. This vital, deep-rooted figure can say 'I am a Nigger' and make the words as true and as rich as the soil from which it springs."

Ever heard of more asinine outpourings in all your life?

Back to the Mayflower!

Unsigned Editorial (1923)

Shortly after its appearance, Lothrop Stoddard's *Rising Tide of Color* became the Bible of the racial revolutionists. Vocabularies of adjectives were exhausted in praise of it. Hearst serialized it in his *Journal* and the white world likewise devoured it. Mr. Stoddard, a political best seller, duplicated the feat in a subsequent work, *The Revolt Against Civilization.* In both books the author [is] presented, not as a sort of Anglo-Saxon-rule-loving Paul Revere, but as a highly specialized journalist who saw and dared to interpret the trend of racial affairs. It so happened that the Africans and the Asiatics, fully race-conscious, had begun to react to the post-war state of affairs, and Mr. Stoddard's findings added vim and vigor to their loose efforts. In short, he was deified as a friend of the rebellious races.

Now, in Hearst's *International* for February, Mr. Norman Hapgood brings documentary evidence to prove that Mr. Stoddard is an Imperial Kleagle in the Knights of the Ku Klux Klan! But wait. That is not all. Mr. Stoddard this very week contributes an article to the *Saturday Evening Post* called "Lo, the Poor American." Veiled in a cloud of subtleties, he hurls a forceful challenge at the radical and progressive group in America. He hits at *The Nation,* the virile organ of liberalism; he lambastes the "Inquiry by the Thirty Americans Into Civilization in the United States." Harold E. Stearns, its editor, is viciously taken to task. Mr. Stoddard does not stop there. He "has blood in his eyes" for the whole school of modern realistic literature. Sinclair Lewis, H. L. Mencken, Ben Hecht, Sherwood Anderson, each comes in for a sound thrashing. Says Mr. Stoddard: "We older Americans will not be browbeaten into scrapping one jot or tittle of our handiwork until we are convinced that it should be done."

This in an "opinion-reflecting" journal like *The Saturday Evening Post,* with its two and a half million circulation, is astounding, to say the least. In short, Mr. Stoddard is an exponent of the doctrine of "white supremacy." He is a Klansman. He is opposed to the strivings of racial minorities who constitute the "New American." Very adroitly he refrains from referring to Negro agitation. He, however, with an amazing love for statistics, goes into the white race complexities in America. "For," he says, "in the last analysis, it is the North European stocks which constitute the predominant force in America." Stoddard says that of the 95,000,000 whites in the Untied States "fully 40,000,000 were descended from the old colonial stock, which was, of course, almost wholly Nordic North European in race, while another 40,000,000 of our population were of the same kindred North European stocks, the great majority being either fully assimilated or in rapid process of assimilation.

He continues: "Only 14,000,000 or 15,000,000 of our population belong to the newer elements from eastern and southern Europe and the Levantine fringe of Asia. To be sure, these newer elements are today increasing relatively faster than the older stocks, owing both to their higher birth rates and to accessions by immigration. Nevertheless, they are still a decided minority, which will be unlikely to gain very greatly at the expense of the older stocks now that our gates have been closed to further wholesale immigration. In fact our recent immigration restriction laws are a striking proof of north European racial ascendancy in America. The passage of those laws was fought tooth and nail, not only by the newer immigrant groups but also by very powerful economic influences like the steamship lobby and industrial interests eager for cheap labor. Nevertheless, the majority of north European descent had made up their minds that wholesale immigration was a bad thing—and the restriction laws went over with a bang!

"So far as can now be judged, therefore, America is going to remain predominantly north European in race, ideals and institutions. That is a fact which should be clearly grasped by those unassimilated persons who dislike certain aspects of our civilization. Whatever changes they desire can be made only by the friendly assent of the older stocks. Certainly any widespread endorsement by unassimilated groups of the anti-native American propaganda now being conducted in radical circles would be an extremely short-sighted proceeding."

The sum up: Mr. Stoddard, a "north" European, is opposed to the radicals, racial and intellectual, who despise everything "Nordic" over against "the dark, swarthy alien—apparently the darker and swarthier the better." Or, to use his own words, "the south or eastern European, and still more the western Asiatic," are to be kept in their places. Along with these are thrust the Catholics, the Jews and the Negroes. Still some of our wiseacres sit by and ridicule the dream of an African empire administered by and in the interest of Negroid peoples. Still Dr. Moton, a cross between Ichabod Crane and the Knight of La Mancha, goes "a-race-co-operating." Still Mr. DuBois in his

Fifth Avenue tower folds his arms and dreams of a lynchless commonwealth.
Still—
    But need we go any further?

Rudyard Kipling

H. G. Mudgal (1922)

Has Kipling Saved His Soul?
    "They (the Americans) have got the gold of the world, but we have saved our soul!" said Kipling to Clare Sheridan.
    Rudyard Kipling is a rare soul. An English soul born and brought up in India and so imbibing all the venom of the Anglo-Indian, half-educated in India and half in England. Really nature meant him to be a rare soul. Kipling made his name and fame and amassed illgotten wealth, the very gold he taunts the Americas for possessing, in India. But what gratitude had he for India? He even could not call himself an Indian, but preferred to style himself as an Anglo-Indian, though he owes so much to India. On the contrary, he slandered and misrepresented India. He called India a "God-forsaken country," the "stony-hearted stepmother of collectors," and by a thousand and one other names. And all the spirit and inspiration he has he got in and through India.
    Kipling is the only great artist in the history of humanity that has proved capable of misusing his art for dark purposes and destructive ends. He is the only poet that has been unable to see the good side of human nature wherever it may present itself. He is the only thinker that has persisted in mis-thinking. In short, his brains have always been revolving in a wrong direction. What a pity!
    When he first visited Calcutta, what was he interested in, do you suppose? What the darkest spots were in the city. What did he observe in San Francisco? Nothing but the Chinese gambling dungeons, the only thing he wrote about. Always his mind is jumping like a fly to find out a filthy spot among a nation or in a people. His is a real, rank, filthy mind, indeed. Only we wonder why he was classed as one of the "great artists." He is a stinking carcass with gaudy clothing and fragrant flowers on.
    Kipling could not be reconciled to any nation that was not subordinated or not friendly with England. That is one of the reasons why he hates the

United States. He has not concealed his feelings on the matter, but has revealed his springing hatred at every opportunity, and that, too, decked in the most radiant array. He could not see anything good in the United States, not event the language, because there was no more the "Union Jack," "the old flag," as he called it, to make the States cultured, superb and refined. Of language he had said: ". . . the American has no language. He is dialect, slang, provincialism, accent, and so forth."

His past career is a sufficient warrant that he must have uttered the recent insults to America. But a coward as he is, he has denied not only the statement but the interview with Mrs. Sheridan. But, unfortunately for him (woe be to the married life!), his wife honestly brought to light the fact that Mrs. Sheridan did have the interview. If she had the interview, he did pass those insulting remarks about America.

Whether the whole British nation has saved its souls is not the concern of this article. But we are much interested in Mr. Kipling's individual soul. Kipling has committed so many sins that even Lucifer had to hang his head down in shame before his "god-embraced" rival. And yet he dares to raise his head and declare, "but we have saved our souls." Can he damn whole nations and peoples without being damned in return? Let us see how widespread and venomous his hatred is. In the words of the *New York World*: "Once Russia was the devil nation—'the bear that walks like a man.' Then it was Germany in the period when German and British militarists were egging each other on. Now it is America, which 'lent us money at 8 per cent, and made good business out of it.' At all times it is India, Ireland and Egypt. If Mr. Kipling were an American he could be a King Kleagle of the Ku Klux Klan."

Such is Kipling, and he is a rare soul. Has he saved his soul?

T. S. Stribling in St. Croix

Unsigned Editorial (1922)

It is clear that Mr. Stribling is out to uphold the torch of American imperialism. It is annoying to him to observe the predominance of black authority in the West Indies. St. Croix ought to be Haitianized. In his articles in the *Evening Post* he shows a distinct prejudice against the black labor agitators led by D. Hamilton Jackson. St. Croix is one of the Virgin Isles which was recently taken over by this country as a naval base for the protection of the Panama Canal. The author of *Birthright* in a very skillful way shows how the Danish capitalists at Fredericksted are conspiring to unionize the black cane hands and so cut the throats of the unorganized planters. All sorts of things creep in to make it uncomfortable for the crackers—obeah, cane fires, terrorism, intermarriage, Garveyism. Of Garveyism in St. Croix Mr. Stribling devotes a good sized paragraph. He says:

"In the meantime a completely new African force is approaching St. Croix. It has already reached St. Thomas. This is Garveyism. The complete name of Garvey's organization is 'The Universal Negro Improvement Association and African Communities League.' Its head-quarters is in New York. Its avowed and widely known object is to seize Africa for the Africans. The spirit of the organization is strongly anti-white and has a semi-religious fervor. The writer interviewed the leader of the African Communities League in St. Thomas. He was a Negro tailor, a smallish chocolate colored man with a flattened nose. He talked for two hours with the pure fire of a zealot about the absolute economic independence of the black man. The slightest dependence upon white men is gall to the Garveyite. Therefore, when the African Communities League enters St. Croix it will form a strong new anti-'Bethlehem' force, and this will tend towards a black absorption of the island."

Yes, the handful of "buckras" are in a sorry plight. And Mr. Stribling, boiling over with rage, cries out to Harding to study the record of his predecessor in Haiti and Santo Domingo, and send an army of marines to "Keep the Niggers in Their Place." It is a good thing to know that Mr. Stribling is laying his cards on the table. Artist that he is, his anti-Negro complex has prevented him from dealing with the Negro in an objective and dispassionate way.

But neither Mr. Stribling nor his lynchers in Texas are going to stop the wave of Negro agitation that is sweeping over the world—a wave destined to disturb the foundations of white civilization and put the black radicals on top!

Stribling on the Women of Trinidad

Eric D. Walrond (1922)

T. S. Stribling, the novelist, contributed an article to the *New York Evening*

Post of Saturday, December 17, 1921, on "Women in the American Tropics," in which he speaks of the lack of "sex solidarity" among white women in Trinidad. For the benefit of those who have never heard of him, Mr. Stribling is the author of that psychological novel, *Birthright,* which is running serially in *Century* Magazine. This is the story of the return of Peter Siner, a Negro graduate of Harvard, to the slush and grime of Nigger Town, a decadent citylet in the heart of Dixie. The author delves into the inner consciousness of the Negro, and is brilliant when he pictures Siner's reactions to his environment. There are times, however, when one is forced to acknowledge the superficiality of his hero. Things he does are open to question, and once more the question is raised, "Who is best able to portray the Negro, a white man or the Negro himself?"

In the article under discussion, Mr. Stribling admits that "the colored women of Trinidad are becoming ambitious for their children. It is a highly interesting and significant fact that nearly all the Rhodes scholarships and the governmental scholarships awarded in Trinidad go to colored boys or Negroes." The author goes on, "a certain Negro woman in Port-of-Spain made her living by peddling mangoes. She was thought half crazy. She went from door to door calling:

T for teef (thief)
An' C for cat
Here are your nice mangoes!

And it turned out that the old Negress really was stealing mangoes for her stock in trade. The mango growers could not stop her. She went to the mango orchards before day and picked up the fallen fruit. There was no way to keep her out, and her condition was such that no one would prosecute her. So she continued making her rounds, shouting the absolute truth.

"This Negress had a son. She kept him in school on the proceeds from the mangoes. He won the Rhodes scholarship and specialized in surgery, and the old Negress aided him even in Oxford with her mangoes. He is now one of the foremost surgeons in one of the King's colonies—it is obviously wise not to say which one.

"Endless tales are current in Trinidad of Negro boys sent to school half starved, half clad, who carried off the colonial and Rhodes prizes. I myself visited the different courts in Trinidad: the barristers were uniformly men of color. Precisely the same conditions prevail in Demerara. Now back of these ambitious black boys are ambitious black mothers. These women are declaring a dividend of energy, and this is the form it takes.

"If there ever comes a woman's development in the West Indies it will be a colored woman's development."

The heroic part a Negro mother plays in the evolution of the race is a story that is not yet written. One of these days a Negro Dickens will come along and, in his realist sweep, take in the whole panorama of irony, tragedy, heroism, sacrifice and achievement, and then the women of the race will come into their own.

The peculiar interest Mr. Stribling's article has for us is that it puts to flight all the lying and prejudiced stories some writers have been publishing about us. When Louis Siebold of the *New York Herald* visited Barbados and St. Lucia a few months ago he created an uproar among West Indians in North America over the lopsided views he expressed of conditions there. Similarly, Isaac F. Marcosson, in his book, *An African Adventure,* paints an ignorant, parasitic Congolese who does nothing but eat and get drunk and run errands for his pot-bellied master. Likewise, H. G. Wells, the British publicist, while admitting interest in the intelligent type of Negro, feels that the diamonds, pearls and priceless riches of Africa are too good for the native. Back of all this propaganda is the purpose—clean cut—to discredit the Negro in the eyes of the world. Marcus Garvey, Casely Hayford, Solomon Plaatje and Dusé Mahomed Ali are living repudiators of it. In a review of Angelina Grimke's *Rachel,* Miss Mary White Ovington, chairman of the Board of Directors of the N.A.A.C.P., regrets that Negroes are prone to look at all literature, especially when it is about them, in the light of propaganda. It might be inartistic and all that, but the Negro is obliged to be suspicious of white people, and no less an authority than Edward Alsworth Ross, professor of sociology, University of Wisconsin, strengthens this contention. Says Professor Ross: "The man who tells us that he feels to all men alike, that he has no sense of kinship, that he loves the Kaffir as he loves his brother, is probably deceiving himself." And don't forget, Professor Ross is a white man, expressing a white man's viewpoint.

Tom Watson

Unsigned Editorial (1922)

The Hon. Tom Watson, Democratic Senator from Georgia, died Tuesday morning, September 26, of acute asthma. He was born as a poor cracker in the sand hills of Georgia sixty-six years ago. Tom Watson became famous because he hated colored people, the Catholic Church and President Wilson as Cato hated Carthage. He was also a Populist candidate for President and wrote a history of the French Revolution.

Tom Watson was one of the most picturesque and versatile of Southern statesmen. Like Ben Tillman and Blease of South Carolina, Hoke Smith and Hardwick of George, Heflin of Alabama and Vardaman of Mississippi, he rode into fame and political power through riding the horse of Negro domination.

Prior to the rise of Senator Ben Tillman, the aristocrats were in the saddle politically in the South, and the poor whites were only camp followers. But through casting upon the canvas the bugbear of Negro domination and riding the hobby of Anglo-Saxon supremacy, representatives of the poor whites were able to ride into the gubernatorial chair and the United States Senate.

Tom Watson differed from most of the Southern leaders, whose stock in trade was cussin' and discussin' the Negro, in that he possessed some literary ability.

He was the author of *Story of France, Napoleon, a Sketch of His Life, Character, Struggles and Achievements,* and *Life and Times of Thomas Jefferson.* While these works are not characterized by the erudite learning and brilliant analysis and description of Hippolyte Adolphe Taine's *The Ancient Regime, The French Revolution* and *The Modern Regime,* they are very creditable pieces of work, considering that they were not written by a professional historian but by a man in public life.

Tom Watson's narrowness and provincialism in his attitude toward the Negro, the Catholic Church, President Wilson and other men and measures that he did not like were due not only to temperamental peculiarities, but also to the fact that he was born in the sand hills of Georgia and reared among the poor whites. It is very difficult for a man to wholly overcome the effects of his early training and environment. If his early environment is provincial and narrow and his boyhood associates are ignorant and illiterate, it will be hard for him to evolve into a broad-minded and broad-gauged man of culture.

But meanwhile the black man, in spite of criticism and handicaps, has been steadily forging forward, winning his spurs and establishing his title clear to recognition.

PART III

REVIEWS

9

Literary Works by Black Authors

The categories of "reviews" and "literary criticism" overlap somewhat. Selections included in the present section were presented as formal reviews or tended to be less wide-ranging, perhaps revolving around a single work of a particular author.

Batouala again dominates, as it did in the "literary criticism" section. Here we can follow some of the commentary, from the first brief excited notices of the book's impending arrival, to three substantial reviews. Eric D. Walrond's is probably the shallowest of the three longer pieces. He sees Batouala *as a great epic, but only hints at the novel's place in the propaganda debate that swirled about it. Walrond did, however, return, not very satisfactorily, to this question in "Batouala, Art and Propaganda," already presented.*

G. M. Patterson saw in Batouala *a straight propaganda novel. J. A. Rogers saw in the work a Ferris-type propaganda, masked on the surface by a cool irony, but too insistent beneath it to go undetected.*

Eric D. Walrond expressed complete love for Claude McKay's poetry collection, Harlem Shadows. *In the process he gave an inkling of the anti-propaganda position he was later to change to. Hodge Kirnon saw the same work as uniformly nonpropagandistic, despite the presence of "If We Must Die" and "Enslaved," to both of which Walrond referred.*

Robert L. Poston, like Ferris, demonstrates the genuine pleasure with which Walrond's fellow editors and columnists greeted his entrée into the major white publications. Poston gave a book-type review to what was in fact a short Walrond article in Henry Ford's Dearborn Independent. *The congratulations of his fellows was to change to disapproval in 1923 as Walrond accelerated his shift away from Garveyism.*

Walrond's own review of William Pickens' Vengeance of the Gods *was as harsh as* Negro World *reviews ever got—harsher than Ferris on DuBois or Hodge Kirnon on the* Messenger *magazine. Pickens' deep involvement at this time in the "Marcus Garvey Must Go" campaign may have had something to do with it. Pickens in his own way also represented, in extreme form, the propaganda position that Walrond was getting ready to abandon.*

Batouala

Anonymous (1922)

Batouala, the thrilling romance written by René Maran, the French Negro, that was awarded the literary prize by the Academy Goncourt, Paris, France, for the year 1921, will soon appear for the first time in the English language.

This is the first story of its kind ever written and for that reason has attracted international attention. It accurately depicts African customs and tells of the corrupt reign of the Caucasian in that country.

Mr. Maran, the author of the wonderful book, is the best-known Negro writer of the present time, the story having been favorably commented upon in every tongue because of its extraordinary features. The novel is tensely appealing to race-loving Negroes in all quarters of the globe.

The author richly deserves the success he has achieved, and his work is certain of an enthusiastic reception in America.

On Reviewing *Batouala*

Eric D. Walrond (1922)

On our desk is a copy of an English translation of René Maran's *Batouala,* published by Seltzer and distributed by Minor & Patterson of our own "belt."

It is a pity our French did not permit us to devour this Africa *Iliad* in its original text, as, according to J. A. Rogers, the Comstocks got hold of it and cut out all the real wild and woolly parts. Well, that is what we get for our Frenchlessness.

Batouala

By René Maran
Distributed by Minor & Patterson

Eric D. Walrond (1922)

Batouala is a series of poetic jungle pictures around which are built a story of savage dramatic interest. It is the historical triangle, but wrought with a vigor, a realism and beauty that stamp Maran the master that he is. One gets up from it with a tumult of emotion. The dark, hot, cold, sensual forest life of Ubangi-Shari; Batouala's hatred of the whites, which, at times, is not divorced from the author's; Batouala's jealous passion, the ceremony of the circumcision, the predominance of sex in the African milieu—all these are sketched with a realism, a lifelikeness that is truly phenomenal.

One sees the sun mounting the skies, and the figure of Batouala meditating as to whether he should get up or go back to sleep. . . . "He did not know." In his mind, omnipresent, is the constant fear that Yassiguindja, his favorite wife, is infatuated with the hemanized Bissibingui. At the festival of gan'zas the lovers dance the dance of love and Batouala is infuriated. From then on the story hinges on the plotting of Batouala to get rid of his rival. . . . "But Bissibingui knew that Batouala plotted revenge, and Batouala knew that Bissibingui knew."

Then—

Bissibingui had no time to hear or think. The barking of the dogs, the shouts of their masters, the glare of the flames, the heat, the drunkenness born of the sight of blood and the sight of the violence to which he and his companions had abandoned themselves—the tumult of light and sound and movement had stunned him. . . . A heavy javelin whizzed close over his head. . . . Who had thrown it? . . . . Batouala. . . . A moment before, however, Bissibingui, to escape the panther as it leapt upon him had thrown himself flat on the ground. When he raised himself, still trembling, the panther had disappeared. . . . But Batouala was there, very close to Bissibingui. . . . The mokoundji lay surrounded by a group of M'bis and N'gapus. . . . His breath rattled in his throat. . . . The panther infuriated by the javelin which he had seen coming—though it was not meant for him—had ripped open Batouala's belly with one blow of his paw. Then he had fled.

To add coals to a consuming fire, Yassiguindja and Bissibingui looked at Batouala and shook their heads.

"Is he dead?" she asked.

"Not yet."

"They smiled at each other. And they understood each other. Alone in the world, masters of their own fate, nothing and noboby could keep them apart. . . . Bissibingui went to Yassiguindja and drew her into his arms. She yielded to his desire."

Enraged at her brazen infidelity Batouala attempts to wreak vengeance on the lovers.

Ah, your eyes are opening, your eyes have opened, and you, you have thrown the covers off your horribly emaciated body. . . . You have risen. . . . You walk, tottering and holding out your arms like a baby learning to walk. . . . Where are you going? To Bissibingui and Yassiguindja?. . . . You're jealous, then, up to your very last gasp?. . . . Couldn't you let them alone, Batouala, seeing that soon you are to die?"

But no, Batouala, with a mighty effort, raises, goes to them, separates them, and leaves them there "glued to the wall, their limbs quaking, their teeth chattering with terror." And the belligerent chieftain, "killed by your own self, you topple over and fall to the ground unbending as falls a tall mighty tree."

It is easy to say that Batouala will go down in history and rest alongside the epics of all time.

Batouala's Author

G. M. Patterson (1922)

René Maran was born in the island of Martinique in the year 1888. At a tender age he was sent to Bordeaux, France, where he received his education. It is said that he spent all his time, even his vacations, in study. While he was an excellent athlete—a good football player, a clever fencer—his chief interests were literary. At the age of twenty-one he published his first book of poems called *The House of Happiness,* which was followed three years later by another volume of poems entitled *Interior Life.* He then turned to realistic fiction, which finally resulted in *Batouala.*

Batouala! The very name suggests, to one of vivid imagination, a weird story. And the tale is, indeed, so strange, so powerful and so unusual that the Academie Goncourt at Paris, France, granted it the prize as the best literary production of 1921; this, despite the fact that it is the most severe, the most bitter and the most caustic indictment of the Caucasian in his relations with black folks yet to appear.

Maran's Purpose

This book has been reviewed by the magazines and newspapers of all countries. I have read many of the comments, the majority of which have been laudatory, but nowhere have I seen expressed the evident design of the author in writing the story. This has been concealed either purposely or because of the difficulty for the Caucasian to interpret that which appears only in the soul of his black brother. Do you think that *Batouala* was written merely for the purpose of diversion, to do something not heretofore attempted, to commercialize talent? Do you think that René Maran spent six years of his life, as he says: "Listening to the conversations of these poor people" (meaning the natives) simply to write something that might amuse or entertain!

No, no! A thousand times NO! René Maran was writing a problem story, food for thought; something to awaken the consciousness of his group everywhere; something to tend to ameliorate the condition under which his African brother is living. His heart bled from the suffering he had witnessed and he determined that he should be the medium by which the cry of anguish he had heard should be disseminated to every part of the globe. His ambition has been realized in *Batouala.*

The preface to the book reveals, in language clear, eloquent and unrestrained the ideals of the writer that are later to be exemplified in the naive, realistic and unaffected story, through which is interwoven the thread of a thrilling romance.

Listen to the energetic language of the preface:

"Civilization, civilization, pride of the Europeans and their charnel-house of innocents! . . . You build your kingdom on corpses! Whatever you wish, whatever you do you move always in an environment of prevarication. You are the force that transcends the right! At your sight tears spring forth and the cry of anguish is heard. You are not a torch, but a raging fire. Whatever you touch you consume."

In this precise manner the reader is prepared for the impression he is to receive by inference in reading the romance.

Highly Educated

And thus, nowhere can one escape the contrast and comparison drawn between the habits and customs of the so-called savage and those of the so-called civilized man, and yet the theme is so simply and convincingly developed that one is ashamed to acknowledge allegiance to the latter group. It must be borne in mind, in this connection, that René Maran is a highly educated gentleman. That he has lived in Paris, the great metropolis of the world. That he knows, as you and I do, after careful reflection, that the so-called civilized man, like the so-called savage, is guided in his life and views by tradition.

Our thoughts are usually molded in early youth, through the reading of text books, in whose authors we place implicit confidence. The school boy recites his essay on a national character or event and is imbued with the truthfulness of what he is saying, without any independent analysis of the facts. And later, his time is so occupied in the struggle for existence that he rarely has the opportunity or inclination to investigate and analyze the falsity of all that by which he is surrounded. He is taught that work is dignified and arduously applies himself to his task. He will be astounded to read Batouala's reflection that "work is for those who will never understand it"; that idleness is not laziness, but the mere taking advantage of all that surrounds us. Meaning, that the Creator has placed within the grasp of the African to acquire without effort all that is necessary to sustain life, including a soil so fertile that abundant crops spring forth as the result of the slightest scratching of the earth's surface. So, why should he toil?

René Maran says, in substance, to throw away the mental crutches, to snatch the veil from the face of truth and look at her as she is, not as you would wish her to be, weighing the facts by the cold analytical process of reason.

And what is disclosed? A civilization guilty of the atrocities of the recent world war, a civilization that has since ruthlessly slain thousands of East Indians; a civilization that teaches and practices the right of the powerful to crush the weak; a civilization that is decimating the natives of Africa; a civilization with its hands on the throat of Haiti and Santo Domingo; a civilization that ties its constituent members to the stake and burns them alive as too frequently occurs here; a civilization whose hands are dripping, as it were, with the blood of its victims—a horrible thing! And, by truthfully depicting the traditions of the so-called savage, one learns that his most abhorrent practices pale into insignificance when compared to those of the so-called civilized man. You will note that I have consistently used the word "so-called" to qualify "civilized" and "savage." This has been intentional, because I believe that the terms "civilized" and "savage," as generally applied, are misnomers; that the one is only partially civilized and that the other is not wholly savage; that each contains elements of the other; that they represent two distinct types, one of which has arrogated to itself the right of classification—flattering in one instance and scandalous in the other. These are the facts. Why try to escape them by equivocation? This is the sociological exposure made by the gentleman about whom I am speaking.

Then the author takes us to what is frequently referred to as the "dark continent." Does the Caucasian go there to help, to uplift and to educate the native? Does he go there with charity and love in his heart for the poor creatures there? René Maran tells us that even the untutored native knows better. That he knows that it is GREED that brings his pale nemesis. That he knows that the attractive forces are diamonds, gold and other metals, and all those other commercial assets that mean dollars. That the native population is being decimated because of the arduous tasks imposed upon it as a consequence of the coming of civilization. René Maran says, in reflecting upon this situation: "They (the natives) suffer, and laugh while suffering."

But ah! some say, Africa and René Maran are far away. We have more intimate problems. And I say to you that the very purpose of this distinguished gentleman is to awaken the race consciousness of his group everywhere. Until we individually can feel the crisping heat of the flames burning South Sea Islands, we will not be in a position to present a united front that will correct the abuses of society we suffer everywhere. Let no one of us condone the mistreatment or misfortune of another member of our group, no matter where the action may take place. What matters it to you or to me the accident of birth? That one is born in Georgia and another in Patagonia, if you will, or in New York? The result of mere hazard. But our consanguinity, because of the blood that courses through our veins, is the stamp of our individuality and should be symbolic of brotherhood, love and affection.

Can you not see, my friends, that the present civilization is only a self-styled one? That it must disappear and is disappearing? That the time has come for you and for me to unfold our arms and do our part toward its reorganization? Let us lay aside our hammers and adopt the slogan of the *Three Musketeers,* by our Alexandre Dumas, "all for one and one for all." The time is at hand when we must stretch our hands, as it were, across the seas to grasp that of our brother, in order that we may together exert to the best advantage all the power that a gracious Creator has placed in our hands for the correction of abuses imposed under the guise of civilization. And the test of support must be, not where does he come from, but is he mine?

My friends, what I have said are not my thoughts. No one knows the little book *Batouala* better than I. Read the book, and in the lines and between the lines you will find expressed and implied the ideas I have tried in my own way to present.

Let us enlist in this struggle for the improvement of existing conditions. The East Indians have enlisted and the Africans are enlisting. Let us support and uphold those who are bold and daring enough to tell the facts as they are. René Maran tells us that the struggle will be beautiful because of the idealism of the objective. He does not mean by that physical force. The experience of the late war teaches the futility of that. There are stronger weapons than the use of arms; but, then, I am digressing. Some day I may have the opportunity to say something on this subject, and then those will be my thoughts, not those of another. Today I am speaking for René Maran.

Because he is ours. Let us acclaim him as such. Let us show him that he is appreciated at least as much by the members of his own group in America, whom he defends, as by the Caucasians whom he excoriates. His book is being released here on a royalty basis and every book purchased is an expression of gratitude.

And bear in mind that long after you and I shall have gone whence we came René Maran and *Batouala* will still stand as guideposts, pointing out the straight and narrow path of truth in a forest filled with winding paths of prevarication.

Sidelights on *Batouala* and Its Reviewers

J. A. Rogers (1922)

The world's verdict has been pronounced. *Batouala* is conceded to be a masterpiece; René Maran, the author, is conceded to be, if not a genius, at least a literary artist of the very highest rank. Even the critics who do not "like" the book admit that it has "poetic" qualities. What most of the reviewers point to are his descriptions of the great native dance and the hunt. They say he "creates an atmosphere of vast spaces and silence and mystery." They admire him because "underneath the fugitive (!) story one catches the heat, the morbidity, the decay of the jungle, the undercurrent of fatality," and so on.

But are these undeniable qualities of *Batouala* the crowning qualities that won René Maran the Prix Goncourt? Are these the qualities that make some readers go back and back to this "astounding book"? Is *Batouala* notable mainly for its vivid descriptions of tropical life? Is it merely that for the first time primitive man has been described by a writer with remarkable powers of visualization and description—by a masterful colorist in words such as Maran undoubtedly is?

No novel that I know of has ever been received with the wonder and delight with which *Batouala* has been received if that novel was strong only in its picturing of nature, manners, customs and the like. These are all outer things. A novel must do more than this. And *Batouala* has done more than this. It has gone beneath the surface, it has gone into the soul of a man. René Maran has drawn the picture of a soul. A single soul? Why, as many souls as there are men, women and beasts for character in his novel.

Innumerable are the things that have been written about man's companion, the dog. But is there any where in literature the laying bare of a dog's soul such as Djouma's, the sorry little yellow cur? And isn't it the universal soul of all the sorry little yellow curs in the world, whether in the Congo or in the streets of Harlem? René Maran even penetrates into the soul of the ducks that live under Batouala's roof.

There is only one thing I miss in the book. Children. We are told that Batouala has children, but we do not see the great mokoundji, the great M'bi chieftain, in his relation to children. We see him in all other relations—to the whites, his head-men, his fellow-chieftains, his beasts, his wives and his friend Bissibingui. Not to his children.

And what sort of a soul is this of the great chieftain Batouala? Is it a soul worth knowing, a soul to be admired or a soul to be despised?

Before answering this question as I feel it should be answered, let me once more turn to what some of the reviewers say. They speak of the "savage as he is" and declare that "man under the equator is shown as nine parts animal with a tenth part composed of weak groupings into the mysteries of nature," and the like.

If that is the way René Maran felt about his Congo tribes I doubt if he would ever have written *Batouala.* He would not have been stimulated to such a work of art. The very harm that civilization has done is to give us false hypocritical values. Tested by the eternal values, the values of simple justice, honor, courage, will Batouala the chieftain stand or fall?

Because René Maran writes with the calm, close restraint of the perfect artist, who never sentimentalizes or holds out an index finger, people have failed to see that for the main figure of his book he has picked out that rarest of creatures in modern civilized life, a man. Batouala, the chieftain, is a man, a sturdy, upright character. Apply the simple tests of justice, honor, courage and he comes through magnificently, in heroic size.

He was a champion of his people and their customs. Nothing could make him swerve in this respect. By contrast, Bissibingui, the handsome young wife-thief, was willing to betray his people and go over to the whites and help them in their cruel exploitation of the blacks. As for Batouala, no amount of oppression could make him yield to the whites in an essential. In non-essentials, where the welfare of his people was concerned, he would yield (see page 85), but in nothing else. He could not be bent. That René Maran means to show this trait clearly in Batouala comes out in the end when he says of him: "He fell to the ground unbending, as falls a tall, mighty tree."

Batouala had a sense of simple justice. Oh, he could forgive the whites everything if only they weren't such hypocrites and if only they would apply the same logic to themselves as to the blacks. He was man enough to know that all people have minor failings which must be overlooked. The major wrongs must not be tolerated.

Batouala was truthful. He had a fine, subtle sense of what truth really means. To embellish naked facts is not to lie. No, that is poetry, that is art. Batouala felt this in his simple, undefiled soul. But the whites lied. They really lied. They lied by method, by rote. This he resented.

Some reviewers and many colored people have expressed disappointment that Maran did not carry out the promise of his preface. They had expected that his book would be an expose. Again they miss his subtle indications. They lose sight of several statements in the preface that are clear pointers.

First, Maran says that his work is purely objective. An expose cannot in its very nature be objective. In the second place, his quotation of Montesquieu is revealing, and especially his characterization of the quoted lines, that they "vibrate with restrained indignation veiled under a surface of cool irony." Do these words not show that we must look for the same thing in the book? And on looking do we not find it? Consider the ironic wind-up of the great native dance. To the blacks it was a sacred feast, and in so far as it was sacred it was beautiful and not bestial. To the whites it was a chance to be vulgar and extort a huge money fine. That grim sardonic wind-up to the dance is one of the most magnificent, ironic contrasts in literature.

There is much more to say to show that the book is not about "savages," but about men, strong, fine, courageous, lovable, humorous, light-hearted, laughing men. Is the native hunt any more savage than the annual grouse-shooting in that country of sharp intellects, Scotland? Batouala and his men risked their lives when they hunted. They hunted like men, not like cowards with rifles. Moreover, they hunted because they really needed their food. The people in civilized lands who really need the food are not the ones who go grouse-shooting in Scotland.

The song of the kouloungoulou is a delicious example of something else in the preface: "Their light mockery proved their resignation. They suffered and laughed at suffering." The whites brought disease to the blacks, the blacks know it, they suffer from it, and—they laugh and make songs.

Does an ugly savage make songs?

Does a brute invent those charming myths about sunstroke, the rhinoceros, and how fire was brought down from heaven for the comfort of shivering mortals?

Batouala is a book about men, not beasts that are half-men, not uncivilized brutes, but men. "It is time," says an eminent ethnologist, "that the gulf between savage or even primitive and civilized be bridged by the understanding that all men upon this earth are, first of all, human beings." It is in this light that *Batouala* must be viewed.

A word about the translation. It is, all things considered, excellent. Each nationality has its own literary style and distinctive mode of expression. Hence it is as difficult, if not impossible, to translate French literary style into English literary style as it would be for an individual to imitate another minutely and in detail. Nor would such a translation be necessary. Sufficient it is to give the substance and the spirit of the work. In the case of *Batouala* this, and more, has been adequately and competently done.

The African question is increasing in importance. Because of the vast untapped wealth of that continent it will undoubtedly hold the center of the stage in the not far distant future. *Batouala,* as Maran himself points out, happens to be timely, it having been made so by the Americans. I feel that no one interested in Africa, or in the relations between white and black anywhere, can afford to miss it.

Harlem Shadows

By Claude McKay
(Harcourt, Brace & Co., New York)

Eric D. Walrond (1922)

After swallowing these poems (as I did), one is able to appreciate why Claude McKay is idolized by lovers of the beautiful in poetry. Every poem is a gem—not a mediocre one is in the entire batch. Yes, we risk saying that, despite our limited knowledge of the fundamentals of poetry. As George Santayana says, Claude McKay "paints in again into the landscape the tints which the intellect has allowed to fade from it."

> Like white moths trembling on the tropic air,
> Or waters of the hills that softly flow
> Gracefully falling down a shining stair.

We have been hearing quite a deal recently about the virtues(?) of the women in Claude McKay's poems. Essentially an artist, it is not always easy to feel the pulse of the master poet. It is not condescending to say that the Negro, educated though he may be, is devoid of the true artistic outlook. Experience is what counts in an artist's life. Lafcadio Hearn used to advise his Japanese students not to bother with books, but to go out in the large arena of life and there get ideas. Super-artist that he is, Claude McKay has done the very thing. Experience has been the mother of his poetry. And this, understand, is foreign—entirely so—to the life and character of the artist. One may be with the mob and yet not be of it!

> Into the furnace let me go alone;
> Stay you without in terror of the heat.
> I will go naked in—for thus 'tis sweet—
> Into the weird depths of the hottest zone,
> I will not quiver in the frailest bone.
> You will not note a flicker of defeat;

My heart shall tremble not its fate to meet,
My mouth give utterance to any moan.
The yawning oven spits forth fiery spears;
Red aspish tongues shout wordlessly my name.
Desire destroys, consumes my mortal fears,
Transforming me into a shape of flame.
I will come out, back to your world of tears,
A strange soul within a finer frame.

There, in so many lines, is the poet-artist's philosophy. It would be well to bear it in mind in passing judgment on McKay, the man.

But the one, next to "If We Must Die," which will probably find a snug place in the enflamed breasts of the propagandists and the black proletariat, is "Enslaved."

Oh, when I think of my long-suffering race,
For weary centuries despised, oppressed,
Enslaved and lynched, denied a human place
In the great life line of the Christian West.
And in the Black Land disinherited,
Robbed in the ancient country on birth,
My heart grows sick with hate, becomes as lead,
For this my race that has no home on earth.
Then from the dark depths of my soul I cry
To the avenging angel to consume
The white man's world of wonders utterly;
Let it be swallowed up in earth's vast womb.
Or upward roll as sacrificial smoke
To liberate my people from its yoke!

Altogether it is a wondrous collection, and indispensable to any representative collection of Negro poetry.

Claude McKay's "Harlem Shadows": An Appreciation

Hodge Kirnon (1922)

This simple appreciation of Claude McKay's poems is done in obedience to an appreciative urge which is too strong and insistent to be ignored entirely. I trust that my readers will try and study it in the spirit in which it is offered. It is not a boost. Indeed, I can lay no claim to this peculiar virtue, if it is really such.

I remember first reading of Claude McKay in *Pearson's Magazine*. I think it was in the summer of 1918. I was then living out of this city. It was an autobiographical sketch with a few of his poems appended. I took no particular interest in the writer or his poems at this time. In fact, I mislaid the magazine before I had the opportunity of rereading the article. Then at a later date I came across a poem entitled "Soul and Body" in Pearson's written by McKay. This poem made a profound impression upon me. From then up to this time I have entertained a profound interest and admiration for the writings of Mr. McKay.

In *Harlem Shadows* Claude McKay appears at good advantage. He exhibits ability and talent of no mean merit. I was suspicious of the soundness of Mr. Eric Walrond's . . . *Negro World* review when he said that there was not a mediocre poem in the entire lot. But I now fully endorse his opinion with added emphasis. In every poem there is exhibited a remarkable and subtle balancing of thought and emotion of a nature that is rare indeed. Nothing really essential to good poetry is over-emphasized or sacrificed. A wonderful sense of harmony and completeness prevails throughout the entire volume. There is nowhere any attempt at being clever, big or showy. There is a complete absence of affection. His power lies in his simplicity. He does not choose "big" themes. He absolutely refuses to be imposed upon by himself with shallow and hollow pretenses. He follows with an unpretentious docility, his natural inclinations in the selection of themes. He seems to write under no other urge than that of natural impulse, and what seems strangely interesting is that his knowledge and impulse seem so strained towards perfection that no subject is being ill-treated by lack of treatment or over-treatment.

It is to Mr. McKay's credit that he does not specialize in any sort of propaganda themes, whether they be racial or otherwise. The big soul is universal. There are very few of his poems that would not make a universal human appeal regardless of time, place or circumstance. The spirit and thoughts expressed in his work are fundamental life experiences in some form or other in all human beings.

In order of arrangement the poem, "America," makes a very powerful appeal to me. I quote the first four lines:

Although she feeds me bread of bitterness,
And sinks into my throat her tiger's tooth,
Stealing my breath of life, I will confess
I love this cultured hell that tests my youth!

The last line truly expresses in a most satisfactory manner what I have always felt and thought to be the main redeeming feature of America. And I daresay many other aliens like myself have felt and thought in like manner without ever giving them expression.

McKay penetrates and probes to a depth not to be easily surpassed, the spiritual isolation and loneliness which many of us—rich and poor, white and black—have felt quite often in the heart of the noise and bustle of this great city in the poem "On Broadway." He speaks for the many lonely, struggling, straggling souls that are stranded in awful loneliness amidst the great crowd.

An outstanding feature of McKay is his poetical fancy for things that appear even to the observant and responsive, meaningless and commonplace. At his hands they live and throb with life. They are humanized. As a typical example I take the "Subway Wind." I select the following lines, for they vividly portray the theme:

Far down, down through the city's great, gaunt gut,
The gray train rushing hears the weary wind;
In the packed cars the fans the crowd's breath cut,
Leaving the sick and heavy air behind.
And pale-cheeked children seek the upper door
To give their summer jackets to the breeze;
Their laugh is swallowed in the deafening roar
Of captive wind that moans for fields and seas.

Another pertinent feature of this volume of poems is that one really cannot be but conscious of the "genuine breath of the tropics," to use Mr. Hubert Harrison's words. A certain mildness and serenity pervades and permeates nearly every poem. McKay is a lover of nature. There are several poems dealing with one or the other aspect of nature. There are "The Easter Flower," "Winter in the Country," "To Winter," "Spring in New Hampshire," "North and South," and others. The last named is of excellent quality, and, in my humble estimation, can stand comparison with some of the best of William Cullen Bryant and the great English singer of nature, William Wordsworth.

But these are not all by any means. McKay touches philosophical themes. He contemplates upon matters metaphysical. In "I Know My Soul" he shows a poetical philosophical bent that was so strongly characteristic of Omar and Goethe.

In conclusion, I wish to say that I am convinced that Mr. Claude McKay possesses an exceptional poetical talent. He is an esthetician in the best sense of the word. He is true to himself. At least, I feel that I am justified in making this statement. An honest work which is expressive of one's individuality is art in the creative sense. Imitation is always superficial at best when not made subordinate to the individual personality. Esthetic beauty is greater and beyond objective beauty. And this McKay seems to know. He records his own deepest soul experience in his most intense moods and, in so doing, he holds before his readers a true picture of their inner life; and in this recognition of self lies the possibility of spiritual growth. To understand and appreciate Claude McKay's poems, one must be capable of studying and understanding life through the emotions; for a sympathetic and appreciative understanding is possible only through the feelings.

An Article Worth Reading

Robert L. Poston (1922)

A very unusual article appears in the May 13 issue of the *Dearborn Independent,* entitled "Developed and Undeveloped Negro Literature," by Eric D. Walrond, Associate Editor of the *Negro World.* Mr. Walrond, in a very condensed but comprehensive way, tells of what the Negro has done as a writer, at the same time suggesting the great possibilities that yet remain for him in that almost untrampled field. This the author has done in about a page, leaving room for two excellent photos—one of Douglass as a young man, the other of Paul Laurence Dunbar—to serve as illustrations. While Mr. Walrond makes no attempt to exhaust his subject, and much of the value of the article must come from what it suggests rather than what it actually brings out, he has given us a wealth of information in the brief treatise, which stamps him the student that he is. In this article he mentions several authors known to us all, and then he mentions some not so well known, and one or two whom he credits with having wrought well in their day are known to just the select few, yet their records speak highly for them.

Those who have been reading after Mr. Walrond in the *Negro World* are somewhat acquainted with the style of writing—a style much more suited to a magazine than to a newspaper. This style of saying much through suggestion is brought out to a pleasing degree in this article in question. He no doubt had in mind the class of readers he would be serving in the *Dearborn Independent,* so he was careful not to burden them with any superfluities, hence the article is void of any excessive decorations.

But quite as unusual as the article itself is the fact that it found its way in a great magazine like the *Dearborn Independent.* Usually the article which gets a hearing in our great magazines is the kind which does us up "scrumptiously"—the minstrel variety. If not that, it is the kind which caters to some established prejudice. We seldom ever have ourselves done up in the great magazines as aspiring, ambitious humans desiring to see the world better, like any other rational souls.

We think the *Dearborn Independent* should be congratulated for giving its readers this side of our life—the side which our thinkers have been holding up, for these many years.

I have written of this article as though Mr. Walrond has written a book when, in fact, the article he has written is scarcely longer than this criticism I am writing of it. But if this weak effort can induce a few readers of the *Negro World* to purchase the May 13 issue of the *Dearborn Independent* and read the article, "Developed and Undeveloped Negro Literature," by Eric D. Walrond, I will have done what I consider a good turn by them.

Vengeance of the Gods

By William Pickens

Eric D. Walrond (1922)

Vengeance of the Gods is a book of pseudo-short stories that are likely to disappoint. In the first place the book has an introduction by a bishop of the

African Methodist Church, the purpose of which is not quite clear to me. I read it twice and failed to get what the eminent theologian is driving at.

Mr. Pickens is an editorial writer of national repute. Weekly he contributes two or three editorial articles to the Associated Negro Press that are widely read and quoted throughout the United States. Moreover, as a secretary and investigator for the National Association for the Advancement of Colored People, he has studied and assimilated every phase of this perplexing Negro problem of ours.

To one who is a student of the short story Mr. Pickens' book will be a tragic disappointment. It is packed from stem to stern with arguings, philosophizings, sociological parallels. This is regrettable. A book of fiction, or a book masquerading as fiction, ought to at least tell a story, and tell it straight. *Vengeance of the Gods* is a theme that is old and hackneyed, and one digging up of which is likely to do precious little good. Imagine an unsophisticated person, not interested in miscegenation or the race question, taking it up and reading it for the sheer relaxation one is likely to get out of it. Mr. Pickens is, of course, a propagandist of the first water. He knows the Negro, the Southern white, the Arkansas swamp, the temper of the mob, the psychology of the man hunters, and all that; but *Vengeance of the Gods* hasn't any art in it. It is a sociological tract. In writing it and holding it up as a book of "real stories of American color line life," Mr. Pickens evidently forgot all about the technique of the short story.

10

Literary Works by White Authors

T. S. Stribling in Birthright *presented the North American literary world with the combination of a popular white author and a Black theme—ingredients which invariably evoke interest and controversy. The book was widely reviewed and discussed. This may be why Walrond, in the review which begins this section, neglected to summarize the book's plot. He was kinder to Stribling than even some conservative Black critics. Here again he adopted the un-Garveyite view of propaganda as a factor detracting from fine art.*

Walrond's synopsis of Don Marquis' Carter *suggests a refreshing twist to the hackneyed mulatto theme, for long so beloved of white authors and their less imaginative Black imitators.*

Mary White Ovington's two reviews introduce a new element into this collection, for Ovington was white. She was also, most surprisingly, chairman of the board of directors of the U.N.I.A.'s arch rival, the NAACP. Nevertheless, her "Book Chat" column appeared regularly in the Negro World *and in it Ovington tried as hard as she could to sound like a Garveyite.*

Walrond, in "Books" seemed much more mainstream Garveyite than in his review of Birthright. *His charge of a white "journalistic conspiracy to suppress every ennobling fact about the Negro" was oft-repeated, in many and various ways, in the* Negro World. *Pushkin, the subject of this piece, also happened to be Walrond's favorite Black author.*

Birthright

By T. S. Stribling

Eric D. Walrond (1922)

Following the trend of the defeatist school of fiction, *Birthright* submits to the preeminence of environment. It exalts it. If anyone is to be upbraided for that it is Mr. H. L. Mencken, who, Brooks Shepherd reminds us, is working strenuously toward the creation of a class of fiction, whose protagonist "is a creature hounded by fate and doomed to misfortune. If he marries, the match is a mesalliance. If he acquires wealth, he loses it. If he possesses a woodpile, it harbors a Negro." Like Carol Kinnicutt, Peter Siner bows to the inevitable. With all the soul-pricks of a martyr he surrenders to it. It is preposterous to imagine that Peter's going off with Cissie Dildine is an argument against the higher education of the Negro. Not at all. All Mr. Stribling does is state his case. Judgement is left to the reader. Niggertown in its dust and dirt and tragic awfulness is presented in a series of striking pictures. Every phase of life in the miserable crescent is looked into—morality, religion, philosophy. Not a word, a gesture of the finger, a suggestion of inflammatory reproach—either against the ignorant blacks or the contemptible whites—is brought in to prejudice us. It steers clear of propaganda. It is a genuine tragedy.

Of Peter Siner one gets the impression of sophomoric weakness. It is difficult to believe that a Harvard man is so abominably effete. But it is the Menckenian law, and Stribling, like the majority of his contemporaries, succumbs conventionally to it. Quite a few critics of *Birthright* are of the opinion that Peter ought not to have married Cissie Dildine. Some feel that a man of his cultural and aesthetic sympathies should have gone North and married a girl of his class. But it was the only thing for Peter to do. Under the circumstances it devolved on him to offer shelter to the outraged woman. Tump Pack had done his part. Indeed, this stage of the book is the tensest. It depicts the gruesomeness of the South, its sterility, its cracker psychology. It is this part that comes to the defense of myriad black mothers of illegitimate mulatto children. A black woman raped!

Yes, Peter is a hero, a hero of the most altruistic sort. Imagine the book ending with Peter going North and leaving Cissie at the mercy of that band of yellow-teeth, tobacco-spitting—Whelps! Outlaws! Rapists! Lepers! Or imagine—But what is the use? *Birthright* is a supreme work of art. If Negroes do not like it, that is all right; but for God's sake, let white people read it; let them read it!

Only A Nigger

Carter, by Don Marquis
(D. Appleton & Co., New York)

Eric D. Walrond (1922)

This is one of thirteen short stories by the columnist of the *Sun.* Carter is a mulatto whose "forebears had signed the Magna Charta; several had fought in the Revolutionary War. There had been a United States Senator in the family and a Confederate general." Seven-eighths of his blood is white. As he grew up he scorned the society of black men. Then he came North—and fell in love with a white girl whose "Anglicized name was Mary." Tortured by the predominance of his Negro blood, Carter decides to confess to Mary. One night, as a golden moon hung low in the skies of Coney Island and the fragrance of lilac blossoms was strong and sensuous, he took the bull by the horns. But Mary was not shocked or horrified or even "up in the air" about it. All she did was to continue chewing her gum while she gazed at the placid waters of Jamaica Bay. This irritated the white in Carter. "Do you mean," he said hesitatingly, "that it will—that it won't make any difference to you? That you can marry me, that you will marry me in spite of—of—in spite of what I am?" "Gee! but ain't you the solemn one!" said the girl, taking hold of her gum and stringing it out from her lips. "Whatcha s'pose I care for a little thing like that?" But this does not satisfy Carter; it only serves to plunge him into the "insufferable gloom" of Edgar Allan Poe. "By God!" he said, suddenly leaping to his feet and flinging aside the startled hand which the girl put out toward him, "I can't have anything to do with a woman who'd marry a nigger!"

Negro Folk Rhymes, With A Study

By Thomas W. Talley.
Published by the Macmillan Co., New York

Mary White Ovington (1922)

The Negro has become so much a part of America that there are certain facts regarding his life that we are apt to forget. One is that Africans were brought to this country down to the outbreak of the Civil War; that African lore was thus being continually renewed among the American-born Negroes. And another fact is that the slave lived two lives, one as a servant of the whites, and the other a life of his own, with much that was African in its traditions and its cultural background. This life was despised or good-humoredly tolerated by the whites, but we are learning that in some respects it was richer and more original than the white European civilization dominating it.

This collection of folk songs shows us a little of the Negro's cultural life. It is unsatisfying because with a few exceptions we have only the words, and the words were of the least account. The pastime songs, the dance songs, need the music and the motion. Without this they compare unfavorably with the songs and games of white children. The songs and games that are still played by street children (though the silly kindergarten and public school songs have largely banished them from our playgrounds) are often medieval in their origin and of lovely imagery. Take our May Day songs or "London Bridge." The African songs, as shown in this volume, are poor in vocabulary and sometimes reminiscent of a Mother Goose tale, as "Goosie, Goosie, Gander," or "Patty Cake, Patty Cake." But this is natural, as English was a foreign tongue to the African, and he had not as yet made himself the master of it that he is today. If it were not for Mr. Talley's lengthy and admirable study of these rhymes, we would not half appreciate them. He interprets for us, for instance, such a song as "Jonah's Band Party:"

> "Setch a kickin' up san'! Jonah's Ban'!
> Setch a kickin' up san'! Jonah's Ban!
> Han's up sixteen! Circle to de right!
> We's gwine to git big eatin's here tonight."

This is a dance rhyme and one must first conjure up the swaying figures in their boisterous dance. The drum, the instrument that was used for the dance in Africa, was absent in America, and so the dancers pat hands and feet to the measure, unconsciously recalling the boom to which they formerly kept time. This is a "Call" and "Response" or "Sponse" verse. "Setch a kickin' up san'" is a solo, and "Jonah's Ban'" the response by the rest of the party.

We have this dance rhyme with the music. We are most grateful whenever the music is given.

"De jaybird jump from lim' to lim'
An' he tell Br'er Rabbit to do lak him.
Br'er Rabbit say to de cunnin' elf:
'You jes want me to fall an' kill myself.'"

Negro Poems, Melodies, Plantation Pieces, Camp Meeting Songs, Etc.

By William C. Blades.
Published by Richard G. Badger, Boston, Mass.

Mary White Ovington (1922)

Last week I reviewed Talley's book on *Negro Folk Rhymes,* and this book of Blades' follows naturally after. It follows, however, a long way after. While Mr. Talley's book is a careful study of Negro rhymes, Mr. Blades' is a hodge podge of verses thrown together without introduction and without sequence. We do not know where the verses come from, how old or how new they may be, whether they are all written by Negroes or not. Some of them sound like the conventional Negro minstrel doggerel, as:

"The darkies weep and the darkies pray,
Brush, oh, brush dem tears away,
Bring in a chicken on a tray,
Brush, oh brush dem tears away."

Chicken, 'possom, hoe cake, hot corn, rabbit, these are the themes of many songs. Georgia watermelon figures once as a slight diversion. "Rastus' Fate" sounds exactly like an "end Man" story at a minstrel show:

The doctor cautioned rest and quiet,
And put a ban on Rastus' diet,
No more chicken, no more pie,
'Stop,' said Rastus with a sigh,
'No more chicken, no more pie?
Go away, Doctor, let me die.

The religious songs tell of David and Daniel and call especially upon Elijah. Elijah is the patron saint of the Negro, doubtless because his chariot is to take him from this weary world into heaven. The River Jordan once crossed and all is well. It is a great comfort to find that, unlike the sour Puritan, the Negro never seemed to doubt that he would enter through the pearly gates to heaven.

"I'm gwine to Heaven on the judgement day—
I'm gwine to Heaven in the good old way,
And come all the rivers and come all the floods,
Come all the fires and come all the floods;
They can't stop the shouting in my soul
When I get there that day."

The love songs to Mandy and Chloe and Dinah are plentiful. Dinah gets an especially large share. I cannot say that they are worthy of being kept in memory. They tell of the smiling moon and the sweetly scented flowers and sound like white folks poetry secondhand. Indeed, that is the impression that one gets of the whole collection. It is done on a white man's model, and the vigor of some of the very simple verse in Mr. Talley's collection is lacking. But it does give us pictures of the plantation, the old mule jogging along, the twittering birds, the white folks strutting proudly by, the black folks decked out for a party. One sees the broken-down wagon and the broken-down black man beside it. One hears the banjo and the fiddle and catches glimpses of kicking heels and elaborate bows. The steamboat comes up the river and the roustabouts are singing. Out of the medley of verse comes a picture of a plantation life, half tragic, half humorous, very sentimental. The sentimentality is the veneer that the white man has put upon it, and it does not improve the black man's songs.

Books

Eric D. Walrond (1922)

In these columns two weeks ago I had the pleasure to review a book called *The Penitent,* by Edna Worthley Underwood. On October 15 Isabel Paterson, in the *New York Tribune* spoke very highly of it. She stressed its political significance and as I expected, minimized it racially. She didn't even say in her two-column review that Pushkin was a Negro!

In the *New York Times Book Review* Section of October 22 the book was also reviewed, and likewise nothing was said of the fact that Pushkin was a Negro.

This is nothing new. Some of us may not be willing to admit it, but there is and has been for years a journalistic conspiracy to suppress every ennobling fact about the Negro.

11

The Race Question

Most books reviewed in the Negro World *dealt in one way or another with the race question. The selections in this section, however, consisted more specifically of collections of essays or sociological treatises directly addressing themselves to this question. Arnold Hamilton Maloney's* Essentials of Race Leadership *and Marcus Garvey's* Philosophy and Opinions of Marcus Garvey *(Volume I—Volume II was published after this review), both included essays published originally in the* Negro World. *Another important collection of essays, Carter G. Woodson's* Mis-education of the Negro, *consisted in part of essays originally appearing in the* Negro World.

Maloney was a professor of psychology at Wilberforce University in Ohio and had been assistant chaplain-general of the U.N.I.A. Norton G. Thomas, the reviewer of his book, was an associate editor of the Negro World. *Maloney's affinity with Garveyite opinions was clearly evident from Thomas' review.*

Garvey's ideas also obtrude very clearly through Dusé Mohamed Ali's review of The Color Question in the Two Americas. *Ali had once been Garvey's mentor and employer on the* Africa Times and Orient Review *in London. Now (1922) he was foreign affairs expert for the* Negro World. *His ideas on the "near white" psychology of the mulattoes of the Americas and the Euro-Asians of India found expression also in Garvey's own thinking. His vigorous defence of Garvey's African program further stamped him a true Garveyite.*

William Ware's review of Maloney's book highlighted an important aspect of U.N.I.A. literary activity. For such activity was not confined to the paper's editors or those with formal qualifications. It was very much a mass activity. Ware was head of the Cincinnati U.N.I.A. and his review took the form of a letter to the editor.

William H. Ferris' review of Garvey's Philosophy and Opinions *is full of the deference that one would expect of an editor commenting on his employer's work. All of Ferris' quotes from Garvey's work illustrated Garvey's central point that, as he himself put it on occasion, "what man has done, man can do." If the African would but harness his energies and self-reliantly get to work, he would astonish the world, himself included. Ferris also underscored an often forgotten fact, namely the unusually youthful age at which Garvey built his great empire. In 1923 when Ferris was writing, Garvey was only thirty-six. Yet he had by then already built the largest Pan-African organization in history.*

The trilogy of reviews on J. A. Rogers' works complement the earlier commentary by Hubert H. Harrison and others. By 1924, the date of the anonymous article on From Superman to Man, *Rogers had moved from Chicago to New York. And despite problems from certain white and Black quarters and the refusal of white publishers to accept his work, his reputation had nevertheless been firmly established. For the rest of his life he continued to publish and promote his own works. Yet the reading public, and humble Black folk in particular, provided him with a popularity not often equalled in the Black community.*

In John Edward Bruce ("Bruce Grit") and T. Thomas Fortune (editor from 1923 to 1928), the Negro World *had a wealth of journalistic experience perhaps unequalled by any other Afro-American publication. Bruce in particular often enlivened his articles with pertinent reminiscences and personal anecdotes. He had known, either personally or by correspondence, a veritable who's who of the Black world for the preceding several decades. Few living persons could have supplied the background information he provided on Alexander Crummell's collection of essays,* The Greatness of Christ.

Essentials of Race Leadership

By Arnold Hamilton Maloney
(The Aldine Publishing House, Xenia, Ohio, 1924)

Norton G. Thomas (1924)

It has been our privilege to read *Some Essentials of Race Leadership,* a new book by Dr. Arnold Hamilton Maloney, M.A., S.T.D., professor of psychology at Wilberforce University, Ohio.

Striking in its logic, rich in phrase artistry, careful and methodical in its array of thoughts, remarkable in its candor, unique in its appropriateness in the light of the needs of the hour, *Race Leadership* is at once a critique and an inspiration, a diagnosis and a prescription, a volume which should occupy an honored place on the bookshelf of all thinking people. Its adder stings, its remorseless vivisection, its disturbing indictments are not the handiwork of the pessimist. Its preachments do not carry the taint of the pedant or the too self-assertive pedagogue. It is an able, masterful appeal to the Negro race, to the masses and to the Intelligentsia, couched in terms which may throw the one into ecstasy and the other into dismay, but which both must, when the shock has passed, clearly comprehend and, conscience willing it, heartily laud.

Dr. Maloney is a new Negro—the kind of a Negro that is not content to cavort in the byways and alleys of the world. That much we deduce from a perusal of his book. He knows that the Negro's inherent potentialities are as strong as any other race's, and he lets all and sundry know that he knows this. He knows it and would have his race show it. He believes "white is white and black is black and never the twain will merge." He believes that the Negro repelling every obstacle should "move forward as one solid phalanx toward the goal of racial hegemony." He feels it is far easier for black men to regain empire in Africa than for white men to "drive out the sense of difference from their consciousness." He wants to see Negroes of the New World and Negroes of the Old in a fervent handclasp, their hearts attuned. He despairs of the old type of leadership and rejoices that the awakened masses are hearkening to the new voice. Let bucket be let down where we are and the logical alternative to racial, economic and social serfdom is miscegenation, he declares. But then—"The Negro will be the loser all along the line, for while the cauldron boils he suffers and when the chemistry ends he will not be." He feels that Marcus Garvey is to peoples of African lineage what De Valera is to Irishmen, what Gandhi is to Indians, what Sun Yat Sen is to China, what Okuma was to Japan, what Stoddard is to the white world. Only cowards, he adds, will side-step the challenge.

Race Leadership is attractively printed. There are twenty chapters and three appendices. Appendix 1 is the reprint of a letter by the author to the *Pittsburgh Courier* which was inspired, we are told, by Prof. Kelly Miller's letter criticizing the conduct of members of our race on Thanksgiving night in Washington after the Howard-Lincoln game. The second is a thoughtful racial questionnaire, and the last is a concise review of the report of the Commission of Investigation sent a year ago from the British Colonial Office to the West Indies and British Guiana. The captions of the various chapters, each chapter a complete essay in itself, but each whetting the reader's appetite for the succeeding one, are illuminating. They are: "Types of Racial Leadership," "The Negro Faces the World," "Leadership That Inspires,"

"Movements and Personalities," "The Rising Tide of Race Consciousness," "The Tragedy of Being Black," "It Can Be Done," "Economic Pressure," "Religion and Prejudice," "The Negro's Political Fate," "The Crucial Race Question," "Face to Face with 'The Right of Might,'" "The Need of Imagination," "The Cry for a Larger Life," "A Plea for Unity of the Negro Church," "Harmony and Efficiency," "Christ in Texas," "Internationalizing the Negro Problem," "Logic and Equality," "The Re-birth of a Race," and "The Victory That Overcometh."

We confess that the chapter on "Christ in Texas" halted us in our reading. We were compelled to read and re-read. Christ in Texas! We shall read this chapter again, and not do prospective readers the injustice of attempting to reveal it here.

Negroes, new Negroes, old Negroes, stand-patters and progressives, get this book and read and digest it. In his preface Dr. Maloney says; "The thoughts set forth in this book had their birth in a fervent desire to help unravel the tangled condition of the race due to superficial and uncritical thinking on the part of those who have taken unto themselves the serious task, and more serious responsibility, of leadership." We think the learned doctor has succeeded admirably. In presenting his *Essentials of Race Leadership* to the public, he has done the Negro race, and especially those of the race domiciled in these United States, an estimable service.

Dr. Maloney's Book
on "Race Leadership"

Able Presentation of the Race's Case by
One of the Great Thinkers of the Race

William Ware (1924)

To the Editor of *The Negro World:*

We in Cincinnati have received a new thrill. It came upon us when we read *Race Leadership,* the new book by Dr. A. H. Maloney, professor of psychology at Wilberforce University. It is no small matter to describe the particular thrill we received, for, like all thrills, it is something that can only be appreciated by the mind.

The least we can say is that *Race Leadership* filled us with a new courage and a new resolve to fight on in the war for justice for the Negro race. In attempting to do justice to this outstanding work of one of our eminent leaders, we will refrain from committing the error of the average reader of books who tries to express an opinion on the work he has read. We will quote little and opine much.

To begin with, the book is delightfully free from the monotonous and useless axioms with which the serious modern writers, especially political economists, scourge their patient readers. To even a casual reader it becomes at once apparent that Dr. Maloney is anything but doubtful about his own race and class consciousness. In this connection, it would be well to caution the prospective readers of *Race Leadership* that "class" and "race-conscious-ness" lose their everyday significance as a result of Dr. Maloney's treatment. The terms become almost interchangeable in this work, and after reading the book, one feels like broadcasting the news that here at least is one of the higher race types who does not dissect hairs in discussing injustices committed against the race by the mechanistic "superior Nordics."

One feels this keenly in the chapter, "The Cry for a Larger Life," where the author fairly shouts: "I love life." I would hold on to it with all tenacity. And when I find my life being attacked, I want all the aid that all the healing arts and sciences can give. I don't care whence comes the desired boon; from the old school, the new school, or no school at all. All I want is life. And what I want for myself, I want for my race. I want for my race the more abundant life, here, there and everywhere. That is the meaning of the cry, "Africa for Africans, those at home and those abroad!"

Although we promised not to quote much and leave the reader to enjoy the full flavor of this refreshing little book, we will take the liberty of quoting the paragraph in which this virile race leader shows us that he fully realizes the lessons of history, and is prepared to accept the responsibilities that the practice of such knowledge would bring.

"Nowhere in the history of the world," declares Dr. Maloney, "is there an instance to be found where the stubborn persistence of a dominant group in its disregard of the basic humanities when supplied to a dependent group [has] been removed by preachments, petitions, vilifications, or recriminations. Dependent groups have always had to match force against force, or else move out and create an environment and a nationality of their own, or die ethnically."

The author of *Race Leadership* is no watery cosmopolitan or pink internationalist on the subject of equality. In the chapter on "Logic and Equality," with rare simplicity he clarifies the subject for us for all time stating, "We must quote this, though it be our last quotation. If A is equal to B the relationship is complete, and no qualifying addenda would be necessary to clarify the relationship. To presume such, would be a prima facie denial of the validity of the idea itself. In the very nature of the case, therefore, 'equality' as an instrument in ideation is within its rights only in the field of discourse."

And elsewhere in this heroic chapter, "Can the word 'equality' admit of adjectives or modifying epithets or phrases? When men speak of 'social equality,' 'political equality,' or 'industrial equality,' are they not under the yoke of a type of sociology analogous to the effete compartment, psychology? Sundering of parts for one as for the other can be only for the purpose of scientific analysis, but not for the reality of life."

Well, we have very nearly overstepped the space provided for us in this one-sided discussion, but we are certain the editorial staff will bear with us in this instance. It is such a great relief to read a book of this kind, a book which we will make so bold as to prophesy will remain a classic of Negro thought, that we could go on in this fashion until all publishing space is exhausted. We can not urge our leaders too strongly to read this clear, fresh, virile book by one of the great minds of our race. We are sure it will prove to be the inspiration it was to us.

The Philosophy and Opinions of Marcus Garvey

William H. Ferris (1923)

At present Marcus Garvey is discussed pro and con. He is not yet forty years old and yet judgement is being pronounced upon his life work.

Usually a man is estimated by the sum total of his deeds and achievements. But this is only a superficial estimate of a man. It only records the ideals, ideas, and dreams that a man has been able to objectify and incarnate in tangible form. A deeper insight into a man's mind and character is gained by discovering what he tried to do and what were the thoughts and ideas that dominated him.

And while persons are discussing the practicability and feasibility of the industrial projects of Marcus Garvey it might be well to read a little book of some 100 pages, entitled *Philosophy and Opinions of Marcus Garvey,* edited by Amy Jacques-Garvey, because it gives an insight into the motive force and basic ideals of the man.

Reference has been made twice in *The Negro World* to the splendid manner in which Mrs. Garvey has edited the attractive book, which also contains the pictures of Mr. and Mrs. Garvey. In 102 pages she has compressed fourteen pages [sic] of Mr. Garvey's views on forty-seven different themes—social, racial, and political; his emancipation speech, his Christmas message, his Easter sermon, his convention speech, and his statement on his arrest. This book contains the most thoughtful passages of Mr. Garvey's feature letters and numerous addresses. It admirably represents a man's thoughts concerning life's supreme issues. We will cull a few passages so that the reader can get an insight into the heart of a man who has launched a world movement.

In his "Dissertation on Man," Mr. Garvey says:

"When God breathed into the nostrils of man the breath of life, He made him a living soul and bestowed upon him the authority of 'Lord of Creation.' He never intended that that individual should descend to the level of a peon, a serf, or a slave, but that he should be always man in the fullest possession of his sense and with the truest knowledge of himself."

In "The Function of Man," Mr. Garvey says, "after speaking of Edison, Stephenson, and Marconi, 'all this reveals to us that man is the supreme lord of creation, that in man lies the power of mastery, a mastery of self, a mastery of all things created, bowing only to the Almighty Architect in those things that are spiritual, in those things that are divine.'"

In the "Divine Apportionment of Earth," Mr. Garvey says: "God Almighty created all men equal, whether they be white, yellow or black, and for any race to admit that it cannot do what others have done is to hurl insult at the Almighty, who created all races equals in the beginning.

"The white man has no right of way to this green earth; neither the yellow man. All of us were created lords of creation, and whether we be white, yellow, brown, or black, nature intended a place for each and every one."

In the "Purpose of Creation" Mr. Garvey says: "The man or woman who has no confidence in self is an unfortunate being and is really a misfit in creation.

"God Almighty created each and every one of us for a place in the world, and for the least of us to think that we were created only to be what we are and not what we can make ourselves is to impute an improper motive to the Creator for creating us."

In "Man Know Thyself" Mr. Garvey says: "For man to know himself is for him to feel that for him there is no human master. For him nature is his servant, and whatsoever he wills in nature, that shall be his reward. If he wills to be a pigmy, a serf or a slave, that shall he be. If he wills to be a real man in possession of the things common to man then he shall be his own sovereign."

One of the most suggestive essays in this interesting book is "The Three Stages of the Negro in Contact With the White Man." The first stage is slavery; the second stage, emancipation. Then Mr. Garvey says: "Now we have entered into the third stage of our existence, wherein we say to the white man, 'After two hundred and fifty years of slavery and fifty-eight years of partial freedom under your leadership, we are going to try our fifty years under our own direction.'

"This new stage calls for all the manhood within the race, and means that we must throw off all the conditions that affected us in the first and second stages and go out and do—acquit ourselves like men in the economic, industrial and political arena."

These quotations give the reader an idea of the idealistic impulses which were back of and behind his movements. Later [we] will take up in detail "The Opinions of Marcus Garvey."

From Superman to Man

By J. A. Rogers

Hubert H. Harrison (1920)

This volume by Mr. Rogers is the greatest little book on the Negro that we remember to have read. It makes no great parade of being "scientific," as so many of our young writers do who seem to think that science consists solely in logical analysis. If science consists fundamentally of facts, of information and of principles derived from those facts, then the volume before us is one of the most scientific that has been produced by a Negro writer. It sweeps the circle of all the social sciences. History, sociology, anthropology, psychology, economics and politics—even theology—are laid under contribution and yield a store of information which is worked up into a presentation so plain and clear that the simplest can read and understand it, and yet so fortified by proofs from the greatest standard authorities of the past and present that there is no joint in its armor in which the keenest spear of a white scientist may enter.

Unlike an older type of scholar (now almost extinct) the author does not go to vapid verbal philosophers or devotional dreamers for the facts of history and ethnology. He goes to historians and ethnologists for his anthropology. The result is information which stands the searching tests of any inquirer who chooses to doubt, and investigates before accepting what is set before him.

From this book the unlearned reader of the African race can gather proof that his race has not always been a subject or inferior race. He has the authority of Professor Reisner of Harvard, of Felix Dubois, Volney, Herodotus, Fimot, Sergi, the modern Egyptologists and the scholars of the white world who assembled at the Universal Races Congress in London in 1911, for the belief that his race has founded great civilizations, has ruled over areas as large as all Europe, and was prolific in statesmen, scientists, poets, conquerors, religious and political leaders, arts and crafts, industry and commerce when the white race was wallowing in barbarism or sunk in savagery. Here he can learn on good authority, from St. Jerome and Cicero, Herodotus and Homer, to the modern students of race history, that cannibalism has been a practice among white populations like the Scythians, Scots and Britons; that the white races have been slaves, that here in America the slavery of white men was a fact as late as the 19th century, and "according to Professor Gigrand, Grover Cleveland's great-grandfather, Richard Falley, was an Irish slave in Connecticut." In short, he will learn here, not that newspaper science which keeps even "educated" Americans so complacently ignorant, but the science of the scientists themselves. He will learn of all that this kind of science has to tell of the relative capacity and standing of the black and white races—and much of it will surprise him. But all of it will please and instruct.

The book also deals with the facts of the present position of the Negro in America and the West Indies; with questions of religion, education, politics and political parties, war work, lynching, miscegenation on both sides, the beauty of Negro women and race prejudice. And on everyone of these topics it gives a minimum of opinion and a maximum of information. This information flows forth during the course of a series of discussions between an educated Negro pullman porter and a southern white statesman on a train running between Chicago and San Francisco. The superior urbanity of the Negro coupled with his wider information and higher intelligence eventually wins over the Caucasian to admit that the whole mental attitude of himself and his race in regard to the Negro was wrong and based on nothing better than prejudice.

This conversational device gives the author opportunity to present all the conflicting views on both sides of the Color Line and the result is a wealth of information which makes this book a necessity on the bookshelf of everyone, Negro or Caucasian, who has some use for knowledge on the subject of the Negro. The book is published by the author at 4700 State Street, Chicago.

From Superman to Man

To Reappear in March

Anonymous (1924)

Readers of *The Negro World* will be glad to learn that the book, *From Superman to Man,* by J. A. Rogers, will be published in book form again in the first week of March. This book, ever since its appearance some years ago, has been well received, not only by Negroes, but a large number of liberal minded white persons as well. Hundreds of complimentary letters have been received by the author, some of which declared it to be "the greatest book" ever written on the Negro. When the edition gave out, two years ago, and the author was unable to bring it out because the plates for the re-printing had been stolen; it was necessary to advertise in *The Negro World* for six weeks, asking that no more orders be sent in for it. Since then many letters from readers of *The Negro World* in all parts of the world have been arriving inquiring about it.

Because of the fearless manner in which this book has dealt with the race question, there has been a determined effort to suppress it in certain quarters. It is generally barred from the public libraries, among them being the Chicago and the New York Central libraries. These libraries, by the way, contain books with the most scurrilous propaganda against the race. The author has encountered the same difficulty with white publishers, who have consistently refused it in spite of the excellent notices it has received.

From Superman to Man answers almost every question. *The Negro World* said: "It sweeps the circle of the social sciences—history, sociology, religion, race intermixture, the beauty of colored women, psychology, economics, politics—which are all worked up into a presentation so clear that the simplest can read and understand, and yet so fortified by proofs from the greatest standard authors of all times that there is no joint in its armor in which the keenest spear of a white scientist may enter."

The *New York Evening Post* said it proves that "the Negro is not a whit inferior to the Caucasian." Profs. Baber and Foster, of the University, both spoke of it as "the best literature" they had read on the subject, and as "being helpful to a better understanding and feeling between the races." The book is now being used in many Northern universities and libraries, among them being Columbia and Chicago Universities.

Among the large number of striking testimonials was one from the Catholic Board for Mission Work Among the Colored People, which said: "There are more objections against the colored race answered in this book more satisfactorily and convincingly than in any book we have read upon the question. We intend using it as a text book for our own advancement in the knowledge of the race question."

The book will be brought out by the Lenox Publishing Co., 2372 Seventh Avenue, New York, a Negro concern. It will be cloth bound, gold stamped and will be sold for $1.50, postpaid.

As Nature Leads

By J. A. Rogers

Hubert H. Harrison (1920)

This is the second book from the pen of Mr. Rogers, the first being the now famous *From Superman to Man.* Like the first this deals with the Negro and is a masterpiece of sociological handling. In it the writer considers "some of the reasons why Negro and Caucasian are mixing in spite of opposition." He first presents the facts of Negro psychology as shown by the ideas and preferences of the black people in their native environment in Africa. The fact that black people there used to exhibit aversion and repugnance and even terror at the sight of a white person is exhibited as proof that the responsibility for bloodmingling does not rest with them.

In this connection our author takes occasion to compare the attitude of the transplanted Negro with that of his brother at home and reaches some radical conclusions. Why do dark men and women prefer to mate with white men and women and vice versa? Do white men and women seek black men and women or the reverse? Which is the more beautiful and attractive, the white or the colored woman? And why? These are some of the interesting questions which this book answers with a wealth of information and a breadth of view unsurpassed by any other author, black or white. He gathers his facts from the best authorities, white and black and the book is thus a treasure house of illustrative material. Whoever wants to know what are the best books to read on religion, psychology, sex, history, politics, aesthetics and philosophy as they relate to the Negro question must come to *As Nature Leads*.

But Mr. Rogers does more than merely digest the information coming from others. He himself makes some competent contributions to the sociology of the race question, in the course of which he very gently but firmly tears to pieces some of the theses of Lester F. Ward. So far as I know, no one has hitherto discovered the part played by "inferior" races in the total process of social evolution. Mr. Rogers states his own law of descansion [sic] all too modestly. He finds a reason for even the daring dresses which white women wear so wantonly. But this reviewer has no intention of transferring that reason to these pages. It must be left as a rare treat for those who read the book.

All in all, this book of Mr. Rogers, together with his earlier work, constitute the greatest contribution yet made by any Negro writer to the race question. The book is published by the author at 4700 State Street, Chicago, Illinois.

The Color Question In the Two Americas

By Bernardo Ruiz Suarez, Published by the Author, New York, 1922

Dusé Mohamed Ali (1922)

The color question, whether in the new or the old world, like the poor, is ever with us. Dr. Bernardo Ruiz Suarez is the latest contributor to a question at once intricate and manysided, and which is destined to shake the foundations of all white civilization. *The Color Question in the Two America* is well written and is pregnant with thought. The doctor tells us of the intricacies of the question in South America, especially Cuba, of which he is native, and of the contending factions who struggle for social and political recognition at the hands of the whites; of the betrayals by some of the colored people; how they have sold each other for personal advantage because of the absence of homogeneity and co-operation. He speaks of the domination of the so-called whites, but unfortunately he does not realize that there are very few, if any, whites of Latin extraction in South America. He does not appear to know that even the reputed pure blooded Castillyano is a rather engaging blend of Carthaginian mulatto with a subsequent injection of Arab and Black-a-Moor-Negro. This lack of ethnic information is no discredit to Dr. Ruiz; even the "whites" of Spanish America, whom he discusses, do not know, and as the doctor obtained his education in the schools of the whites he cannot possibly have more information than they possess. The servant cannot be above his master.

The psychology of the "near whites" and the other colored grades in Latin America which he so minutely describes bear a striking resemblance to their English-speaking prototypes. It is a peculiarity among these colored people that they, along with Euro-Asians of India, are the only people with whom I am familiar who, for the most part, glory in their bastardy as represented by the illicit white element in them which is used as an evidence of superiority and would be ludicrous but for the underlying tragedy. The doctor is not so happy in his deductions when he discusses the "back to Africa" ideal. He says:

"Illustrative at once of the real influence of the go-to-Africa movement and of the black people's ability to appreciate and tolerate good, high-priced humor, is the fact that no enthusiastic migrant, traveling at his own expense, has got anywhere nearer to Africa than the one hundred and thirty-fifth highway running straight east and west in New York. Along this route some few are said to be awaiting passage. One or two have crossed the Atlantic Ocean at the expense of the crowd, but they lost no time in recrossing to bring back the news that blackwater fever is no respecter of black persons born outside of West Africa. And this is about as much as the go-to-Africa association is likely to accomplish for the creation of an enduring nation of black people, respected and recognized by all civilization. So far as black Americans are concerned, their nation is within the boundaries of the United States. If they must be independent, they must find a sphere for the exercise of their independence within the union, for they are not going elsewhere."

The doctor is still young. He lacks vision and he has much to gain for mature reflection. He is apparently unaware of the fact that the whites have thrown down the gauntlet before the black, brown and yellow peoples. That the whites have themselves divided the world into two camps—black and white. That the colored people of Negro origin must inevitably have a separate and distinct entity in their own homeland. That those who have "lost no time in recrossing" to America are neither a credit to American nor any other kind of civilization. The white man has built up his civilization on the remnants and out of the debris of the black, brown and yellow civilizations. If the colored man is too lazy to build for himself, that is no fault of Africa. The white man has succeeded in taking millions out of Africa, East, West,

North and South, and he has not permitted "blackwater," nor any other fever, to deter him from doing so, but has had to work to accomplish this end. The colored man must do likewise if he hopes to cope successfully with the economic struggles which face him in the new world.

Doctor Ruiz suggests a black nation within a white nation. This looks very pretty and idealistic and will no doubt, be very alluring to the black man who thinks white, but it is not practical in the work-a-day world of the West. The doctor seems to overlook the fact that his nation within a nation would have to depend upon the white dominant branch for its support; that the Negro, being for the most part a parasite, the question of economic competition would arise, and economic competition would and will eventually lead to black pauperism, starvation and extinction. It is to be regretted that the exigencies of space do not admit of a more lengthy review. I have said the book is well written and although I cannot follow the doctor all the way, he is entitled to his point of view.

The Color Question in the Two Americas is published by Dr. Bernardo Ruiz Suarez at 229 West 140th Street, New York City.

Alexander Crummell,
The Greatness of Christ;
and a Word on Henry Timrod

Bruce Grit [John E. Bruce] (1922)

It is to be regretted that so few of our people are familiar with the books and pamphlets of the late Dr. Alexander Crummell, acknowledged and acclaimed in his day as one of the most scholarly and cultured clergymen in America. I did not say "Negro clergymen," although he was a Negro and proud of the title. I have purposely used the phrase "most scholarly and cultured clergy-men in America" because it states a fact well known to his white and black contemporaries. . . .

In his book, *The Greatness of Christ* [recently republished] is a chapter under the caption: "The Black Woman of the South." It is the third article in the book and I wish to tell my readers a few facts concerning it. The article was prepared at the request of the Rev. Dr. Rust, secretary of the Methodist

Episcopal Church, and was delivered at a crowded meeting of the members of that church at Asbury Park, August 15, 1883. The address attracted wide attention and was at once put into print. The Methodist Episcopal Foreign Society printed and published four (4) editions of 10,000 copies thus making in all 40,000 copies.

Dr. Crummel himself published a large edition of it. The True Reformers of Richmond, Va., published and circulated over 8,000 copies. Somewhere between forty or fifty thousand copies of this address have been circulated. One of the signal results of its publication as stated by Mrs. Rust to the author, is the fact that one million ($1,000,000) dollars had been received by the Methodist Foreign Missionary Society for the purpose outlined by Dr. Crummell in this address, and that a large number of Industrial Schools for Colored Girls were established and put into operation by the Methodist Church in the South.

More than a million copies of this address was subsequently published and circulated throughout the country. I hope *Negro World* readers, especially the ladies, will get this book, *The Greatness of Christ,* and read the noble tribute paid to the black woman of the South by Alexander Crummel, D.D.

Henry Timrod, said to have been in his day one of the greatest poets the South had produced, was a native of South Carolina and a man of mixed blood.

South Carolina erected a monument to his memory in 1837. Later on South Carolina stopped producing great statesmen and poets, producing instead, bullies like Preston Brooks, who struck down Charles Sumner in his seat in the Senate, with a bludgeon, and foul-mouthed black-guards and Negro baiters like Ben Tillman, who advocated lawlessness from his seat in the United States Senate, and shrewd, calculating politicians like M. C. Butler, who was made a senator by fraud and force, and a whole regiment of others of their calibre who were kept so busy suppressing and bullying Negroes that they have had no time to rise above the low level which characterizes nearly every State in the South, from whence there has not come a great statesmen, poet, novelist, scientist or scholar in the past fifty years.

It is now so busy holding down Negroes and burning and lynching them that it hasn't the time for mental improvement and development which have a Christianizing and civilizing effect even upon Crackers, once they are brought under the influence of the above mentioned condition.

12

Black History

Black history was central to Garvey's program. The rehabilitation of the Black past, the refutation of the distortions of alien historians and the propagation of an Afrocentric historical perspective were all necessary ingredients to the racial self-esteem which Garvey sought to build. The U.N.I.A.'s Declaration of Rights of the Negro Peoples of the World in 1920 demanded the teaching of Black history in schools.

Both Ferris and Arthur A. Schomburg brought a great wealth of historical knowledge to bear on the reviews included in the present selection. Ferris' two volume The African Abroad *(1913) was a compendium of historical and other knowledge. Schomburg's reputation as a bibliophile and amateur historian was already well-established.*

Ferris, in "Books On Liberia," revealed the inadequacies of Jessie Fauset, book reviewer for the rival Crisis, *and not for the last time.*

Even his cursory reading of the main work in question revealed plagiarisms and mistakes of fact that had escaped Fauset. Schomburg, in his plodding style, was painstakingly and meticulously devastating to Carter G. Woodson's The Negro in Our History. *Schomburg and Woodson were simultaneously friends and rivals, for Woodson's later Association for the Study of Negro Life and History (1915) had overtaken the Negro Society for Historical Research, formed by Schomburg and John Edward Bruce in 1911. Schomburg was also understandably peeved at Woodson's failure to acknowledge his indebtedness to the Negro Society for Historical Research for some of the book's illustrations. Schomburg was a frequent contributor to the* Negro World *and his Woodson review was one of the longest formal reviews ever published in the paper.*

In his very sympathetic treatment of John Wesley Cromwell's The Negro in American History, *Ferris attempts a preliminary explication of the role of*

150

history in an organization such as the U.N.I.A. He sees history as heightening Black self-respect, forcing respect from Caucasians and instilling confidence to deal with the contemporary world. He also interestingly sees the New Negro movement as beginning with William Monroe Trotter's Boston Guardian *in 1901 and culminating in the Garvey Movement. Ferris had been an associate of Trotter.*

Eric D. Walrond, in the fourth review in this section, is unusually kind to an amateur historian.

Books on Liberia

William H. Ferris (1922)

In addition to Sir Harry Johnston's, Prof. Frederick Starr's and Mr. Maughan's books on Liberia another book has recently been published and another will soon be published. Rev. Dr. Thomas H. B. Walker's *History of Liberia,* with foreword by J. A. Simpson, missionary to Liberia, published by The Cornhill Co., Boston, Mass., is the latest addition to the field. It is a very readable and interesting book, but we do not know whether it merits the high praise of Miss Jessie Fauset, the accomplished book reviewer of the *Crisis.*

Miss Fauset says of Dr. Walker's book in the March number of the *Crisis:* "For the rest it is a work of careful though uninspired research, and the student of Africa who wishes to clear-up his ideas about the Dark Continent, beginning with Liberia, would do well to put in two or three hours reading Mr. Walker's efforts."

Since Mr. Hubert H. Harrison, the contributing editor of *The Negro World,* began a weekly review of books in *The Negro World* two years ago, other writers have followed suit. And of the number Miss Mary White Ovington and Miss Jessie Fauset have written some very clever reviews. But they say that Homer sometimes nods and Miss Fauset evidently nodded in the March number of the *Crisis.*

While an interesting and readable book, Dr. Walker's work in some parts is a rehash in briefer compass of Sir Harry Johnston's larger two-volume work, without giving the author credit. We only read cardfully one chapter of Dr. Walker's work as we glanced through it while calling on a friend. Now,

152 AFRICAN FUNDAMENTALISM

one swallow does not make the ocean, but this is what we discovered in that one chapter: Part of Chapter XXIII of Dr. Walker's *History of Liberia,* dealing with "Population in 1853, Border Troubles and Annexation of Maryland," is a paraphrase of Chapter XIII of Sir Harry Johnston's *Liberia,* which deals with "President Roberts."

Not only does Dr. Walker paraphrase Sir Harry Johnston without acknowledging his indebtedness to him, but also on pages 115 and 116 of Dr. Walker's *History of Liberia,* nine sentences are practically quoted verbatim et literatim from page 236 of Sir Harry Johnston's *Liberia* without giving him credit. Not only so but Dr. Walker quotes Sir Harry Johnston blindly, referring to Mr. George T. Downing of New York as Mr. George S. Downing.

As we did not have the time to make a critical and analytical study of Dr. Walker's entire book, we do not know whether Chapter XXIII is a sample of the entire work. We do not believe that the Rev. Dr. Walker would consciously and deliberately plagiarize, and believe, rather, that, his stenographer or the printers omitted the quotation marks, and that the proof-reader or Dr. Walker overlooked the same in reading the galley and page proofs. But it is an unwritten law in the literary world that where a writer follows a path that was blazed by another pioneer, he ought not only to acknowledge his indebtedness to the pioneer, but also give him credit for the discoveries that he has made. Some of our colored writers overlook this and work overtime the ideas of other writers, especially colored writers, without the merited praise. Still, Dr. Walker has given us a readable and interesting book.

We have also received by mail the table of contents and prospectus of Mr. Henry F. Downing's forthcoming *A Short History of Liberia.* In nineteen chapters Mr. Downing gives the history of Liberia from 1816 to 1908. Then follows an appendix in which "Natural History," "Civilized Liberians," "Aboriginal Liberians" and "Miscellany" are treated. But, best of all, there is a supplement dealing with "Opportunity Liberia Offers to Negroes for Self-Advancement" and "Hints to Those Who Propose to Emigrate to Liberia." It is not only a readable and interesting book, but is written by one who has lived for years in Liberia and has an intimate and not a bird's-eye knowledge of Liberia, without having to run to the dictionary or encyclopedia every half-hour to hunt up the meaning of some word or reference.

The Negro in Our History,

By Carter G. Woodson Associated Publishers, Washington, D.C., (1922)

Arthur A. Schomburg (1922)

We expected, upon opening Dr. Carter Woodson's *The Negro in Our History,* to find the treatment of the Negro in Africa from "a cursory examination" based on the people who were in touch with them—Ibn Battuta, Leo Africanus, al-Idrisi, and Dr. Barth's excellent works, not to mention others. His premises are not based on a careful examination and research of the sources, but rather on speculative opinion and findings of latter-day writers.

The people of Africa at one time were, according to certain records, such as to compel Dr. Woodson to reach a conclusion that they were largely of the mulatto type. Whereas, any one who has traveled extensively in Africa must reason against the author, for it appears that the masses of Africans must have been decidedly of pure black stock, becoming lighter by degree and time. "The Axumites or Abyssinians may always be distinguished from the original natives of Africa." Ludolph (Hist. I. i. c. 4) is of the opinion that in the colony of Abyssinia race as well as climate must have contributed to form the Negroes of the adjacent and similar regions. "The hand of nature has flattened the nose of the Negroes, covered their heads with shaggy wool, and tinged their their skin with inherent and indelible blackness" (p. 150). The word culture is used with much freedom and looseness in the treatment of the movement of people in their relation to early civilizations. It is too big a subject to be condensed in a paragraph. Dr. Woodson would have us believe "Drawing no color line these Arabs blended readily with the Negroes and gave rise to the prominence of certain Arabised blacks represented by Antar" (p. 9). Gibbons in his *Decline and Fall of the Roman Empire* relates that the believer in Mohammetanism has no scruple between his wives and the female attached to his harem. It is not a question of drawing lines but of religious belief and peculiar toleration of cult. A little further on the same page we find "Carrying their civilization later into Spain, the Africans attained distinction there also, for a Negro poet resided at Seville and in 1757 a Negro founded a town in lower Morocco." We know there was a famous Latin poet of Negro blood in the city of Granada by the name of Juan Latino who, born during 1515 in North Africa, was brought a slave to Spain, where his master Gonzalo de Cordova resided. To state that Latino resided in Seville is to put the results of students' information which is incorrect. An examination of Antonio's *Bibliography* (p. 716), Ticknor's *History of Spanish Literature* (3 vols.) or any Spanish encyclopedia, would have helped to correct the error. The fact that he attained to the distinction of being a learned professor at the University of Granada and printed two books during 1573 makes it more painful why an exhaustive investigation was not made. That "a Negro founded a town in lower Morocco" is nothing of consequence unless definite information is given to lift it to the realm of fact worthy of being chronicled.

The opening of the book dealing with Africa is unfortunately too fragmentary to give the reader a grasp on the early culture of that vast continent in whose bosom the most important vestiges of civilization [are] embodied in her many epochs of history. The book takes for granted opinions, whereas the historian should of necessity deal with naked facts.

"A man in need of labor purchases additional wives to supply that need, and a wife is usually worth so many cows. As very few slaves are required and there is often a scarcity of meats, cannibalism is practiced as the taste of human flesh does not differ materially from that of other animals" (p. 4).

It is unfortunate for a history in the form of a text book for school children to be marred by such improper statements. Can Dr. Woodson believe that the young mind should face the comparative remark that the taste of human flesh does not differ from other animals?

Dr. Woodson would have us believe that Negroes were "so common" in the city of Seville, Spain, in 1474, that Ferdinand and Isabella nominated a celebrated Negro, Juan de Valladolid as the "Mayoral of the Negroes" in that city. The writer has quoted this as from W. E. B. DuBois's *The Negro* (p. 146). As this is somewhat misleading let us examine the source, Diego Ortiz de Zuniga, author of the *Ecclesiastical and Secular Annals of Seville, 1246-1671* (Vol. XII, 1475; p. 374), Madrid, 1677, gives us the transcript of the patent creating Valladolid a Negro Count. Arthur Helps in his excellent work *Spanish Conquest in America,* etc. (Vol. I; p. 32), London, 1855, commenting on the case, says, "But the above merely shows that in the year 1474 there were many Negroes in Seville, and that laws and ordinances had been made about them." Dr. DuBois in *The Negro* (supra) says, "We find, for instance, in 1474, that Negroes were common in Seville." Dr. Woodson goes one better on Dr. DuBois when he said "they were so common." Neither Dr. DuBois nor Dr. Woodson can show any right for adorning language at the expense of fact. Diego Ortiz de Zuniga in his able work only stated from the records that outside the small Negro village with its Roman Catholic Church and its brotherhood there was nothing to show that they were as common as we find them in Harlem. Sometimes paraphrasing is a dangerous thing.

Here we have another instance. It would have been more appropriate for the Doctor to have called the discoverer of the city of Cibola, Esteban, as his foot-note from Channing's history (p. 75, Vol. I) proves, rather than for him to have dubbed him diminutively Estevanecito; even George Parker Winship in his elaborate work on the *Coronado Expedition, 1540-1542,* printed in the fourteenth annual report of the Bureau of Ethnology (p. 348), holds to the dignity of the proper name of "Esteban" (or Stephen).

Delving into the slavery of the West Indies, while he states that it "was most unfortunate" (p. 25), he says it can not be compared with the slavery of our own borders. For slavery in the West Indies was not carried out in a uniform system of cruelties; it was modified according to the government under whose control the island was subject. There was a great deal of religious toleration due to the tradition and customs of the nation involved. But Dr. Woodson, no doubt, while he is conversant with his *Journal of Negro History,* seems not to be acquainted with Baron de Humboldt's *Travels to the Equinoctial Regions of America* (3 Vols.). It seems as if the statement is prompted by U. B. Phillips' *American Negro Slavery,* but it is a matter of fact that the Latins did not practice interbreeding for the purpose of selling their own offspring in the market places. Calvin Fairbanks, in *How the Way Was Prepared,* was careful to relate the facts. They practiced miscegenation because the economic conditions existing in those days made possible the intimate relations with slaves. A peep into Coke's *West Indies,* Bryan Edwards' *West Indies* (5th edition), Southey's *Chronological History of the West Indies* (3 Vols.) would have aided Dr. Woodson to a more stimulated and definite understanding of the slavery of the West Indies.

We do not feel like going into 340 pages to show omissions and palpable errors and enter into conflicting conclusions for a book seeking to enter the school room as a text-book with subject unsuited for the immature scholar in quest of positive information, not after controversial arguments leading to endless discussion. For instance we question the propriety of the extensive treatment of miscegenation [in a text intended for school children]. We need not parade before their eyes the palpable sins of omission and commission for which they are, as a race, irresponsible. Perhaps Dr. Woodson forgot that Dr. James W. C. Pennington, a runaway slave of Maryland, printed at Hartford in 1841 a *Text Book of the Origin of the Colored People.* But why claim that William C. Nell and William Wells Brown are the "first factual historians produced by the race?" What proof is there that Denmark Vesey was born in St. Domingo whereas it is known he was born in St. Thomas, Virgin Islands? Why didn't Rev. John Marrant, who converted the Indians around the State of New York, receive that meed of praise he is entitled to in preference to a good many living persons who adorn the pages of the history?

A charitable appreciation for those who helped Dr. Woodson with rare prints, engravings, etc., would not have in any way harmed him in the preface. It is one of the few books lacking this feature of long-established custom.

The book is splendidly and profusely illustrated, but unfortunately out of tune with the rules of chronology. There is much information promiscuously scattered through the 342 pages for those who may want to read and enjoy the "dry bones of history."

Missing Pages in American History

By Laura E. Wilkes, 85 Prentiss Street, Cambridge, Mass.

Eric D. Walrond (1922)

Here is a book that is of peculiar interest at this time. Only a few weeks ago Miss Ernestine Rose, of the 135th Street Library, organized an association for the "Study of Negro History." This is decidedly a step in the right direction, and it would be well to bring out books that throw light on the Negro's mysterious past. Miss Wilkes, who is a teacher in the colored schools of Washington, has undertaken a very strenuous task. While the book is alive with information about the achievements of Negroes ever since they were brought as slaves to this country in 1636 [sic], quite an improvement may be made in the matter of style and classification. It is undoubtedly the result of idefatigable labor, and is a book that ought to be in the possession of every Negro interested in his race's glorious past.

The Negro in American History

By Prof. John Wesley Cromwell
(Washington, D.C., American Negro Academy,
1439 Swann St. NW.)

William H. Ferris (1922)

In 284 pages Prof. John Wesley Cromwell, of Washington, D.C., has given a very instructive and interesting work on Negro life and history in America. Interest in the Negro's contribution to civilization, past and present, and his development in his native land and his evolution in Western civilization is now something of a fad among Negro leaders, although some of them seen to have forgotten who first called attention to the value of Negro history fifteen or sixteen years ago.

The study of Negro history has a threefold value. First, it will heighten the Negro's self-respect when he learns that his race first discovered the art of smelting iron, used wheeled vehicles in Africa, built up vast empires in the Dark Continent in ancient and medieval times and produced eminent men in modern times. Then, again, it will teach the Caucasian, proud of his world supremacy, that black and brown men first evolved the germs of civilization, which he has so successfully developed, by the waters of the Nile, the Tigris, the Euphrates, on the isle of Meroe and on the plains and plateaus of Ethiopia. It will also teach the white and black world that the Negro not only has his roots in the historic past, but has shown marvelous ability in absorbing and assimilating the complex modern civilization.

No man is more fitted by training and experience to unravel the Negro's course in American history than Prof. John Wesley Cromwell. He, Prof. Richard T. Greener, the first colored graduate of Harvard University, and Mr. John E. Bruce, the writer, known as "Bruce Grit," are the three living men who knew intimately the antebellum leaders and were in close touch with reconstruction events—Prof. Greener and Prof. Cromwell as actors and Mr. Bruce as a young newspaper correspondent. Prof. Cromwell has passed the threescore and ten mark. He was one of the early graduates of the Institute for Colored Youth in Philadelphia; taught school in Virginia for a few years and in the national capital for nearly forty years. He edited two newspapers, was a prominent layman in Bethel A.M.E. Church, Washington, D.C.; a prominent factor in the celebrated Bethel Literary; served for over a score of years as secretary of the American Negro Academy and is now the president emeritus of the organization. Thus for half a century he has been in close touch with the religious, political, educational and literary life of the Negro and knew as a young man some of the leaders of the generation who preceded him. All these things combine to make Prof. Cromwell, a scholar possessed of common sense and high ideals, eminently qualified to write of the evolution of the Negro in American history. I found his advice helpful while I was preparing *The African Abroad.*

The full title of Prof. Cromwell's book is *The Negro in American History: Men and Women Eminent in the Evolution of the American of African Descent. . . .*

It is divided into thirty-five chapters. The seventeen early chapters deal with discovery, colonization, slavery, national independence and emancipation, slave insurrections, early strivings, the anti-slavery movement, the Civil War and reconstruction, educational progress, the Negro as a soldier and the Negro church. The last eighteen chapters consist of biographical sketches, summing up the careers of Phillis Wheatley, Benjamin Banneker, Paul Cuffe, Sojourner Truth, Daniel Alexander Payne, Henry Highland Garnet, Alexander Crummell, Frederick Douglass, John Mercer Langston, Blanche Kelso Bruce, Joseph Charles Price, Robert Brown Elliott, Paul Laurence Dunbar, Booker Taliaferro Washington, Fanny M. Jackson Coppin, Henry Ossawa Tanner, John F.Cook and sons (John F., Jr., and George F. T.) and Edward Wilmot Blyden. There are eight appendices, dealing with Holly, the Somerset case, the Amistad captives, the underground railroad, the Freedmen's Bureau, medal of honor men and the Freedmen's Bank. The book is also well illustrated, containing seventeen illustrations, which comprise pictures of colored Congressmen and other eminent Negroes, colored schools and interesting events in Negro history.

Of the 284 pages a little more than one-third deal with Negro history per se and nearly two-thirds deal with biographical sketches of distinguished Negroes. This arrangement will undoubtedly please the general reader.

Very little of the book deals with the happenings and leading figures of the past twenty-five years. Only seven of Cromwell's 20 heroes and heroines extended over into the twentieth century. And the fame of all of these was won in the nineteenth century. A very brief mention is made of the antagonisms and the criticisms of Dr. Booker T. Washington's policies as a leader, but Prof. Cromwell does not go into the merits of the controversy or deal with the various phases of the evolution of the New Negro, which began when William Monroe Trotter launched the *Boston Guardian* in the fall of 1901 and culminated when Marcus Garvey launched the *Negro World* in the summer of 1918 and started the U.N.I.A. upon its marvelous career. Still this is no defect of the book, that it practically ignores present problems and largely deals with men and measures of the past three generations. Prof. Cromwell's book claims to be a historical rather than sociological treatise, and lives up to its title.

Considerable valuable information is packed in the pages of Prof. Cromwell's history. The student and specialist will learn much from Prof. Cromwell's illuminating pages. And the clear, simple, lucid style renders the work interesting and acceptable to the general reader. We regard Prof. Cromwell's book as a distinct contribution to Negro literature.

13

Non-Fiction by White Authors

In these two selections Hubert H. Harrison proves that he was not only the first regular book reviewer for an African-American publication, but one of the most accomplished. His style is as elegant and polished as his analysis is incisive. And always, barely beneath the surface, are the subtle wit and irony that are hallmarks of his writing. Here too, as elsewhere, he demonstrates the encyclopedic quality of his knowledge, for which he was justly famous in his own time. He could write with authority on a multiplicity of subjects, from politics to literature, from theology to drama to history.

In his comments on The Influence of Animism on Islam *Harrison also deftly demonstrates the Afro-centric perspective, of which he was a prime exponent. In fact he was a major popularizer of the term "race first" which Garvey also used.*

The Influence of Animism on Islam

By Samuel M. Zwemer

Hubert H. Harrison (1920)

The way of the reviewer, especially in a weekly newspaper, is not always an easy one; and a book like this one makes it even harder than usual. For, here is a learned book in which Robert Smith and El Shibli, Al Burkhari and Brinton Meinhof, Wallis Budge and Sir J. G. Frazier elbow each other across the printed pages. Yet it deals with a subject which is conceded to be with a single exception the most popular subject on earth, viz, religion. But this is not a treatment of religion which would commend itself to the average believer; and anyone who gets Professor Zwemer's book in the belief that it will strengthen his faith, whether Christian or Mohammedan will find himself sadly mistaken.

This is essentially a learned work and it is written for men of learning. For such its theme is full of interest. For it deals with a tendency which exists in all great religions, namely, the tendency to partake of the nature of the common dirt of superstition on which most religions are grounded. It is a study of the religion of Mohammed not as it was promulgated in its original purity, but as it finds itself today, compelled to adopt and assimilate the various local superstitions and magical practices which have developed within the area over which it holds ostensible sway.

Prof. Zwemer, however, pointedly ignores the fact that what is true of Islam in this respect is just as true of Christianity. It is here in New York that people who go to church on Sunday refuse to put the number 13 on their doors, but compromise on 12A; it is here that people go to fortune tellers for divinations and witch-craft; it is here that we pursue "familiar" spirits by the way of the Ouija board and the spiritualistic seance; it is here in the very center of Christian civilization that fine ladies and gentlemen walk all around a black cat rather than let it cross their path and that folk who expect to go to heaven depend for luck upon the left hind leg of a graveyard rabbit. But Prof. Zwemer is in good company, for most of the white men who write on these subjects like Elmore, Brinton, DeGroot and Skeat can see a certain significance and value in the religious practices of "inferior" folk while remaining as blind as bats to exactly similar things in the religious practices of their own "superior" people.

Prof. Zwemer follows the crescent into Africa, Asia and Europe, and studies the way in which it adopts its ritual to that lower religion which is the actual belief of the various populations that come under its sway. Demons, stone-worship, magic, the prayer-bead or rosary, and other animistic elements in prayer and practice run riot over the Muslim world—so Prof. Zwemer tells us; and the illustrations in the book help to make good his contention. The part which should be of particular interest to the New Negro is that which shows the kinship between native Negro West African practices and similar practices among Muslims and Jews. What the obeahman does in the delta of the Niger is shown to be spiritually akin to what the muezzin does in Cairo, the Rabbi in Kishnivev and the Roman Catholic priest under the dome of St. Peter's.

In some respects as regards scholarship and breadth of view, this work of Prof. Zwemer's is deserving of high praise. It is undoubtedly a very great improvement over some of the silly judgements which are wont to do duty as "scientific" and "scholarly" interpretations of Islam in the days of Dr. Blyden and against which that African scholar had to contend. And that fact marks a great advance in the respect shown by white men for the culture products of men who are not white. For such as may be interested in a scholarly treatment of religion and superstition, this work will be found to be a genuine service. It is published by the Macmillan Company.

The Folly of Nations

By Frederick Palmer,
Dodd, Mead and Co., New York, 1921

Hubert H. Harrison (1922)

The war drums throb no longer, though the battle flags are furled. Their martial music has been "changed by request" to the soft cadence of a funeral dirge, and all the world prays sniffingly at present for deliverance from the sins of patriotism and vain-glory. That veteran war correspondent, Mr. Frederick Palmer, has given us his "Musings on the Mutations of Mars," in the key of Penitence, which would be interesting reading if Messrs. Wells, Perrero, Gibbs and Irwin had not preceded him on the concert stage. To one who has read Mr. Palmer's great polemic against war, "The Last Shot," written early in 1914, before the outbreak of the great war, it is somewhat of a shock to listen to the childish treble which has taken the place of the powerful bass of the earlier days. It is another proof that men grow old.

It isn't that friend Palmer's argument is wrong; it is that it is so weak. He uses the soft pedal when he needs the full diapason. It is as though the old man's fires have burnt low. And no lily-handed touch on the collar of steel-clad Mars will check that monster in his mad career.

The impressions of war which Mr. Palmer gives us from his wide experience in Turkey, Greece, the Philippines and Manchuria are valuable as firsthand records. He knows the dirt and cruelty, the whoop-las and the lies, the cynical indifference of statesmen drunk with power to the miseries they invoke. He sees them through a haze of pathetic optimism and futile sentimentality, and he attempts to analyze them with the means at his command. But the deep underlying causes seem to escape him altogether. Imperialism, which puts the war-making powers of the modern state in the hands of those who own the earth and its products, and sends its millions of men to die abroad for markets when they lack meat at home—to this the old war reporter remains blind to the last. He is a humanitarian who sees that war is all wrong and wasteful, and his testimony on that head is clear and refreshing. But he lacks the insight of the seer, the probing power of the physician, who diagnoses the disease and points to its hidden causes before prescribing the remedy.

And so long as those who write dodge their duty of diagnosing the cause of war, so long will they fail to exert any appreciable influence on the recovery of a sick world. For it is as true today as when Shakespeare wrote that "diseases desperate in their nature grown require desperate remedies."

PART IV

POETRY

14

The New Negro Spirit

The literary output of the Garvey Movement was most marked in the field of poetry. Dozens of poems appeared each month in the "Poetry for the People" and other sections of the Negro World. The U.N.I.A. poets came from all over the world. They ranged from rank and file members of the organization to historically important political figures. Some of them achieved wide recognition as leading literary figures of the mainstream Harlem Renaissance. Garvey himself was a prolific poet. His poetical works are collected elsewhere.*

U.N.I.A. poetry gave clear expression to the Garvey aesthetic. It was very much a fighting poetry, a New Negro poetry. It was a fitting complement to the overtly political side of Garveyism. Carita Owens Collins' "This Must Not Be!" was published in 1919. This was the year that the Black soldiers came back home, to Afro-America, to the Caribbean, to Africa, to England. They brought with them many a painful memory of discrimination, not from the enemy, but from their own white compatriots. They were not prepared to suffer silently at home. This was the year of the "Red Summer" in the United States, when Black communities fought back bravely against the forces of lawlessness and disorder. Similar scenes were enacted in Trinidad, in British Honduras (Belize) and in Britain, where the New Negro showed a similar willingness to do battle in the streets if necessary. Nineteen nineteen was also Garvey's year. It was the year that his Black Star Line Steamship Corporation and his rapidly mushrooming organization made him the best known African in the world.

Carita Owens Collins provided a rousing battle cry for the New Negro of

---

*Tony Martin, ed., *The Poetical Works of Marcus Garvey* (Dover, MA: The Majority Press, 1983).

166

1919. Unlike Claude McKay's famous sonnet, "If We Must Die," also written in that year, she paid scant regard to the prospect of dying. The Lusk Committee into "revolutionary radicalism" in New York State in 1919 was scandalized by her poem. It preferred to see in such sentiments a cause rather than an effect of violence.

Robert L. Poston's "When You Meet A Member of the Ku Klux Klan" was as violent an anti-racist statement as it was possible to make. The New Negro was afraid of no one. Poston was a secretary-general of the U.N.I.A.

Lucian B. Watkins, in his "Prayer of the Race that God Made Black," provided a nice contrast to the poems of Collins and Poston. He was subdued, even prayerful. But through it there still shone the unmistakable light of the New Negro—calm, resolute, unafraid. Watkins was one of the Negro World *poets to achieve wide acclaim in the mainstream of the Harlem Renaissance.*

T. Albert Marryshow's "And Yet—!" illustrates the universality of the New Negro phenomenon. Marryshow was a journalist and major political figure in Grenada and the Caribbean.

Ethel Trew Dunlap was the most prolific of the U.N.I.A.'s poets for the people. Her "Black Bards" is an important statement of the Garvey aesthetic. Hers was a total commitment to the struggle. She was quite willing to sacrifice popular acclaim in the interest of racially uplifting verse.

Lester Taylor, in "The West Indian Student in New York," rendered tribute to an important, though oft neglected contributor to the New Negro movement, namely the West Indian immigrant to the United States. Taylor paints a heroic picture of the young immigrant, "The sum of his belongings in his hand," as he prepares to do battle with a hostile metropolis, all Goliath like in its threatening massiveness. Yet the immigrant prevails, for there is "A wealth of calm resolve behind his eyes." Garvey had been such an immigrant, a mere three years before Carita Owens Collins wrote her poem. Others were to be found in every political movement in Harlem, whether Garveyite, Communist, socialist or mainstream.

Andrea Razafkeriefo's "The Rising Tide" took its name from Lothrop Stoddard's popular work, The Rising Tide of Color Against White World Supremacy. *Here was a warning to the Anglo-Saxon to hearken to the path of righteousness, or be engulfed. Ethel Trew Dunlap brought this message on home in "To the Sons and Daughters of Ethiopia." "It won't be long now," she seemed to say—"The U.N.I.A. will free you."*

This Must Not Be!

Carita Owens Collins (1919)

This must not be!
The time is past when black men,
Laggard sons of Ham,
Shall tamely bow and weakly cringe
In servile manner, full of shame.

Lift up your heads!
Be proud! be brave!
Though black, the same red blood
Flows through your veins
As through your paler brothers.

And that same blood
So freely spent on Flanders fields
Shall yet redeem your race.
Be men, not cowards.
And demand your rights!

Your toil enriched the Southern lands;
Your anguish has made sweet the sugar cane
Your sweat has moistened the growing corn,
And drops of blood from the cruel master's whip
Have caused the white cotton to burst forth in mute protest.

Demand, come not mock suppliant!
Demand, and if not given—take!
Take what is rightfully yours;
An eye for an eye;
A soul for soul;
Strike back, black man, strike!
This shall not be!

When You Meet a Member of the Ku Klux Klan

Robert L. Poston (1921)

When you meet a member of the Ku Klux Klan,
Walk right up and hit him like a natural man;
Take no thought of babies he may have at home,
Sympathy's defamed when used upon his dome.
Hit him in the mouth and push his face right in,
Knock him down a flight of stairs and pick him up again.
Get your distance from him and then take a running start,
Hit him, brother, hit him, and please hit the scroundrel hard.
Pour some water on him, bring him back to life once more
Think of how he did your folks in the days of long ago;
Make a prayer to heaven for the strength to do the job,
Kick him in the stomach, he, a low, unworthy snob.
Call your wife and baby out to see you have some fun,
Sic your bulldog on him for to see the rascal run.
Head him off before he gets ten paces from your door,
Take a bat of sturdy oak and knock him down once more.
This time you may leave him where he wallows in the sand,
A spent and humble member of the Ku Klux Klan.

Prayer of the Race
That God Made Black

Lucian B. Watkins (1920)

We would be peaceful, Father—but, when we must,
Help us to thunder hard the blow that's just!

We would be peaceful, Lord, when we have prayed,
Let us arise courageous-unafraid!

We would be manly, proving well our worth,
Then would not cringe to any god on earth!

We would be loving and forgiving, thus
To love our neighbor as Thou lovest us!

We would be faithful, loyal to the Right—
Ne'er doubting that the Day will follow Night!

We would be all that Thou has meant for man,
Up through the ages, since the world began!

God, save us in Thy Heaven, where all is well!
We come slow—struggling up the Hills of Hell.

And Yet—!

T. Albert Marryshow (1920)

A cup of cold water,
    A crust of bread
A stone for a pillow,
    Bare earth for a bed

And yet I'll be happy
    With Truth comforted.

Poor rags and all tatters
    My portion might be,
And yet robbed in Manhood
    No slave dwells in me;
The world's dearest mantle
    Is true Liberty!

'Mid walls of a prison
    For God and my kind;
On wood-pile or gallows
    Of Force that is blind,—
And yet not the body
    Is Man, but the Mind!

It may be some Judas
    May sell with a kiss
That some willing patriot
    May die to a hiss;
And yet, what love greater
    Hath Mortal than this?

The Romans may threaten
    The might of their spears
And gloat o'er repression,
    And banish their fears,
And yet the great verdict
    Is left with the years.

Great nations of history
    Stood proud for the Wrong,
And held men in bondage
    As fast as 'twas long,
And yet they have crumbled
    And Right is more strong.

Hold fast all ye people
    Who feel the red rod,
Ye are the Promise,—
    Not masses of clod,—
For yet comes the glory,
    The day-smile of God!

Black Bards

Ethel Trew Dunlap (1921)

Poets who are seeking for a wreath,
    If your ancestors are of dark descent,
Consider, ere you dip your pen in ink
    Or to the muse your earnest ear is lent,
The obstacles that you will meet ahead,
    The entrances that will be closed to you;
The exits that will furnish no egress
    Where progress points the bard he must go through.
Consider criticism's searching eyes
    That turn the X-ray on the trembling soul;
Consider all the stately ships that pass
    The frailer bark bound for success's goal.
And worse the silence which thou must endure
    Until hope droops her weary, lagging wing,
And jaded thoughts all hollow-eyed surround
    Thy soul aspiring that had hoped to sing,
And then, dark bard, if thou canst patient be—
    If it will not be to thy soul distress,
While others wear the laurels, to confine
    Thine appetite to flavor of success—
Dip pen in ink and loose the prisoned thoughts
    That shall go forth to set a nation free—
Burn evil's rubbish piles with virtue's torch—
    And thou indeed a noble bard shall be!

The West Indian Negro Student in New York

Lester Taylor (1921)

The sum of his belongings in his hand,
    Strong with the strength of honest enterprise,
Bravely he steps into the stranger's land
    A wealth of calm resolve behind his eyes.

The great skyscrapers glare unfriendly down,
    The busy city's clangor frights his ears;
Naught for unfamiliar faces' frown,
    Naught for the half-guessed scorn or gibe he cares.

Resolved to conquer, struggling day by day,
    His hours of study snatched when best he can;
Tried in the fires of the "Melting Pot,"
    Behold emerge, aye, in God's truth, a man!

Breed more of such as these, Oh, thou, my Race,
Then shall indeed the nations give thee place!

The Rising Tide

Andrea Razafkeriefo (Andy Razaf) 1920

Look around you, Anglo Saxon
    At the rising color tide,
How it rushes to engulf you—
    You, with all your power and pride.
See the restless waters, joining;

    Brown and yellow, black and red,
Seeking wider, better sources
    And a smoother ocean bed.

Gaze above you, Anglo Saxon,
    See the clouds that swiftly form
Do you not, with all your wisdom
    Sense the coming of the storm?
Will your dykes of race-subjection
    Stop a long imprisoned sea;
Every drop of it determined
    To possess its liberty?

Heed the warning, Anglo Saxon
    To the words of reason, hark
And take justice as your pilot—
    That's if you would save your bark;
Without her, the port of safety
    Soon will close to you for aye
For the rising tide of color
    Is the menace of to-day.

To the Sons and Daughters of Ethiopia

Ethel Trew Dunlap (1923)

Write to me, O sons and daughters
    Of a race that is oppressed;
For your letters thrill my spirit—
    Through your messages I'm blessed.
Write and tell me of your sorrows;
    Write and tell me of your woes.
How is Georgia, Alabama?
    Write from where Miami flows.
Write to me from o'er the ocean—
    Winds grow tired and free the waves;
But the captor never wearies

Of oppressing weeping slaves.
Ah! I know you bear a burden
    And I seem to hear you sigh;
But the U.N.I.A. will free you—
    And the time is very nigh.
Slavery's hand is growing rigid;
    Soon its monster corpse shall be
Cast away to fire and brimstone,
    And the slave shall be set free!

15

To Marcus Garvey

Marcus Garvey was the single most popular theme for Negro World *poets. He was the subject of constant adulation in prose as well. In both prose and poetry he was routinely likened to a prophet, a divinely inspired deliverer of a long suffering people. His followers practically worshipped him, and the unshakable loyalty of many of them was legendary.*

The present selection provides a representative sample of these Garvey-inspired praise songs. There is a certain similarity of imagery and language running through these poems. For D. T. Lawson, Garvey is "This chosen leader inspired by our Lord." For Ethel Trew Dunlap, too, Garvey is "Inspired by God." Charles S. Bettis considers him the greatest of humans save only Christ. C. H. D. Este, head of the Montreal U.N.I.A.'s literary club, clothes Garvey in supernatural powers.

The Hon. Marcus Garvey

D. T. Lawson (1923)

A man of wisdom with wondrous vision imbued,
A benefactor of a multitude,
A lover of his race whose tongue and pen
Are ever battling for his fellowmen.

He stands unbribed in these degenerate times,
When public horror wait on public crimes;
A grateful world will consecrate his fame,
And mankind reverence Marcus Garvey's name.

We who have caught that inspiration here,
Of his brave spirit something fresh and clear,
Catch something of a charm and flame and glow,
Which all the Negroes of the world should know . . .

Justice shall guard him with righteous sword,
This chosen leader inspired by our Lord;
Fraternal love and unity divine
Shall render homage at its hallowed shrine.

Within the precincts of our meeting place,
Shall be no difference of creed or race;
But one religion and one cause shall bind,
To help each other and to serve mankind.

Then poverty and crime shall disappear,
And peace and virtue reign for Negroes everywhere,
And lowly merit and down-trodden worth,
And love and friendship rule supreme on earth. . . .

Dedicated to Marcus Garvey

Charles S. Bettis (1921)

Some names are large and some are small
    Upon the scroll of Fame,
And which is greatest of them all,
    I know not, but I claim
Were Christ to walk our earth again,
    Rerisen in Galilee,
You are the first of living men
    Whom he would go to see.

To Marcus Garvey

C. H. D. Este (1921)

The night was cold the wind was high;
    The path I trod was rough and drear.
No voice I heard; no friend was nigh,
    My mind was filled with doubt and fear.

And thus I sat beneath a tree;
    The clouds were pale, the showers fell
The thunder roared, the sky was free,
    And echoes wild rolled through the dell.

When mid the ire of the night,
    A gentle voice breathed in my ear;
And bade me look toward the right
    To see a star in twinkling there.

I looked across the pasture wild,
    And there I saw you robed in white.
'Gird up your loins O little child,'
    The voice replied in language bright.

At this the night grew calm and bright.
    A yellow light illumed the way;
And all the shades of gloom and fright
    In sudden rush were chased away.

In Respect to Marcus Garvey

Ethel Trew Dunlap (1921)

He loosed the shackles from the hand
    Bound for three-hundred years.
His voice resounded through the land
    'Til millions sent up cheers.

He led his race out from the tomb
    Of darkness and despair,
That crushed hopes might revive and bloom
    In liberty's pure air.

He did not heed the cynic's sneer—
    His soul fell in a dream.
And critics could not hush the lips
    That spoke of freedom's theme.

He saw his mother country free—
    Behold her rising star,
And begged his countrymen to flee
    Where kin and loved ones are.

Inspired by God, one hundred years
    Became to him a day;
He saw his kinsmen, heard their cry
    When future tyrants sway.

He saw them swept like driven tide
    To Canada's retreat,
Confined there by the ocean bars,
    And trampled under feet.

He saw his people pass away
    Like clouds that tempests send.
While idlers criticised and smiled,
    He was the black man's friend.

Fired with a patriotic zeal
    That fanned his loving heart,

He yearned for native land ties
   That aliens tore apart.

He saw a flag eyes could not see—
   A nation yet unborn—
A land where black men might be free,
   The dawn of freedom's morn.

He did not deem the price too dear
   (whatever it might be)
For black men to regain their soil
   And set their country free.

A Paul Revere that God hath raised
   Of Ethiopian fame,
To rouse a nation and to fan
   Its fire into flame.

In Respect to Hon. Marcus Garvey

Ethel Trew Dunlap (1922)

He is drawing back the curtain
   That has veiled three hundred years.
He is bidding those who languish
   To take heart and dry their tears. . . .

He is leading Egypt's daughter
   From the captor that defiled
Back to where her royal kinsmen
   Wait for their abducted child.

And his eyes are keen and searching;
   They behold the only path
Where he may escape the tyrants
   Who are filled with hate and wrath.

He is sending forth a message;
   When its echoes shall arise

They will shake the ocean islands,
    And disturb the stars in skies.

Flee with him, O dark-browed maiden,
    Egypt's daughter—grasp his hand!
He will bear thee safely over
    And restore thee to thy land.

16

Black Man in the White Man's War

The First World War had a lasting impact on the African world. This was the "war to end all wars" and the war "to make the world safe for democracy." Black men as well as white were caught up in the skillful Allied propaganda that sent them to willing deaths in the mud and mustard gas of the European battlefields. From Senegal, South Africa and Morocco they came, from the British West Indies, Afro-America and Bermuda, in their hundreds of thousands. Those who were British and United States subjects participated mostly as members of labor battalions. This was a white man's war and the powers that be were quite explicit in their reluctance to let Black soldiers kill white ones, even when the latter were the infamous enemy "Huns" of Allied propaganda.

The few Afro-Americans who served as regular soldiers did so in the French army. The few units of the British West Indies Regiment who did so got their chance in the Middle East, near the end of the war. At the beginning of the war, the British War Office had even tried to prevent Afro-West Indians from volunteering. The French were more generous to their African troops. They used them as shock troops and cannon fodder. Senegalese blood copiously nourished the poppies of Flanders field.

The war experience rankled in the minds of African peoples for many years. Its aftermath could easily be seen in the spirit of resistance and even aggression displayed in the 1919 race riots in Afro-America, Britain and the West Indies. The bitterness engendered by that war experience was still fresh in these verses, published three and four years after the war ended. They are among the most moving of the U.N.I.A.'s poetical offerings.

Ethel Trew Dunlap in "He Sleeps in France's Bosom," encapsulated the cruel dilemma of the Afro-American soldier, unfree at home yet forced to pay the supreme sacrifice in an alleged struggle for freedom. Each stanza posited the contradiction in a manner poignant and powerful. And, supreme irony, the soldier's ancestral homeland of Africa, still unfree, loomed almost within reach as he vainly expended his life in Europe.

Rosalie Phyfer's "Lines to Needham Roberts, Who Won the Croix de Guerre in the World's War" (1922) was a tribute to one who came back alive. Needham Roberts and Henry Johnson, both members of Harlem's celebrated "Old 15th" were Afro-America's most celebrated war heroes of the period. Badly wounded, they nevertheless routed a force of twenty-four German attackers. There were scenes of great jubilation as they rode an open car up Fifth Avenue as the Old 15th returned to Harlem in 1919. Garvey was among the multitude who watched the "Hellfighters" as they marched into Harlem on that winter's day in 1919. He is said to have returned to his office and wept. "As for me," he announced later, "I am tired dying for the white man." Any dying he did in the future would be to set Africa free. Rosalie Phyfer alludes to Garvey's sentiments here when she bids Needham Roberts live on until he shall hear the cry of "Africa for the Africans" "resounding throughout the globe."

Ernest E. Mair, a Jamaican-American, was evidently very familiar with Britain's record of duplicity and ingratitude to its Black soldiers. Apart from everything else, his "Hypocrisy" is an accurate account of this episode in Caribbean history.

He Sleeps in France's Bosom

Ethel Trew Dunlap (1921)

He sleeps in France's bosom!
    The faithful, loyal slave;
He tilled the soil and then he gave
    His life across the wave.
He sleeps in France's bosom!
    He never saw the sky
Of Africa; for he was brought
    To toil and then to die.
He sleeps in France's bosom!
    Midway his humble grave,

Between the land where dwelt his sires
    And here where he was slave.
He sleeps in France's bosom!
    Perchance he has a dream
Of sires who writhed beneath the lash
    Or peon's stifled scream.
He sleeps in France's bosom!
    O wish him not awake,
While innocence is martyr
    To mob law and the stake.
He sleeps in France's bosom!
    The colors o'er him fly;
They were his prison stripes and then
    They sent him off to die.
He sleeps in France's bosom!
    His life was term of toil,
By chance escaped his captor
    To die on foreign soil.
He sleeps in France's bosom!
    Thank God he had one life;
For if he had a million
    They would have fed crazed strife.
He sleeps in France's bosom!
    Peace made his bosom swell;
It was his Afric heritage,
    But for the mad he fell.
He sleeps in France's bosom!
    His primal land not far,
By Gihon's classic river,
    Where Eden loaned her star.
He sleeps in France's bosom!
    Columbia claimed his brawn;
France stole his ashes, but his soul
    Goes sweeping grandly on.
He sleeps in France's bosom!
    The Afric breeze comes far
To sigh above the captive's grave
    Beneath a foreign star.
He sleeps in France's bosom!
    By yonder lonely wave,
Where tragedy and God have vowed
    To vindicate the slave!

Lines to Needham Roberts

Who Won the Croix de Guerre in the World's War

Rosalie Phyfer (1922)

Brave youth and hero of the race
The world in thee doth see
The spirit of the Negro interpreted.
In thy conduct o'er yonder land,
When determined thy apart to play
Confronted with enemies, whose
Aim was death, to those who dare impede

Their march across the Rhine,
Just then amid the unbearable blow
And shots that wrecked thy frame
In thee was seen the warrior's heart,
Resolved to do or die.

And when in bruises and blood thou lay
That hand uplifted still struck
The fatal blow, that caused the enemy to retreat,
When the cold hand of death seemingly
Had touched thy youthful brow
E'en there the warrior's attitude
Was still enveloping thee.

When in the death chamber thou wert
Placed, to be numbered with the dead,
The hand of the summoning angel
Did soothe and bade thee for thy race to live.
Live on, brave youth, till thou shall hear
Resounding from valley and hill
The slogan resounding through the globe,
"Africa for the Africans!"

Hypocrisy

Ernest E. Mair (1922)

O England! You are horror-struck because your Gallic neighbor
Has placed black soldiers on the Rhine
To keep the Hun in order.
You prate aloud of outrage and you shout about the crimes
Your lying tongue invented for those men of Afric climes.
'Tis a shame that stinks to heaven,
And it makes you sick to think
Of the depths to which such action
Makes the dear good Germans sink.

But pause a minute, England,
While a hand of sable hue
Steers the ship of your remembrance
Back a wee short year or two.
Let's go back to 1914,
Month of August, day the fourth,
When you hurled your proud defiance
There across the Firth of Forth,

When you told the cruel Teuton
To the bitter end you'd fight
To uphold the faith of England
And to vindicate the right.

"'Tis impossible!" you thundered,
"That I sit supinely quiet
While the ruthless hordes of Prussia
Over Belgium run riot."
So you seized your sword and rifle
And you rushed into the fray,
Backed by Gaul and helped by Russian.
"Soon," you thought, "I'll win the day."
Then, to hearten up your soldiers
And to win the world's consent,
Tales of fiendish German cruelty

Around the world you sent:
To America and Asia,
To the islands of the seas,
To East and West and North and South
Your cry was on the breeze;
."They have murdered little children,
Killed the suckling at the breast:
They have ravished Flemish women,
They have spread the noxious pest;
They have violated treaties
And their word is good for naught,
Hymns of hate and hellish kultur
In their infant schools are taught."

How you counted up their vices
While you swore they virtue lacked,
Reams of anti-German stories
In creation's ears you quacked;
But the Germans kept advancing,
Charged and broke your wavering line,
And while hell was loose in Flanders
All was peaceful on the Rhine.

When your hardy black colonials
Their aid at first did proffer,
You told them, "'Twas a white man's war"—
You scorned their noble offer.
But, ah! the fight grew fiercer,
And the battle grew so strong
Your mushroom hopes of victory
Died, and your face grew long;
Chill terror gnawed your vitals,
Despair was in your soul,
Defeat loomed near, and far away
Receded vict'ry's goal.

Your life blood flowed like water,
The ghost was at the feast,
The stiff-necked Anglo-Saxon
Sought delivery from the East!
His boastful words of yesterday—
"This is a white man's war"—
Were dropped, and in the race to die
Down went the color bar!

Forth from the East and from the West,
From North and South they came,
The captives' sons arose to save
Their captor's race from shame!
Nobly they fought and nobly died:
Dupes of autocracy,
They shed their rich red Afric blood
To save democracy.

And now the fearful strife is o'er,
Now that the battle's won,
Oppression is the base reward
Of every Afric son.

The German that but yesterday
Was held a creature vile
From Negro contact must be saved
Or we will him defile!

O England! queen of hypocrites,
That wields the cruel rod
Which bleeds the Ethiopian's back,
Prepare to answer God!
For though his mills grind slowly,
They grind exceeding small;
Your kingdom built on blood and tears
Is rushing to its fall.

Sure as the rising of the sun
Dispels the gloom of night
Your paths of wrong to darkness lead
While Negroes from your bondage freed
Shall rise to greet the light!

17

Poems of Home

Harlem of the 1920s was a land of immigrants. According to the census of 1920, approximately seventy percent of its residents were born in the South or the Caribbean. Several of the poems of this section express that universal note of nostalgia which hovers over all immigrant communities. Augusta Savage and Zora Neale Hurston were immigrants from the South while Ernest E. Mair and DeVere Stuart were from the Caribbean. For each of them home was an idealized, halcyon place, a secret place of refuge from a care-filled world. DeVere Stuart spoke for nearly every immigrant in the world when he recalled how hard it was to leave and how much he longed to return some day. Only Augusta Savage, in these selections, actually returns home to confront the idealized dream with a less flattering reality—a reality which, nevertheless, still cannot quite dispel the dream of an ancient remembrance.

Ethel Trew Dunlap, unlike the others, emigrated West from Chicago to Los Angeles. Here was a slightly different variant of the immigrant experience—the lingering feeling of guilt associated with departing the ghetto for more congenial surroundings. She assuaged her guilt by promising to return if the Black Belt should ever summon her back.

The Old Homestead

Augusta Savage (1922)

I visited today the old Homestead,
    Deserted now for many busy years,
Explored again with memory laden tread,
    The birthplace of so many hopes and fears.

The windlass seemed to creak a doleful tune,
    The mocking birds that used to sing so gay
Seem all forgetful of the month of June,
    The time to sing their merriest roundelay.

The meadow that to childish eyes did seem
    To stretch into the distance mile on mile,
Is but a glen, and now the raging stream,
    Is just a little brook that tries to smile.

The brier vines are trailing o'er the ground,
    The old red barn will never look the same,
And nothing seemed familiar till I found
    The maple bough whereon I carved my name.

It used to stretch far out before the door,
    Where through its leaves the sunbeams used to play
And make a dappled shadow on the floor,
    Of porches fallen now into decay.

And down my time scarred cheek there crept a tear,
    For those who sleep beneath the ocean's foam,
And then a sigh for other hearts so dear,
    That rest so gently 'neath the sand of home.

The Green Hills of Saint Ann

Ernest F. Mair (1923)

There's a place I love to think of
    Through the busy hours of day,
There's a place I love to dream of
    When at night in sleep I lay;
A place brimful of memories
    Of my childhood days gone by,
Where prone upon my back beneath
    Its glorious skies I'd lie.
A desired home of refuge
    To a travel-wearied man
Is my old home town that nestled
    On the green hills of Saint Ann.

When my soul is overburdened
    With the dreary cares of life,
When I fear that I will falter
    And must perish in the strife,
In some sweet, secluded corner
    I recline and take a trip
By the railroad of Remembrance
    Or Imagination's ship
To that place where in my boyhood
    I would long to be a man—
Santa Gloria, that nestles
    On the green hills of Saint Ann.

Near Point Olivet's fair homestead,
    By the old naseberry tree,
Just below the big grape arbor,
    With that wondrous view to sea,
Was my fav'rite spot of garden,
    Shaded from the noonday sun—
Oftentimes I've lain there reading
    Till the day was almost done,

"Ivanhoe," "Sir Nigel Loring,"
   "Sailors' Yarns of Yucatan;"
On such mental food I feasted
   Years ago in old Saint Ann.

How my young imagination
   Dreamt about the coming time
And the laurels I would win as
   Up the dizzy heights I'd climb!
Fame and wealth I knew were certain
   And the joys that they could bring;
Those were days when sheer existence
   Made me lift my voice and sing,
Those were days before my travels
   Out into the world began,
Ere I left my earthly heaven
   On the green hills of Saint Ann.

O land of woods and waterfalls,
   Of moonlit nights enthralling,
Here in the cold and cheerless North
   I hear you softly calling
To yonder sweet remembered scenes,
   To faces bright and sunny,
To blossoms sweet whence busy bees
   Are sucking nectar honey.
Your tropic blood stirs in my veins,
   And the ocean's but a span
[?] my restless spirit leaps
   To the green hills of Saint Ann.

Now I feel my strength returning,
   Now my courage is renewed,
Once again I am pursuing
   Where before I was pursued;
Vanished is my melancholy,
   Buoyant once more is my tread,
Back among the vibrant living
   Comes a spirit almost dead,
For the confidence of boyhood
   Nerves with steel the tired man
When I travel back in fancy
   To the green hills of Saint Ann.

Good-Bye, Black Belt

**(Lines written just before leaving Chicago for Danville, Ill.,
en route to Los Angeles, Cal.)**

Ethel Trew Dunlap (1921)

Good-bye, Black Belt, my duty calls
    And I must say good-bye;
But if you call me, I'll return—
    I'll hearken to your sigh.
I'm going down to make a call
    On Danville, Illinois,
Where country air brings back the bloom
    And there are simple joys.
I want to see the Afric son
    Who led me to God's grace;
And chat with him like Jethro did
    With Moses 'bout his race.
The voice of Ephraim seems to call;
    "Oh, Ethel, come to me,
Where Bibles may be read by stars
    And milk and eggs are free."
Black Belt, you cannot nurse a rose,
    And poets long for flowers.
I've tried to hide it and be brave,
    But, oh, I long for bowers—
Some place like Danville, Illinois,
    Where there's a waving tree,
Or rustic seat in shady nook
    For Ephraim and me.
Some flower to yield us its perfume,
    To rapture aching hearts,
Beneath God's canopy to heal
    The worldly thrusts and darts;
Some flitting bird on soaring wing
    To tell of freedom's flight;

Or rosy dawn like eastern blush
    That follow Afric's night.
Some twilight that is all serene,
    Where Ephraim and I
Forget the White Curse when we gaze
    Into God's starry sky.
So farewell, Black Belt, for a while;
    But if I hear you groan,
Back on the wings of love I'll fly
    To dusky, barren zone.

To the Ethiopian Sons and Daughters of Chicago

Ethel Trew Dunlap (1921)

O Windy City, fare-thee-well!
I've left the Black Belt's zone;
I stole away—you will not care—
You never heard my moan
That poverty and Ephraim's woes
Heaped on the heart of me;
But God looked down and, merciful,
My suff'ring heart set free.
O never shall my soul forget
The weeping, outcast slaves,
Mine eyes shall watch with him 'till dawn
Suffuses land and wave,
And I shall haunt the Black Belt's zone
With memory for guide,
And when the winds of winter blow,
I'll walk by Ephraim's side;
I'll feel the stinging winds that chill
His ill-clad, shiv'ring frame;
I'll fast to feel his suffering

That's caused by hunger's pain,
While I am in the land of sun,
The happy, Golden West,
How can I joy while misery
Clasps captives to her breast?
But hark ye slave! the frowning sky
That Michigan's shores wear
In winter time, and poverty,
Will make you do and dare!
'Tis wind that chills and hand that binds
Which rouses sleeping slaves
To drastic measures that will build
An Empire o'er the waves;
Ah! those who walk in paths of ease
Will never free their race!
It is the outcast slave that seeks
A better, safer place.
The Empire that your race shall build
Across the briny sea
Shall emanate from hardy hands
That struggled to be free.
Hamitic sons and daughters all,
Of Windy City fame,
Who turn your eyes to Africa
Where you might win a name,
Oppression's corpse is growing cold,
And soon its glassy stare
Shall loose Goliath's evil hold
Because you chose to dare.
I left you where I humbly dwelt
With your beloved race,
That in the future I might serve
You with a better grace.
When Michigan sends up a sigh
From out that giant lake,
Remember how I walked with you
All for the captive's sake;
How I endured the stinging cold
That I might closer be
To suff'ring slaves whose dreams have built
An Empire o'er the sea.
And I will hear your troubled cry—

Write from the Black Belt's zone;
When wolves of ease pursue your steps,
Bear not the cross alone.

Home

Zora Neale Hurston (1922)

I know a place that is full of light
That is full of dreams and visions bright
Where pleasing fancy loves to roam
And picture me once more at home.

There nothing comes to mar my days
And dim for me the sun's loved rays
To shake my faith in things divine
And bare the cruelty of mankind.

Ah, that I to that spot might flee
That peace and love may dwell with me
To brush away the somber shrouds
And show the lining of the clouds.

Barbados

De Vere Stuart (1924)

In the west there lies an island belted by a sapphire sea
Over which the ocean breezes ever blow caressingly.
Skies that pale the deepest turquoise, woods and fields of

varied green
Make as fair a panorama as can anywhere be seen

There the gorgeous bougainvillea and the coroleta bloom,
And the balmy air is ever redolent with the perfume
Of the trailing stephanotis and the jasmine's star-shaped
     flowers,
Which with every flirting zephyr flutter, down in fragrant
     showers.

Fifty feet or more above you with the passing of each breeze
Aeolus makes plaintive music in the casurina trees.
Such the softness of that music touched by those aerial fingers,
That the ear is all uncertain if the strain has stopped or lingers.

Humming birds and butterflies like radiant gems go flashing
     by:
And wherever fall your glances some attraction meets the eye:
Honey bees 'mong flow'ring trees are sipping nectar all day
     long:
And from the stately cabbage palms soft comes the
     wooddove's tender song.

And at sundown! O, the opalescent glory of the sky!
Then it seems as if celestial vistas meet th' enraptured eye.
Palest rose to deepest carmine, lightest green to darkest jade:
Flaming gold and softer saffron on a turquoise bed inlaid.

Now the sun greets Oceanus! And the passion of his kiss
Turns the Caribbean sapphire to a shim'ring sea of bliss.
Next he burns an amber pathway from the skyline to the
     shore—
Pauses on the brink a moment—sinks as if to rise no more.

With the motion of his sinking Twilight drops her dusky veil,
And low in the western heavens Hesper sets his silver sail.
For a moment all seems silent: then melodiously clear
Comes the chirping of the cricket cutting through the ambient
     air.

And, then, Night! Night in the tropics! Ah, but mere words fail
     to tell
Of the soul-entrancing beauty that enwraps you in a spell
When the silver beams of Luna bathe in light the island scene
Till the very leaves and flowers scintillate beneath the sheen.

O, Barbados! Sun-kissed, moon-kissed! Nestling in your
    sapphire sea,
Dearest, fairest of all fair spots on God's earth thou art to me.
Isle of peace! Sweet isle of sunshine! Hard it was to say adieu.
But some day, my lovely homeland, some day I'll return to you.

18

Africa

Freedom for Africa was an overriding concern of the Garvey Movement. This concern was inevitably reflected in the poems of Garvey's followers and sympathizers.

Interest in Africa began with an interest in its history. John Edward Bruce's "Africa" (1921) revealed the reverence for Africa exhibited by Greeks and others in classical and biblical times. George Wells Parker, an activist and student of African history, predicted a return of Africa's pristine might, much as Garvey frequently did.

The desire to return to Africa was often voiced within the movement. Sometimes Garveyites envisaged sending over skilled and ambitious personnel to help in Africa's development. At other times he and his followers hinted at mass repatriation. Several strands within the repatriation theme are given expression here. Arnold W. Ford in "O Africa, My Native Land" (1920) likens the African in the West to a prodigal child seeking to return home. Ford, musical director of the U.N.I.A., himself emigrated to Ethiopia in 1930. Ford's "Legion's Marching Song," anthem of Garvey's Universal African Legion, envisaged the possibility of military assistance to Africa in its struggle against colonialism. After the Italian invasion of Ethiopia in 1935, many Garveyites and others did in fact offer their services to Ethiopia. Charles W. Cranford in "The Spirit of '23" (1923) explicitly ties the return to Africa to the experience of the World War. He feels, as does Ethel Trew Dunlap in "Good-Bye, America!" (1921) that, as the nationalist Bishop Henry McNeal Turner used to say, there is no manhood future for the African race in the United States.

Dunlap in "Onlys" (1922—probably her rendering of "onliest") introduces a different aspect of the African question. She sees "Black English" as a charming evidence of African cultural survivals in North America.

Kobina Sekyi's "The Sojourner" (1922) was the second longest poem to appear in the Negro World, *after Garvey's "The Tragedy of White Injustice" (1927). Sekyi was a Gold Coast (Ghana) lawyer and his poem demonstrated that some Africans born on the continent, too, could usefully imbibe Garvey's African propaganda. Sekyi's long epic, probably autobiographical, at least in part, showed that the European educated African, like his African-American and Afro-Caribbean counterparts, needed to "go back to Africa" culturally and spiritually. The sojourner, having travelled the long and weary road to attempted assimilation, discovers at length that he has been enticed by a lie. European civilization proves, on close examination, to be a corrupted entity hiding behind a facade of technological progress. Disillusioned, the sojourner retreats into his Negritude and stretches forth his hands to Africa, much like the prodigal child of Arnold J. Ford. Sekyi, like his fellow Garveyite poet T. Albert Marryshow, was a major nationalist political figure in his country. His appearance here as a poet is likely to prove surprising to many.*

Africa

John Edward Bruce (1921)

A land of mystery, and famed
For sheltering the son of God;
Rich in tradition, and thy name,
Is mentioned in His Holy word,
Called Egypt, Ethiopia, Ammon, but—
"Africa" for thee is oftenest heard.

When Africa Awakes!

George Wells Parker (1923)

When Africa awakes! and from
The crushing centuries of studied wrong,
Base defilement, lust and thong,
Lifts up her voice and cries aloud
Her right to rule herself! Methinks the crowd
Of gold-greedy men will laugh and say:
"Not now, thou backward race! This is our day!
Yours yet to bow and meekly pay
The price of weakness.

But Africa will ponder well these words,
Her sons shall seek the shadows of the hills
And vow, as they recount the rosary of ills,
That their fair land of summer sun and mien
Must not forever be the Midas dream
Of self-made masters, who even loath to give
The one last human right, to live.

Africa bides her time! But from the ocean strand,
O'er jungle, mountain, vale and mead,
That sweet word, "Unity!" will speed
On wings of winds, and woo her fretful folk
Into one dream, one voice, one heart, one hope!
And yet again she'll claim her sacred right
To rule herself, apart from alien might;
But if, once more, the pale-faced men shall say:
"Not yet, thou backward race! Still thine to pay!
I quake to think how swarthy arms shall hurl
Thundering terrors at a gasping world!
When Africa awakes!

O Africa, My Native Land!

Arnold J. Ford (1920)

O Africa, my native land,
A forlorn prodigal I stand,
Torn from thy breast by cruel fiends
To consummate their selfish ends—
    Only a slave to be.
I now arise with solemn mind,
The haven of thy shores to find,
Grievous and heavy is my load,
And dark and dreary is the road;
      Stretch forth thine hands to me—
      Stretch forth thine hands to me.

O Africa, my native land,
Let me once more in honor stand
Upon thy shores, our battles won,
Bath'd in the light of God's bright sun,
    A nobleman and free,
Where forests green luxuriant grow
Where lordly rivers ebb and flow,
Where strength and beauty had their
    birth—
Mother of greatest sons of earth—
      Stretch forth thine hands to me,
      Stretch forth thine hands to me.

Legion's Marching Song

Arnold J. Ford (n.d.)

The Legion here, will fight for Africa there,
We are going to avenge her wrongs,
We are coming, oh, Mother Africa,
We are four hundred millions strong.

CHORUS:

We are coming, oh Mother Africa,
We are coming to avenge your wrongs,
We are coming, oh yes, we are coming,
We are four hundred millions strong.

We will fight, we will fight,
With all our might, we are sons of liberty,
We will fight, oh yes, with all our might,
We are sons of liberty.

We are here, because Mother Africa calls,
She wants us to avenge her wrongs,
We are here because Mother Africa calls,
We are four hundred millions strong.

We are going to fight our foe, blow for blow,
We won't stop until we have knocked him down,
And when at last he has hit the ground,
We will show him who is the clown.

We shall fight our foe, from coast to coast,
For Africa must be free,
I am a soldier, Mother Africa,
You can depend on me.

Travel on, on, on, my good brother,
And keep within the law,
No cracker will dare to slap our Mother,
Or we will knock him on the jaw.

No cracker will dare to seduce our sister,

Or to hang us on a limb,
And we are not not obliged to call him mister,
Or to skin our lips at him.

Good-Bye, America!

Ethel Trew Dunlap (1921)

Good-bye, America, good-bye!
    We're leaving, Uncle Sam!
You stole us, but we're going back
    Into the land of Ham.
You told us that we were baboons,
    And that we came from trees,
But we are getting wise enough
    To sail across the seas.
You told us Africa was wild
    In red and glaring lines,
But you forgot to tell our folks
    About the diamond mines.
You painted pictures of wild beasts
    In Afric jungle lair.
You fooled us and you kept us here
    While you went over there.
Now we are black, but if we're fools
    It's you who made us so.
But you can't keep us on this shore—
    We simply have to go.
Since J. D. Barber crossed the sea
    And grasped the Crown Prince's hand,
We know just why you try to keep
    Us in this hoodlum land.
The lions didn't eat him up—
    He came back looking fine!
Black men, we've been fools long enough—
    Let's take the Black Star Line.

Some Negroes say they never lost
    A thing across the sea,
But some things here that we have found
    Don't look so good to me.
You say America's your home,
    But if it is I dare
For you to make yourself at home
    Or take a parlor chair.
Good-bye, America, good-bye!
    We cannot wait to be
The President since Barber saw
    That Queen across the sea!
Good-bye, America, good-bye!
    We cannot wait to dust
The White House, blue room and its chairs—
    Those diamonds might rust!
Good-bye, America, good-bye!
    You can have all we own,
But don't forget Liberia
    Needs quite a little loan.
Good-bye, America, good-bye!
    Your slave we cannot be
When they need statesmen who are black
    Beyond the briny sea.
Good-bye, America, good-bye!
    We can't forget the hours
Together, and you'll think of us
    When you pick cotton flowers.
Good-bye, America, good-bye!
    We've lived beneath Old Glory;
You've cooked us, too, beneath its stars—
    The whole world knows the story.
Good-bye, America, good-bye!
    Blame Garvey for the end!
And if the foe insults the flag
    Your hand will have to mend!

Onlys [Onliest?]

Ethel Trew Dunlap (1922)

I'll teach you English, how to cast
    Aside your Negro dialect;
But there's a word I hesitate,
    In spite of grammar, to reject;
'Tis onlys. Ephraim, of course,
    You never knew you spoke it so.
It sounds peculiarly sweet—
    And so, I think, I'll let it go.
Pronounce it only when you speak
    To others; but when lights are low,
And we converse as heart to heart
    Let onlys through your language flow.
And the world should look askance
    When from your lips it falls like sigh,
Blush not—it is thy mother tongue,
    The accent 'neath the tropic sky.
Let onlys be a word to bind
    Thy mem'ry to thy native land—
Thy soul to mine—the world may smile;
    But we alone may understand.

The Spirit of '23

Charles W. Cranford (1923)

1

The war was fought and peace was bought,

But at a staggering price.
Great men with brain were gassed insane,
    And nations lowered to vice.

2

Black men fought, too, the whole war through,
    To save the powers that be;
They gave their lives to make the world
    Safe for democracy.

3

They thought their stand would make this land
    A living Paradise.
When they perceived they'd been deceived,
    Toward home they turned their eyes.

4

For there alone we'll build a home
    Where we can live in peace;
Our lives thus spent we'd die content,
    While Hamites would increase.

5

So spread the news of a great man's views
    Of something that must be;
Install in them that grit and vim,
    The spirit of '23.

The Sojourner

Kobina Sekyi (1922)

Untravelled

A product of the law school, embroidered by the high,
Upbrought and trained by similar products, here am I!

I speak English to soften my harsher native tongue,
It matters not if often I speak the Fanti wrong.
I'm learning to be British, and treat with due contempt
The worship of the Fetish, from which I am exempt.
I was baptized an infant, a Christian hedged around,
With prayer from the moment my being was unbound.
I'm clad in coat and trousers, with boots upon my feet,
And tamfurafu and Hausas I seldom deign to greet;
For I despise the native that wears the native dress,
The badge that marks the bushman who never will progress.
I like civilization, and I'd be glad to see
All people that are pagan eschew Idolatry.
I reckon high the power of Governors and such,
But our own Kings and Chiefs, why they do not matter much.
I soon shall go to England, where I've been often told,
No filth and nothing nasty you every may behold.
And there I'll try my hardest to learn the English life,
And I shall try to marry a real English wife!

Abroad

Far from my home, I sojourn in a land,
    Where the day's course may see the season's changes,
Where Morn may see me, with a steady hand,
    Veiling my eyes to view the distant ranges,
And evening bring me misery and doubt,
And shivering limbs within and cold without!

My inner-self, unused to sudden turns,
    Swayed here and there by atmospheric frolic,
Now sad, since dull without, it pleasure spurns,
    And breathes laments, becoming melancholic;
Now gay, because of sunshine warm and long,
It grows in cheerfulness, and I am strong.

And being strong, I walk in crowded streets,
    And watch the people, white, some grave, some merry,
Some prosperous and some with many needs,
    Some free and careless, others very wary,
For money shortens distance and mishap,
Speeds o'er the ways, the reckless to entrap.

When June permits the country to display
    The sunny plants hot-housed since the autumn,
When Palm may thrive and feel the breath of day,

And plantain leaf above its fleshing column,
Then is this land most like to my dear home,
Then may I joy and let my spirit roam.

But when stern autumn lays bright summer low,
        And spoils the trees of all their verdant beauty,
Heralding sterner winter bleak and slow
        To alter, then I would betray my duty.
And quit the seats of learning, which, alone,
        To these inclement climes can we atone.

It is a land of Freedom held in chains
        By Trade, the sire of Mammon and Oppression,
And comrade of Deceit, whose crooked gains
        But jeer at doting Law's effete aggression,
And satisfy Religion's earthly greed,
Whilst Labor languishes in very need!

Deep Poverty ranged by the side of wealth,
        Is this what thou would'st call Civilization?
Or many ills that view excessive health,
        Yet, where may reach to such realization?
What tho' thy care for sickness is extensive,
        If arrogance doth blight the gift's receipt,
Whilst much that's necessary is expensive,
        And crime is fed, whilst Merit lacks to eat?

What tho' thy massive cities stand erect
        On concave streets that throb with life and action?
What tho' thy noble buildings are bedecked
        With art that gives aesthetic satisfaction?
What tho' thy wisdom soars on rigid wings,
        Speeds over iron, burrows through the deep,
And hath created many wondrous things,
        If some may laugh whilst others needs must weep?

Gaunt Misery, filling her sunken cheeks
        With curses and derisions of thy splendor,
In bitter tones, with strident voice, she speaks:
        "Behold the victory of cant o'er candor,
Of Science over Nature, and of Wealth
O'er human welfare and o'er social health!"

Retrospective

I.

Thus spake the wakening spirit:
"Give honor but to merit,
And credit not the folly
Of warp or melancholy!

"Should Ignorance or Bias
Appropriate the dais
Of Wisdom or of Knowledge,
Face imprudence with courage.

"And credit not the folly
Of warp or Melancholy,
But learn to think unbidden,
And seek, thyself, the hidden!"

II.

"But written parchment History knows,
And what old monuments disclose;
She knows no race that must have nursed
The race in hieroglyphics first.

"Are records of the days gone by
All brought to sight of human eye?
What nation by itself alone
To full maturity hath grown?

"How much may mortals not forget,
When on the craved meridian set?
'Tis thus plebian nobles scorn
The arms that pulling them had borne."

III.

"Immortal Caesar once essayed
To strengthen Rome's divided State,
And humble Rome's increasing pride
By spreading franchise far and wide.

"Corruption broke his noble scheme,
And soon was rampant and supreme
Within the Empire's wide domain,
Whose risen star began to wane."

IV.

"Some ruder men, down from the North,
To storm and plunder sallied forth:
With vicious zeal he rent the foe
That once had dealt him many a blow.

"An Eastern faith nursed by the West,
His savage soul at length possessed;
And bade him train his bloody hand
In conquest of an Eastern land.

"Of liberty by nature fond,
Some freed them from a Catholic bond,
Their young, with newer thoughts imbued,
Each his peculiar creed pursued.

"Religion to Oppression grew,
And soon a fervent few withdrew;
They found a home, beyond the seas,
To worship, there, their God in peace."

V.

"Of liberty now fonder grown,
They kept it for themselves alone,
Thus, Freedom, to one race combined,
Another race in chains could bind!

"They turned a man into a brute,
His human soul they'd fain uproot:
They sought to foist a spirit mean
Where once a human soul had been!

"Grim Slavery, in the hideous shape
That fostered torture, murder, rape,
Went hand in hand with Christian grace,
And would deform a human race!

"The day of reckoning did arrive,
And, with a mortal civil strife,
The Furies did avenge the wrong
A race had suffered for so long."

VI.

"Yet yet, who felt the shame and pain

Of slaving in a milder strain,
Have lost your milder heritage—
Your manhood—in a fractious age!

"Ye heed the wild barbaric boost
Of fickle Fortune's present host,
And deem your surprise social state
An object meet for Christian hate!

"Inconstant Fortune favored Rome
When caves and grottoes formed his home,
That now both had the enlightened van,
Of tutors of the African."

VII.

"But we are black,' and hear you say,
Yea! Ye are black, flatnosed, yea!
Your lips are thick, your hair is fleece
Ye are not Gods of Ancient Greece.

"'And they are ape-like,' adds your guide,
What then? There were the greater pride
Therein: a swinish skin and snout
And fur might put a Darwin out.

"The ape hath gained a fleecier wig,
And grown a thicker lip; the pig
Retrains the fur and skin, but he
Hath turned his nostrils southerly.

"Let mutual fools themselves amuse
With such-like gibes. The varied hues
Of men decide their inner worth,
But for the churls of peevish birth.

"From black to brown, from brown to white,
Civilization spread her light,
And added lustre gained from each
That once herself did guide and teach.
"Hence, wherefore pride and smug conceit,
That but proclaim a mind replete
With travesties of Clio's scroll,
And make a boasted wisdom droll?"

VIII.

"So credit not the folly,
Of Warp or Melancholy,
But learn to think unbidden,
And find, thyself, the hidden.

"And learn that man may borrow
The wisdom of tomorrow,
Who, yesterday, was teaching
The sage that now is preaching.

"Awake thee from thy slumber,
And quickly disencumber
Thy manhood of the fetters
That make thine equals betters."

Home Again
(To Africa)

Resplendent as the noon-day sun art thou,
　　Fresh as the wind that blows,
And unto thee eternal love I vow,
O smile from thee were recompense enow,
Queen of my heart, to give me love's repose.

Once, in my foolish days, I thought thee vile,
　　And bound my faith to her,
That cloaked thy virtues with her ancient guile,
And strove thy mellow beauty to defile,
With masks of shame that she had painted fair.

She made thee faithless to thy beauty's slaves
That gave their heart to thee,
And bade thee deem thy many suitors knaves
And some betray to most untimely graves,
That offered life itself to make thee free.

To make thee free from falseness and disgrace,
And shield thee from the greed
Of subtle lovers of another race—
The vampires whose devotion would efface
Thy charm, and drain thy plenteous wealth with speed.

Thy gold, thy sunshine and thy shady palms,
Thy forests thick and grand,
Have drawn thee faithless wooers; and thy qualms

Were charmed with gilded gifts; the praise that calms,
The future prey did gain thy wavering hand.

Thou hast thy faults, but some are tender faults:
Thy freeness with thy trust,
Hath laid thee open to the base assaults
Of foreigners. Thine openness exalts
In needless gifts, that but increase their lust.

Thou hast thy faults, Beloved, thou shouldest know,
Wherein thy goodness fails,
True love with open eyes alone can grow,
But sees far deeper than the outward show,
And thrives on truth, that chides but never rails.

I've watched thy pageant of the strange address
That hath replaced thine own:
I've watched thine earnest strivings to repress
Ancestral manners lest they e'er digress,
Thee from the ways for which thy love hath grown.
I watched thee slighting laws thy sires obeyed,
And since thou dost aspire,
To gain the praise of aliens, thou hast prayed
Unto an alien God. Thine own life hath decayed
Since thou dost strange observances desire.

Thy children, born in wedlock here unknown,
Before the strangers came,
Are bastards most of whom have shameless grown
As such: their graceless bastardy is shown
In meekness mean to gain a father's name!

Thou should'st improve thine own, if it be short
Of perfectness: 'tis thus
One's powers should increase; but if then court,
Approved from without, then may'st distort
Thyself with toil and kill thyself with fuss.
Behold, rebuffs and gelding ridients
Attend the days of all
That are displeased with what they have and pale
For strange things. Disappointment's biting rule
Waits at the end to aggravate their fall.

Thy native charms are many: wherefore waste
Thy needed energy,

In learning foreign ways that are in haste
But in the foreign land; O, wherefore haste
To spoil thy charm with foreign finery?
Resplendent in thy native grace art thou,
Fresh as the native rose,
Unforced in hot-house, and to thee I vow
Eternal love. Thy smile were balm enow
My aching heart to comfort and compose.

19

The Black Woman

The question of the Black Woman was one on which Garvey himself had waxed poetic—"Black queen of beauty, thou hast given color to the world!" It was inevitable that an organization such as the U.N.I.A. should preoccupy itself with this question. The sexual exploitation of the slave woman was a memory that still rankled in the consciousness of the New Negro generation. Such exploitation had by no means disappeared, especially in the South, where near-slavery lingered on in the guise of peonage. These unfortunate realities were compounded by the widely disseminated white stereotype of the Black woman as a person of easy virtue. Prevailing standards of physical beauty made matters even worse. Garvey often admonished Black men to take down the white pin-ups from their walls. He also encouraged the manufacture of Black dolls for children. On the other side of the coin, the problem of prostitution was one that agonized sensitive Black leaders of varying ideological persuasions. Black leaders in Philadelphia, for example, had in 1904 founded the Philadelphia Association for the Protection of Colored Women.

The poems in this section illustrate responses to some aspects of these problems. Estella Matthews in "The New Negro Woman's Attitude Toward the White Man" (1922) militantly rejects the legacy of slavery and the submission bequeathed by that institution. The New Negro Woman will defend her virtue, however high the price. Matthews was an official of the Philadelphia U.N.I.A. and doubtless therefore in a good position to articulate the organization's views on this subject.

Ethel Trew Dunlap's "Sweet Afric Maid" (1922) and Ernest E. Mair's "O Afric Maid" (1922) both take a different tack. They exalt the Black woman. They make of her an object worthy of veneration and love. Leonard Brathwaite, in his usual incisive, witty and moralizing way, deals quite frankly

216

with the touchy question of intra-racial color prejudice. Brathwaite's prose poems were often miniature short stories, complete with plot, suspense, denouement and moral. This is demonstrated with telling effect here.

The New Negro Woman's Attitude Toward The White Man

Estella Matthews (1921)

Laugh with your lustful eyes,
    We will never bend our knees.
The shackles ne'er again shall bind ,
    The arms which now are free.

Some strike for hope of booty,
    Some for the hope of pride;
We battle to defend our all,
    For which our mothers died.

We loath you in our bosoms.
    We scorn you with our eyes;
We despise you with our latest breath,
    And fight you till we die;

We ne'er will ask you quarters,
    And we ne'er will be your slave;
But we will swim the sea of virtue,
    Till we sink beneath its waves.

Sweet Afric Maid

Ethel Trew Dunlap (1922)

Sweet Afric maid, sweet Afric maid!
Thou daughter of the Southern Queen!
Oh, let me lift thy cross of care
And be thy Simon of Cyrene!

Sweet Afric maid, sweet Afric maid!
Come, like Rebekah did, at eve,
When weary I pause by life's well,
To minister, that I may believe.

Sweet Afric maid, sweet Afric maid!
Be my Zipporah, fond and true.
As Moses fled to Midian,
A fugitive, I come to you.

Sweet Afric maid, sweet Afric maid!
The words of Jethro's lips have ceased;
But they are written on thy heart,
And thou shalt be my dusky priest.

Sweet Afric maid, sweet Afric maid!
Be thou my Rachel! I have fled
From Esau's anger, Bethel's fear,
To worship where you dwell and tread.

Sweet Afric maid, sweet Afric maid!
Be thou my lotus of the Nile;
The fragrance of my motherland,
To cheer a soul that's in exile.

O Afric Maid

Ernest E. Mair (1922)

O Afric maid whose beauteous eyes,
    Whose voice, whose smile I idolize;
Whose name enchantment spells for me
    O Afric maid, I dare love thee!

Doth not the flower love the sun
    That burns its petals one by one?
So painful though affection be
    O Afric maid, I dare love thee!

Doth not the North Wind kiss the sea?
    Proud sea! She answers angrily
With foam and spume and angry roar
    She hurls her billows on the shore.

Such bold presumption makes her rise
    In dreadful wrath toward the skies—,
Thou art the sea; the North Wind—I
    I'd gladly kiss thee once and die!

O Afric maid, thy priceless love
    The vaulted deep doth light above
Like some bright star beyond the ken
    Of me; the lowliest of men.

But strong desire lends me wings
    And hope to cheer me sweetly sings
"Mount up!" He only wins who dares
    Cast off these base unmanly fears

That clog thy soul's ambitious rise
    "Toward this godness of the skies."
Hope's words I drink and lightly soar
    For now I'm strong, I fear no more.

And oh, my soul what joy 'twill be
    O Afric maid, when thou lov'st me!

At The Masked Ball

Leonard Brathwaite (1922)

She was a beauty in her mask and costume.

Her shapely contour, her agile carriage, lent grace to her make-up.

Her deep, resonant but exceedingly mild voice—a voice heated by the suns of Africa and tempered by the bleak ozone of these United States of America—would have wooed and charmed anyone. She would have made Ponce de Leon exclaim "I've found it!"

She waltzed and waltzed like the whiff of a zephyr—her, yes, her Afro-American, Negro American, colored American (pick your choice) partner was just delighted with her.

Anyone would have been, after peeping through a mask on those dreamy, amorous eyes of hers—eyes that pierced, eyes that drew, eyes that seemed to say, as they looked into her partner's, "I am virtue itself."

The waltz was through. The ball was over. They had exited to go home. She had removed her mask. "Horrors! She's black. I thought I was dancing with and would have been escorting home a high-yallah!"

But she was black. And wouldn't it show sense on the part of Afro-American, colored American, Negro American (pick your choice) men if they, instead of having silly delusions about "high-yallahs," seek out intelligence and virtue in women, whether they be brown, black, "pink" or "high-yallah"?

20

Race

The race question naturally entered into a large number of Negro World poems, whatever their ostensible subject. H. David Murray's "The Kindred Racial Flame" (1923) goes to the heart of Garvey's "race first" doctrine. Every group, he says, has a collective spiritual existence unique to that group. Some people, reformers and racists alike, have called this the "race soul." The idea was often implied in the works of the Francophone "Negritude" poets of the 1930s and beyond.

The poetical exchange between Ethel Trew Dunlap and H. A. Nurse provides yet another twist to the old "tragic mulatto" theme. Dunlap was not only the Negro World's most prolific poet. She was also very light of complexion. Her "If I Should Die Tonight" (1922) is in reality an anguished plea for help—help in her predicament, caught as she is between the rock of Afro-America and the hard place of the white world. She has bravely cast her lot with the Black side of her ancestry and she needs help.

H. A. Nurse's assistance was almost instantaneous. Negro World poets often carried on conversations through their verse. These two poems together provide one of the most eloquent examples of this. Nurse follows Dunlap very closely in meter, structure and overall length of his poem. "We need your clinging faith," he says. The two poems cannot be separated, the one from the other.

The Kindred Racial Flame

H. David Murray (1923)

Humanity! Humanity!!
    O'er all the world the same;
There dimly burns within each breast
    A kindred racial flame.
Tho deadly dormant it may be,
    Entirely hid from sight,
But at the cry of peril
    It becomes a beacon light.
It stirs each group to action,
    O'er all the world the same;
This little hidden something,
    Called the kindred racial flame.

If I Should Die Tonight

Ethel Trew Dunlap (1922)

If I should die tonight, perchance
    Someone who is born fair
Might gaze into my face and see
    The lines of sorrow there,
And whisper: "She was freedom's child;
    She loved the outcast slave."
And those who chided me in life
    Might pity by my grave.

If I should die tonight, my race
    That madly passed me by,

Might pause beside my bier and ask
    Black men the reason why
I clasped the Red, the Black, the Green
    While solemnly I slept;
Some patriot might speak a word
    For which in life I wept.

If I should die tonight, perchance
    Columbia's blue-eyed son
Who scorned by Negro friends and me
    Might say: "Her crown is won;
She saw the man and not the skin—
    Her love gushed o'er the wave."
Columbia's son and Menelik's
    Might clasp hands by my grave.

If I should die tonight, perchance
    My racial foes might hush,
And change the word of hate to love,
    When death had stole life's blush.
Lips that said: "Traitor" when I spoke
    My love for southern Queen,
Might speak in accents soft and low
    Of Red, the Black, the Green.

If I should die tonight, perchance
    The Red, the White, the Blue
Might shed its light upon my grave
    If liberty but knew;
And those who said: "She loved the slave
    More than her kindred fair,"
Might say: "She was a patriot,
    And she shall have our prayer."

If You Should Die Tonight

To Miss Ethel Trew Dunlap

H. A. Nurse (1922)

If you should die tonight
    And never more should sing,
The Sun's ethereal light
    No joy to me would bring;
'Twould be a sorry world,
    How could I deem it right
If god should claim your soul
    Before you've won your fight?

If you should die tonight
    Perchance you then will know
The love we bear—despite,
    We dare not tell you so;
Perchance the Infinite
    Our secrets would disclose;
Then you could read aright
    What He already knows.

If you should die tonight,
    The alien race may learn
The righteous way to fight
    And cease to lynch and burn;
Perchance they'll recognize
    The common rights of all;
If Ethel Dunlap dies
    Before the dewdrops fall.

Yes, should you die tonight,
    A million hearts would break
For in this noble fight
    We need your clinging faith;
Your songs to speed us on,
    Unto that woeful day;

When every dark-hued son
    'Thiopia's call obey.

Then, sing not solemnly,
    Bring me no fault'ring note.
Freedom and Liberty
    Are worth the songs you wrote;
So think not, dear, of death;
    'Twill come too soon, I fear,
But shout with one full breath
    Redemption day draws near.

21

Poems Of Love

The Negro World *poets were not so highly political as to be oblivious to life's more tender aspects. Some of the authors of the following poems of love— Mair, Sekyi, Ali—were among the most political of people. Yet, here they reveal a side of their personalities that was sentimental and charming.*

Zora Neale Hurston and Lucian B. Watkins were two of the better known literary figures of the Harlem Renaissance who published in Garvey's newspaper. It is difficult to tell whether Watkins' "Loved and Lost" (1921) was meant to be taken literally or whether it was intended as an allegory on his life. For Watkins wrote this sadly beautiful swan song practically on his deathbed. Perhaps there were elements both of literal experience and of allegory running through this melancholy masterpiece.

To My Antidote

Ernest E. Mair (1922)

When my heart is heavy laden
And I'm feeling sore oppressed,
When my trouble-tossed spirit
Wars within my aching breast,
When I sleep to dream misfortune

226

And awake to find it true,
When the skies of my mentality
Take on a leaden hue;
When life hardly seems worth living
And everything goes wrong;
When my ears attuned to weeping
Find no more their joy in song—
Then to you, my sympathizer,
All my woes and griefs I bring;
And I find with you that solace
That takes away their sting.
Oh, it's wonderful to have a friend
Who understands your mood,
Whose gentle pressure of the hand
Uplifts you when you brood.
God bless you, little comforter!
When your time to grieve shall be
God provide you a supporter
Such as you have been to me.

To A Pair Of Married Lovers

Kobina Sekyi (1922)

Long have you together trod
Matrimony's winding road,
Wedded at the shrine of God.

Motherly, you seek his good:
For you loved him ere you stood
At the gates of parenthood.

Fatherly, you guard her life
That hath been so good a wife
From affliction, care and strife.

As of old, may you and he,

Held by love in harmony,
Longer yet together be!

Passion

Zora Neale Hurston (1922)

When I look back
On days already lived
I am content.

For I have laughed
With the dew of morn,
The calm of night;
With the dawn of youth
And spring's bright days.

Mid-summer's bloom
And autumn's ripening glory
My youth rejoiced.

And when winter bleak
Spread melancholy 'round
I still smiled on.
And I have loved
With quivering arms that
Clung, and throbbing breast—
With all the white-hot blood
Of mating's flaming urge.

My cool, white soul
Has oft fared forth
In Astral ways,
For none may lag
When star dust hides the earth.

The wings of dreams
Have swept me up

To touch my feet on cloud
And wander where none
But souls dare climb.

The Poppy

Dusé Mohamed Ali (1921)

I drank of the juice of the poppy,
    The juice on your ruby lip.
That fount of intoxication
    From which you have let me sip.

But leagues and leagues divide us,
    Though I yearn like the thirsty soul,
The soul in the arid desert
    Who pants for the water bowl.

How long must I bear this parting?
    How long shall the thirsting be
Ere the juice of that ruddy poppy
    Be once more given to me?

Loved and Lost

By Lucian B. Watkins (1921)

My fallen star has spent its light
    And left but memory to me;
My day of dream has kissed the night.

Farewell; its sun no more I see;
My summer bloomed for winter's frost;
　　Alas, I've lived and loved and lost!

What matters if today should earth
　　Lay on my head a gold-bright crown
Lit with gems of royal worth
　　Befitting well a king's renown?—
My lonely soul is trouble-tossed,
　　For I have lived and loved and lost!

Great God! I dare not question Thee—
　　Thy way eternally is just;
This seeming mystery to me
　　Will be revealed, if I but trust:
Ah, thou alone dost know the cost
　　When one has lived and loved and lost!

22

In Memoriam

The dialogue that went on through the medium of Garveyite verse naturally extended to panegyrics on the death of colleagues and friends. John Edward Bruce was an associate editor of the Negro World. *He was one of Afro-America's most experienced journalists and a respected father figure to his younger colleagues on the paper and in the movement generally. Ernest E. Mair's majestic verse does justice to the impact of his passing.*

J. R. Ralph Casimir's "Marcus Garvey—Dead," was published in a Harlem magazine in 1946, six years after Garvey's death. Casimir's poems and reports from Dominica, West Indies, had appeared regularly in the Negro World. *Casimir's poem is at once a memorial and a defence. His loyalty to Garvey's program was clearly undiminished after a quarter of a century.*

Zora Neale Hurston's "Journey's End" (1922) is of a different stripe. It is a beautiful but self-indulgent attempt at an auto-epitaph.

Sir John Edward Bruce

E. Egerton Mair (1924)

Old Ethiop's head is bowed upon his breast,
Dulled his desire for sleep and food and rest;

231

I heard him moan—"This sense of loss I feel,
Pierces my heart like blade of tempered steel."

Womanly tears coursed down his manly cheek,
Sobs rose and choked him when he tried to speak;
"Oh, cruel death," he cried, "give back my son!"
The echoes answered mockingly "My son!"

Why did he die who lived to serve our race?
We know no other who can fill his place;
Had we not griefs enough to bear till now,
That 'neath this greater grief our heads must bow?
Mute are the lips that gave us counsel sage,
Courage of youth and wisdom of old age;
At one fell swoop Death took the strength of ten,
When mighty Bruce laid down his trenchant pen.

He knew no narrow bounds of nationhood.
For universal brotherhood he stood;
They shared his heart who hailed from distant lands,
Equal with brethren of his native stands.

"Break down the barriers of might," he sang,
Ever his voice against injustice rang;
And, like the preacher who was Auburn's pride,
"Even his failings leaned to Virtue's side."

Upright in conduct, courteous in mien,
His bearing dignified, his humor clean;
Free from the taint of biased clique or clan,
He bore the stamp of Nature's nobleman.

Though he is gone, his memory remains,
To show success means more than ill got gains
Of filthy lucre, and to cheer us on,
The while we fight the fight he fought and won.

Journey's End

Zora Neale Hurston (1922)

Ah! let me rest, when I have done,
Beneath a warming, stirring sun,
Beneath a flower-studded sod
That shows the smiling face of God.

In kindly earth that comfort gave,
A kindly couch where dreams the brave,
Where longing hurries weeping grief,
Where halting goes the gilded chief.

Sweet spring will trail a bridal veil,
Grim frost shall lose his howl and wail,
And summer flowers deck my breast
And sunlight gild me from the west.

But I shall rise with verdant spring,
And I shall speak when song-birds sing,
And laughing ripple in the streams,
And flit and flicker in the beams.

Ah! let me rest when I have done.
When I my earthly course have run,
And wake me not to shame or blame,
Nor stir my dust with flore of fame.

Marcus Garvey—Dead

J. R. Ralph Casimir (1946)

Some say he was an upstart,
      A silly ne'er do well;
Some praised him to high heaven,
      Some cursed him down to hell.
Persecuted by white folk
      And cheated by his own,
He fought for Afric's welfare
      To cowardice not prone.

And nations raved and plotted
      But Marcus fought unbowed,
And e'en behind prison bars
      There Garvey was uncowed.
I drank from Afric's fountain
      Of pride of race a lot
By following his teachings
      And inspiration got.

Bow down in shame ye traitors
      Who tampered with his plan,
What plan have you to offer
      To help the African?
Call him a cheat, how dare you,
      Nordic, Saxon, and knave?
What of your "democracy"
      Black mortals to enslave?

Peace be to thee, O Marcus,
      Away beyond the grave;
Diligently you laboured
      Benighted blacks to save!
Rest thou from care and labour,
      What now if foes still rave?
Thou wert a true patriot,
      Leader, ebon, and brave.

23

Moralizing

Many Negro World *poems painted a moral, but few as interestingly as Leonard Brathwaite's. Brathwaite's avant garde mixture of free verse and occasional rhyme, interspersed with his almost mock-serious little sermonettes, made him the* Negro World's *most original poet. In form, though not in spirit, his poetry resembled that of the better-known Fenton Johnson. "Big Negroes" and "Poise" are mainstream Brathwaite.*

Big Negroes

Leonard Brathwaite (1921)

The "Big Negro,"
   *   *   *
Is he really big?
   *   *   *
The "Little Negro,"
   *   *   *
Must he stay little?
   *   *   *
It would be well

* * *

For all concerned
* * *

If the would-be
* * *

Big Negroes
* * *

In the process
* * *

From Little to Big
* * *

Brighten their intellects
* * *

And curb their egos
* * *

And get real big
* * *

And "broad";
* * *

Help and co-operate
* * *

With the Little Negroes,
* * *

"As a man's a man
* * *

For a' that,"
* * *

And the Little Negro,
* * *

Then,
* * *

Could and should
* * *

Be proud
* * *

Of
* * *

His big brother,
* * *

Instead of
* * *

Having to criticize

```
     *   *   *
```
His sometimes
```
     *   *   *
```
Ignorant and bombastic
```
     *   *   *
```
Actions.
```
     *   *   *
```
Be big
```
     *   *   *
```
Before God;
```
     *   *   *
```
Be big
```
     *   *   *
```
Universally!

Poise

Leonard I. Brathwaite (1922)

There is the individual who, when one approaches,
Tries to seem dignified, owlish, cultured and learned;
And when one gets close to him, if his head he has turned,
He's sure to seem spasmed; then contracts and gives a smile,
As if he were a Colossus and one looked up at him awhile.

There is the individual who is so much nerved and poised
That he's completely lost to the world around him—be it ever
    so noised.
When one gets close, and, to him, tries to speak
About things, sundry, the weather and life,
He gives a sharp grunt, and away would sneak,
As if one was devoted to curiosity, malice, hatred and strife.

There is the individual of all whom I detest:
The individual who insists on being a pest—
Keeping his "poise"—when all around him
There are mirth, happiness, laughter and noise.

He is blind and deaf to the cuddling and wooing of lovers—
It may be that he thinks his are the more serious things of life,
And the only two who, peradventure, understand him
Are himself and his Maker, or himself and his wife:
If this individual to the spice of life is dead,
What are the uses of his eyes and ears and head?

Poise is just another word for simplicity; with the coming of civilization and its eccentricities, along with its good, one must "appear poised" to "seem" unaffected.

Many a man in the army of life thinks himself a general when, in fact, he's only a private.

There is many a one who thinks his or her education is an oak when it's just an acorn; probably it would be a stalwart oak, but the chances are his or her ego will stunt it and trample on it.

24

Nature

Vivid descriptions of nature have already been seen in such poems as Ernest E. Mair's "The Green Hills of St. Ann" and Augusta Savage's "The Old Homestead." In Zora Neale Hurston's "Night," however, nature comprises the total subject matter. It is not incidental to a larger theme. Hurston was the Negro World's *most completely apolitical poet.*

Night

Zora Neale Hurston (1922)

When night opens her shining eyes,
    And spreads her velvet gown;
She softly paints the purple skies
    In grays of cloudy down.

25

Parodies

Parodies of well-known poetic standards appeared from time to time in the pages of the Negro World. *Some of the bitterest of Garveyite poetic invective came clothed in this device. Longfellow would scarce have recognized "The Village Lynch-Smith" that Andrea Razafkeriefo (1922) fashioned from his all-American blacksmith. The mean, hateful, hypocritical, raping, "red-eyed cracker" with his lynch rope in his hands is the very antithesis of the picture of sanctimonious piety that was his blacksmith counterpart. Razafkeriefo, as it were venting the pent-up anger of a long-suffering people, rips the smugly self-satisfied veneer from the blacksmith and reveals the lynch-smith lurking inside.*

T. Thomas Fortune is hardly less bitter in "The Black Man's Burden" (1921). This time it is Rudyard Kipling's "White Man's Burden" that is the object of the poet's parody. Kipling captured the whole spirit of an age in his justification of British imperialism. Fortune saw that same imperialism from the perspective of the victims—slain, raped and enslaved. His was a cry of vengeance. Fortune later edited the Negro World, *from 1923 to his death in 1928. This 1921 poem marked his initial appearance in the paper.*

Norton Thomas' "With Apologies to Shakespeare" (1924) used parody for a different purpose. His was a more normal use of parody, as a vehicle for ridicule. The object of his ridicule was W. E. B. DuBois, who had recently described Garvey as "A Lunatic or a Traitor." Thomas, an associate editor of the Negro World, *leaned on Shakespeare's* Julius Caesar *for a reply. This piece appeared as an editorial.*

The Black Man's Burden

T. Thomas Fortune (1921)

What is the Black Man's Burden,
Ye hypocrites and vile,
Ye whited sepulchres
From th' Amazon to the Nile?
What is the Black Man's Burden,
Ye gentile parasites,
Who crush and rob your brother
Of his manhood and his rights?

What is the Black Man's Burden,
Westward to Eastward Ind,
But Japheth's broken pledges—
Faithless master of his kind?
He robbed Ham of his manhood,
His brotherhood he's slain,
His woman he has raped,
Her children sold for gain!

He got them in the darkness—
He shuns them in the light—
The children of "the first fruits,"
The "off-ends," of his might!
The Lord-Masters shall perish,
The unnatural parents die,
Because they wronged the widow
And the widow's son deny!

White Christians of the Nations,
Ye slumber in the light,
But the Father of us all
Shall rouse ye in the night!
The God who rules the Nations,
"O, Hypocrites and vile!"
Shall search ye out as serpents
And blast ye in your guile.

What is the Black Man's Burden,
Westward to Eastward Ind,
But Japheth's broken pledges—
Faithless Master of his kind?
But, now, the even cometh;
The even now is here;
And all the Christian Nations
Are rived with dread and fear.

With Apologies to Shakespeare

Norton Thomas (1924)

Act XCIX. Scene IX. Harlem. Seventh Avenue.
Enter William Pickens, William DuBois and Weldon Johnson.

Pickens.   DuBois, I do observe you now of late:
   I have not from your eyes that gentleness,
   And show of love, as I was wont to have.

DuBois.   Be not deceiv'd, William. Vexed I am
   Of late, with passions of some difference,
   Conceptions only proper to myself,
   Which give some soil, perhaps, to my behaviors:
   Afric's memories doth worry me.
   But let not, therefore, my good friends, be griev'd
   (Among which number, Pickens, be you one);
   Nor construe any further my neglect,
   Than that poor DuBois, with himself at war,
   Forgets the shows of love to other men.

Johnson.   Tell me, good Willie, can you see your face?

DuBois.   No, Weldon; for the eye sees not itself,
   But by reflection, by some other things.   [Shout
   What means this shouting? I do fear, the people
   Choose Garvey for their king.

Johnson.   Ay, do you fear it?
　　Then must I think you would not have it so.

DuBois.   I would not, Weldon, for I hate the man:
　　He dwells too much on "Afric's rising sun."
　　But what is it you would impart to me?

Johnson.   I cannot tell what you and friend Pickens
　　Think of this life; but, for my single self,
　　I had as lief not be, as live to be
　　O'ershadowed by a bearded commoner.
　　I was born free as Garvey; so were you:
　　We three have fed as well: and we can all
　　Endure the Tropic's heat, as well as he.　　　　　　　　　[Shout

DuBois. (Nervously.)   Another general shout!
　　I do believe, that these applauses are
　　For some new honors that are heaped on Garvey.

Johnson.   Why, man, he doth bestride the world of Negroes
　　Like a Colossus; and we petty men
　　Walk under his huge legs, and peep about
　　To find ourselves dishonorable graves.
　　Men at some time are masters of their fates:
　　The fault, dear DuBois, is not in our stars,
　　But in ourselves, that we are underlings.
　　DuBois and Garvey: What should be in that Garvey?
　　Why should that name be sounded more than yours?
　　Write them together, yours is as fair a name;
　　Sound them, it doth become the mouth as well;
　　Weigh them, it is as heavy; conjure with them,
　　DuBois will start a spirit as soon as Garvey.
　　Now, in the names of all the gods at once,　　　　　　　　[Shout
　　Upon what meat doth this our Garvey feed,
　　That he is grown so great?

DuBois.   Enough, faithful one. (Sighs.) What you have said,
　　I will consider; what you have to say,
　　I will with patience hear: and find a time
　　Both meet to hear, and answer, such high things.
　　Till then, my noble friend, chew upon this:
　　DuBois had rather be a Nordic
　　Than to repute himself a son of Ham
　　Under these hard conditions as this time

Is like to lay upon us.

[Exeunt DuBois and Johnson.

Pickens.   Well, DuBois, thou art noble; yet I see,
Thy honorable metal may be wrought
From that it is disposed: therefore, it is meet
That noble minds keep ever with their likes.
. . . . . . Let Garvey seat him sure;
For we will shake him, though worse days endure.

Exit.

The Village Lynch-Smith

(With apologies to Longfellow)

Andrea Razafkeriefo (1922)

Under a spreading chestnut-tree
    A red-eyed cracker stands
(A champion of democracy)
    A rope is in his hands
And a veteran warrior is he
    Of southern Ku Klux Klans.

His head is hammer-shaped and long
    And brainless as a pan
His brow is wet with moon-shine sweat
    He loves to "rush the can"
And boast that common decency
    He owes no colored man.

Week in, week out, from morn till night
    You can hear him madly blow
Against social equality;
    Yet he will slyly go
And hound some helpless colored girl
    When the evening sun is low.

He goes on Sunday to the church
    And makes a lot of noise
Proclaiming Christianity—
    Yea, you can hear his voice
Singing in the village choir
    And it makes his wife rejoice.

It sounds to her like her father's voice
    Coaxing a pair o' dice
She needs must think of him once more
    How in the jail he lies,
And with her powder puff she wipes
    The eye-balls from her eyes.

Raping, hanging and burning
    Onward through life he goes;
Each morning sees some crime begun
    Each evening sees it close;
Hatred attempted, hatred done
    Has earned a night's repose.

Thanks, thanks to thee, my cracker friend
    For the lesson thou has taught
And it is this: your southern pride
    Means absolutely naught—
Unless it means illiteracy
    And the evils you have wrought.

PART V

DRAMA, THEATRE, FILM

26

General Considerations

The Garvey aesthetic naturally extended to drama as it did to other art forms. This aesthetic is inherent in William H. Ferris' plea for variety and dignity in the portrayal of Black folk on the stage. The Emperor Jones of this world may be all right up to a point, but, he argues, it becomes difficult to justify such stereotypes on artistic grounds when the portrayal of Black people is confined to such negative roles.

The Negro in Dramatic Art

William H. Ferris (1922)

Miss [Jessie] Fauset . . . justly says, "To say that the average Negro is the Negro artist's hardest critic would be undoubtedly to state a truism whose deepest meaning would not be immediately apparent. Thus among many theatregoers Charles Gilpin's rendition of the Emperor Jones caused a deep sense of irritation. They could not distinguish between the artistic interpretation of a type and the deliberate travestying of a race, and so their appreciation was clouded."

This is quite true and there is also a psychological reason.

When the average Negro sees a Negro comedian with blackened face, red lips and grotesque garb, shuffling and shambling and galloping and cavorting on the stage or playing "Emperor Jones," he realizes that he witnesses "the artistic interpretation of a type." But he resents it, because he feels that it is a low type rather than a high type of a Negro that is interpreted. And hence he regards the "artistic interpretation of a type" as a "deliberate travestying of a race." And the average Negro feels that when a Negro artist portrays a Negro in his grotesque and ludicrous aspects, to get the applause of the gallery gods, that he is catering to a race prejudice for a few dimes and shekels. The Negro no more regards the darkey and coon who plays the monkey as the typical Negro than the Jew regards the rag pedlar as the typical Jew or the Italian regards the banana vender as the typical Italian or the Irishman regards "Pat" with his broken vogue as the typical Irishman. Of course he realizes that a poet, writer, painter or actor can produce more dramatic and picturesque effects by portraying the unusual types.

Just a few years ago some prominent Jews protested against "The Merchant of Venice" because they felt that the character, "Shylark," was a libel, a slander and a travesty of the Hebrew race. They realized that the character was artistically interpreted by Shakespeare and the actors. But they felt that Shylock was a caricature of the Jew and not a typical Jew. And they felt that the portrayal of that character upon the stage would have a psychological effect upon the audience and would result in a lowered estimate of the Jew.

The average Negro is not narrow. He doesn't object to the Uncle Toms, the mammies, the pickaninnies, the buck and wing dancers, etc., being depicted on the stages. But he wants the higher type of the Negro also depicted. He regards Toussaint L'Ouverture, Sir William Conrad Reeves, Henry Highland Garnet, William Howard Day, Frederick Douglass, Alexander Crummell, Edward Wilmot Blyden, Dusé Mohamed [Ali], Marcus Garvey, William Monroe Trotter and Dr. W. E. B. DuBois as worthy of presentation on the stage as the banjo players and "Shuffle Along" dancers. If ever the career of a man offered abundant material for the dramatist, the career of Toussaint l'Ouverture certainly did.

27

U.N.I.A. Dramatic Club

The U.N.I.A. Dramatic Club again illustrates the genuine love for the arts evident at all levels of the organization. The Poston brothers, Ulysses and Robert, were both in the highest echelons of the U.N.I.A. Yet they somehow found the time to direct the Dramatic Club's 1922 production of "Tallaboo." Ulysses Poston also acted in the play. Ferris' evaluation of this performance contrasts nicely with his earlier remarks on the "Emperor Jones." This is his conception of a worthwhile play—one that educates and furthers the interests of the race, in addition to being entertaining.

The Negro in the Drama

William H. Ferris (1922)

Next week if Providence permits we will elaborate at length upon the great race drama, "Tallaboo," which was presented by the U.N.I.A. Dramatic Club under direction of U.S. and R. L. Poston and Lester Taylor in Liberty Hall, New York City, on Thursday evening, January 12. This drama was composed by the late N. R. Harper of Kentucky.

Not only did the play entertain a large audience on a stormy night, but it also brought words of praise from Dusé Mohamed, a poet and playwright; A. Lincoln Harris, a playwright; the Rt. Hon. Marcus Garvey and Mr. Harper, the son of the author of the play, who came all the way from Holyoke, Mass., to New York to witness it.

From the days of Sophocles, Aeschylus, Euripides and Aristophanes of Greece, from the days of Plautus and Terence of Rome, down to the immortal Shakespeare and the present time, the drama has not only entertained the public, but has been an educational and moral force.

Through Dunbar, James Weldon Johnson, Fenton Johnson, Georgia Douglass Johnson and Lucian B. Watkins in poetry, Chesnutt in the novel and Dr. DuBois in *The Souls of Black Folk,* the Negro has artistically portrayed his higher longings and aspirations.

And in "Tallaboo" the lesson of the race pride and race respect is taught in a natural and spontaneous manner. "Tallaboo" is not heavy and labored as so many race novels and plays are. But the story runs easily and naturally. The characters are strong and interesting. The audience enjoys the play as a play. And after it is all over the spectator realizes that his racial vision has been broadened and his racial ideals uplifted.

"Tallaboo" Scores a Huge Success

V. L. McPherson (1922)

The U.N.I.A. Dramatic Club assumed a great task—risking its life in staging "Tallaboo" under such unfavorable circumstances. It may well be proud of having done sufficiently well to hold the attention of the audience, thereby causing the critic to forget the absence of artistic setting seen on a first-class stage. These things considered, "Tallaboo" scored a huge success.

Mr. E. R. Matthews as Mr. Smithford was very good, and with a little more naturalness he would be excellent, equalling Clarence Muse, of the old Lafayette Players. He was undoubtedly one of the best actors, almost bordering on professional acting.

Miss Morris as Mrs. Smithford would do very much better if she had given a better interpretation of a wife and mother. The acting of Mrs. Jaycox as housekeeper was flawless.

Miss Sybil Bryant as Tallaboo was perfect, putting her whole soul in the part. Evella (Miss Cornell) was every bit of a society college girl.

Mr. U. S. Poston as Chapman Smithford, in love with Tallaboo, knows how to love. He "says it with his eyes." His part was well acted. In the villain scene, however, he should have gripped his revolver more firmly, showing more fight, in defence of the girl he loved.

A very brilliant piece of acting was done by Mrs. Mae F. Robinson as president of the Yorkville Club, in the Yorkville Club scene. Tallaboo's (Miss Bryant) acting in this scene was also very good.

Mrs. A. Dazong Tobias playing in the roles of Chink, Chinaman, and Mrs. Giles showed good acting.

The U.N.I.A. Dramatic Club has scored its first goal. There is no reason why it should not play to a full house at the Lafayette for one week, instead of one night. If, under conditions such as there were at Liberty Hall, they made good, their success at the Lafayette is assured.

28

Black Actors and Actresses

The four sketches contained here cover a considerable period of early Afro-American drama. Ira Aldridge was the dominant figure of the nineteenth century. He probably had no serious Black challenger in the field of Shakespearian acting until Paul Robeson, who eventually became an equally famous "Othello." Dusé Mohamed Ali, so fulsome in his praise for Madame Maud Jones, had himself for many years been an actor on the international stage. Bert Williams and Florence Mills are two of the major figures of the twentieth century. Both died relatively young, while still at the height of their careers. Eric Walrond's article on Williams came in the year after his death in 1922. Florence Mills died in 1927, five years after the present article appeared.

Several important recurring themes can be extracted from these brief accounts of four Black stage personalities. Aldridge found success easier in Europe than in his own homeland. Williams, a West Indian by birth, succeeded in the United States, but at a price. He longed to be a serious actor. He, too, would have liked to play "Othello." Instead, he had to settle for blackface, in order to please his white employers and audiences. Walrond tells us that Bert Williams agonized over having to make so unpalatable a choice and presumably died an unfulfilled artist.

Ira Aldridge

John Edward Bruce (1922)

"The heights by great men won and kept.
Were not attained by sudden flight;
But they, while their companions slept,
Were toiling upward in the night."

Ira Aldridge was a black man of humble origin who succeeded in reaching the highest niche ever before or since attained by any member of his race in dramatic art. He made himself one of the world's great tragedians because "he toiled upward in the night." He was born in Bellaire in the State of Maryland, early in the nineteenth century, and started out in life as the valet of the great Edwin Forrest, who in his day was regarded as one of America's leading tragedians. He accompanied Forrest on one of his tours to England and, while there, made during his leisure hours an intensive study of the Shakespearian dramas and tragedies. In saying this I mean to imply that he put his soul, his whole being, into the characters, which he afterward so successfully portrayed, so skilfully delineated when he appeared before critical and exacting audiences in the great capitals of Europe, where he was honored and idolized for this transcendent genius as an interpreter of the Shakespearian drama.

Aldridge was so realistic, so true, and so much in harmony with what must have been the thought of Shakespeare that whenever he appeared he carried his audiences by storm, because he spoke the speech "trippingly on the tongue."

I am going to let my old friend, Wm. Wells Brown, who saw and heard him in England in the 50's, tell my readers about this wonderful Negro tragedian's interpretation of "Othello," as given at the Royal (Haymarket) Theatre, in London. He says:

"Though the doors had been open but a short time, when I reached the theatre, the house was soon filled, and among the audience I noticed Sir Edward Bulwer-Lytton, the renowned novelist; his figure neat, trim; hair done up in the latest fashion, looking as if he had just come out of a band-box. As the time approached for the curtain to rise it was evident that the house was to be jammed. Stuart, the best 'Iago' since the days of Young, in company with 'Roderigo,' came upon the stage as soon as the green curtain went up.

'Iago' looked the villain and acted it to the highest conception of the character. The scene is changed, all eyes are turned to the door at the right and thunders of applause greet the appearance of 'Othello.' He seemed to me the best 'Othello' I had ever seen. As 'Iago' began to work upon his feelings the Moor's eyes flashed fire, and, further on in the play he looked the very demon of despair. When he seized the deceiver by the throat and exclaimed: 'Villain! Be sure thou prove my love false! Be sure of it! Give me the ocular proof or by the worth of my eternal soul thou hadst better have been born a dog, Iago, than answer my waked wrath' the audience with one impulse rose to its feet amid the wildest enthusiasm. At the end of the third act 'Othello' was called before the curtain and received the applause of the delighted multitude. I watched the countenance and every motion of Sir Edward Bulwer-Lytton with almost as much interest as I did that of the Moor, and I saw that none appeared better pleased then he.

"The following evening I went to witness his 'Hamlet' and was surprised to find him as perfect in that as he had been in 'Othello,' for I had been led to believe that the latter was his greatest character. The whole court of Denmark was before us, but till the words: 'Tis not along my inky cloak, good mother,' fell from the lips of Mr. Aldridge, was the general ear charmed or the general tongue arrested. The voice was so low and sad and sweet, the modulation so tender, the dignity so natural, the grace so consummate, that all yielded themselves silently to the delicious enchantment.

"When 'Horatio' told him that he had come to see his father's funeral, the deep melancholy that took possession of his face showed the great dramatic power of Mr. Aldridge. 'I pray thee, do not mock me, fellow student,' seemed to come from his inmost soul. The animation with which his countenance was lighted during 'Horatio's' recital of the visits that the ghosts had paid him and his companions was beyond description. 'Angels and ministers of Grace defend us.' As the ghost appeared in the fourth scene it sent a thrill through the whole assembly.

"Mr. Aldridge's rendering of the 'soliloquy on death,' from which Edmund Kean, Charles Kemble [and] William Macready have reaped such unfading laurels, was one of his best efforts. He read it infinitely better than Kean, whom I heard at the Princes but a few nights previously. The vigorous starts of thoughts which in the midst of his personal sorrows rise with such beautiful and striking sadness from the over wakeful mind of the humanitarian philosopher are delivered with that varying emphasis that characterizes the truthful delineator when he exclaims: 'Frailty, thy name is woman!'

"In the second scene of the second act, when revealing to Guildenstern the melancholy, which preys upon his mind, the beautiful and powerful words in which 'Hamlet' explains his feelings are made very effective in Mr. Aldridge's rendering:

" 'This most excellent canopy, the air, the brave o'er hanging firmament, this majestical roof, fretted with golden fire—'what a piece of work is man! How noble in reason! How infinite in faculties! In form and moving how express and admirable! In action, how like an angel! In apprehension how like a god!'

"In the last scene of the second act, when Hamlet's imagination, influenced by the interview with the actors, suggests to his rich mind so many eloquent reflections, Mr. Aldridge enters fully into the spirit of the scene, warms up, and when he exclaims: 'I would drown the stage with tears and cleave the general ear with horrid speeches, make mad the guilty and appall the free,' he is very effective, and when his warmth mounts into a paroxysm and he calls the king:'Bloody, bawdy villain! Remorseless, treacherous, lecherous, kindless villain!' he sweeps the audience with him.

"I thought 'Hamlet' one of his best characters, though I saw him afterwards in several others."

I have here given the reader a tolerably fair idea of the great Ira Aldridge by a man who knew him, saw him act and admired him; a man who was fully competent to appraise him at his true worth.

In eighty years there has not been produced among us his equal anywhere on the dramatic stage.

Madame Maud Jones, The Colored Ellen Terry

Dusé Mohamed Ali (1922)

On the 9th [of March] I was accorded the pleasure of being present at a recital in New York at the Mother Zion Church, given by Madame Maud Jones.

In the course of my dramatic and literary experience, extending over a period of some thirty-five years, I cannot remember to have been so enthralled as I was at Mother Zion Church.

Madame Maud Jones is a genius.

I have named her the Colored Ellen Terry, because I have never heard a dramatic reciter or actress whose tones or elocutionary expression more nearly resembled that of the celebrated English actress than Mme. Jones. Her tones are musical, her expression intensely dramatic, and, although she does not possess depth in what might be termed, for convenience, the lower register, her technique and artistry surmount many of the most difficult cadences in the elocutionary register.

This lady has been so well trained and her dramatic instinct is so intense that the few minor faults which she possesses are so clearly glossed that only the artistically trained ear could discover them.

It was the first time that I had heard a recital of the "Ode to Ethiopia," by Paul Laurence Dunbar. I had read the ode, but I confess that I had not appreciated the fullness and richness of its beauty until I heard Mme. Jones recite it.

"The Bells" of Edgar Allan Poe I had heard before, but I have never previously heard one who gave the lines of that morbid poet with such telling effect as Mme. Jones.

She was not quite happy in the purely Negro dialect poems of Dunbar. For some inexplicable reason, although an American, she did not seem to quite get the dialect of the Negro, which, to me, was extremely disappointing; but, in the "Cremation of Sam McGee," by Robert W. Service, she lifted us to the heights of tragic intensity only to land us in a tempest of laughter at the humorous conclusion of this tragi-comedy poem.

In the two scenes from "Romeo and Juliet," she not only proved her familiarity with the poet's lines but she also succeeded in bringing out all of those poetic beauties which the average—and some of the so-called prominent—Shakespearian impersonators have failed to produce. Her finely proportioned body enabled her ot speak Romeo's lines with manly dignity, carrying conviction, and her exquisitely modulated voice enabled us to visualize her Juliet, and as the Nurse in the fifth scene of act two she gave us a proof of her unquestioned versatility.

I should say that the real metier for Mme. Jones is the tragic muse rather than the humorous. I know she would give an excellent account of herself as Lady Macbeth or Emilia in "Othello."

Were she Caucasianed, I have no hesitancy in saying that she would be accounted among the foremost classical dramatic expositors of the day.

I have seen and heard, as stated at the head of this critique, many actresses and reciters of the first flight, but I do not remember having listened to any possessing such all-around excellency as Madame Maud Jones.

I repeat, Madame Maud Jones is an artist and a genius.

Bert Williams Foundation Organized to Perpetuate Ideals of Celebrated Actor

Eric D. Walrond (1923)

On March 4, 1922, at the very height of his career, Bert Williams, the Negro star actor, died—a martyr to his art. This and other illuminating facts are graphically set forth in a volume just issued by the English Crafters, 12 West Sixty-ninth Street, New York City, called *Bert Williams, Son of Laughter.* The author, Mabel Rowland, for sixteen years was the comedian's publicity expert and secretary. More than any one who had the distinction of being closely associated with him, she knows the ups and downs of his celebrated career— the bitter and the sweet portions of it. In a richly sympathetic volume, Miss Rowland has preserved for posterity the priceless heirlooms of Bert Williams' character, both on and off the stage, and as an actor, a partner, a husband and a celebrity. Through it all there runs a poignant strain—a strain of melancholy—a nostalgia of the soul—of the blackface comedian who wanted to follow in the footsteps of celebrated Negro actors like Ira Aldridge, who wanted to play "Othello" and other non-comical pieces. In this book Williams is made to live. One sees him, a handsome youth, just from Antigua, West Indies, where he was born, coming to America; later shuffling about San Francisco as a singer, a cabaret entertainer.

On to Chicago and later to New York as a headliner. Crowning it all is the command to present "In Dahomey" for the artistic tasting of the late King Edward of England. It is a biographic treasure. For—there is no doubt about it—Bert Williams will go down in history alongside the great artists of the theatre of all time. To us, to whom he meant so much as an ambassador across the border of color, his memory will grow richer and more glorious as time goes on. For Bert Williams blazed the trail to Broadway for the Negro actor. It was he who made it possible for shows like "Shuffle Along," "The Plantation Revue," "Liza" and "Strut Miss Lizzie" to go on Broadway. Not only that, but serious dramas of a tragic-superstitious nature which require a great deal of emotional acting, like "Taboo" and "The Emperor Jones," of which Charles Gillpin, a contemporary of Williams, was star—plays of this sort Bert Williams was directly responsible for bringing to Broadway.

One of the things that we get on reading this book is Bert Williams' dominant melancholia. Some day one of our budding story writers ought to sit down and write a novel with a Negro protagonist with melancholia as the central idea. Bert Williams had it. Although it was his business to make people laugh, there were times when he would go into his shell like cave of a mind and reflect—and fight it out.

"Is it worth it?" One side of him would ask, "Is it worth it—the applause, the financial rewards, the fame? Is it really worth it—lynching one's soul in blackface twaddle?"

"But it is the only way you can break in," protests the other side of the man. "It is the only way. That is what the white man expects of you—comedy—blackface comedy. In time, you know, they will learn to expect serious things from you. In time."

With that Bert Williams bore the brunt of ridicule—of ridicule from the Negro press—and fought his noble fight. Today the results are just coming to light. The demand for Negro shows on Broadway is taking a number of Negro girls and men out of kitchens and pool rooms and janitor service.

Bert Williams' tree—to him one of gall—is already beginning to bear fruit, and there is no telling how long the harvest will last.

Some of those who knew Bert Williams well and who contributed reminiscent sketches of him and his art are David Belasco, the great producer; Charles W. Anderson, Negro Collector of Internal Revenue of New York; Heywood Broun, columnist; Ring Lardner, humorist; Percy Hammond, dramatic critic; Geo. M. Cohen, producer; E. F. Albee, Jesse Shipp, Alex. Rogers, W. E. B. DuBois and Jessie Fauset.

In connection with an ideal—the ideal that art knows no color line . . . "The National Bert Williams Foundation," has been organized. This foundation is being pushed by a distinguished group of artists, intellectuals and philanthropists. Its officers are W. H. Vodery, president; J. Finley Wilson, vice-president; Mabel Rowland, secretary, with an Advisory Board consisting of Charles W. Anderson, chairman; A. Baldwin Sloane, Alex Rogers, Jesse Shipp, Hamilton Russell and J. A. Jackson, Negro editor of the *Billboard*. The foundation is at 12 West Sixty-ninth Street, New York City.

On Florence Mills

Eric D. Walrond (1922)

It was our good fortune to witness the opening of "The Plantation Revue" at the 48th Street Theatre Monday night. Florence Mills is decidedly the most charming comedienne the race can well be proud of.

Shelton Brooks, who acted as master of ceremonies, is positively irresistible. Brooks is a born fun-maker, and, as one critic prophesies, is to replace Bert Williams on Broadway. Apart from Brooks, who is an institution of humor in himself, the entire revue palpitates with the spirit of Florence Mills. Although there is a "Hawaiian" number that evidently whetted the palates of the "aristocratic" audience, the grace, the refinement of Miss Mills' dancing and her nightingale singing dominated the entire production. Certainly Florence Mills is the Gilpin of her sex. There is no getting away from that. And "The Plantation Revue" is irrefutably one of the best shows—white or black—on Broadway today.

29

Black Shows on Broadway

Broadway's first tentative steps towards giving Black shows a hearing were met with mixed reactions in the Negro World. It seemed to the paper's editors that Broadway had by-passed the best Black shows, perhaps deliberately. Broadway's probable motives are not spelled out in the two following selections. But there is a broad hint that these early Black successes were motivated by white America's love of stereo-typical Black buffoonery, rather than by any genuine desire to seek out and applaud outstanding Black talent.

Strut Miss Lizzie

Eric D. Walrond (1922)

Outside of Spain Blasco Ibanez is feted as the best of the Spanish "best sellers." At home, however, the Spaniards—and they ought to know—don't think a dickens of a lot of Ibanez's works. Likewise, the Negro artists—with the exception of the "Shuffle Along" company—who desert Negro audiences, pack up, and hit the trail for Broadway, are on the lowest rung of the comic and dramatic ladder. This is especially true of "Strut Miss Lizzie," which opened Saturday night at Minsky's National Winter Garden, Second Avenue at Houston Street. Because the Negro is associated with the traditional buffoon legends of this country, and is a curio, this is no reason for bad actors and painful chorus girls to go downtown and make asses of themselves. In the entire show there were two single redeeming features—the handsome Mexican—looking a la Rudolph Valentino, Mr. Halliday [?] and Creamer and Layton's delightful singing. Oh, those chorus girls! And those black-faced comedians! The lady with us is blasé, and is a diligent connoisseur of the theatre. "I've seen some bimbo shows," she declared, "a whole lot of them, I want to tell you, but this one beats all. I can't even get up a laugh."

The songs were old—"Dear Old Southland," for example; the jokes were stale, the actors stiff, stilted, amateurish.

If it lasts longer than a week it will be a positive miracle.

The Negro Theatre

Unsigned Editorial (1922)

After a year on Broadway "Shuffle Along" has commenced its tour of the United States. That leaves yet two Negro plays on Broadway, "Strut Miss Lizzie" and "The Plantation Revue." This is significant. It means that the white world is waking up to the wonderful dramatic possibilities of the Negro. In the days that were Bert Williams held sway. Although it was his passionate desire to play Shakespearian parts, Williams had to play the blackface comedian. America was not ready at that time to see an Ira Aldridge in the role of Othello. But we are getting away from the narrow point of view. In England Paul Robeson, the Rutgers football demon, is starring in a voodoo play, "Taboo," which is being produced by Mrs. Pat Campbell. And the white people who have the opportunity to see the Negro on the stage have no fears about his dramatic future. Whenever a Negro play is to be put on, rest assured it will not open to an empty house. But it is our honest opinion that at home, in the Negro quarter, the plays produced in the Negro theatre are far superior, with few exceptions, of course, to those one sees elsewhere. One must visit places like the Lafayette Theatre on Seventh Avenue to appreciate the high quality of plays—and distinctly Negro pays—produced by us.

30

Black Shows
in the Black Community

The preceding Negro World *editorial contrasted Black shows on Broadway with the superior dramatic fare to be found in community playhouses such as the Lafayette Theatre in Harlem. But it was not necessarily so, as Dusé Mohamed Ali so incisively pointed out in his critique of a Dunbar Player's production. As an African he felt less inhibited about going to the heart of a problem that many African-Americans politely sought to ignore, at least in public. The Dunbar Players, he argued, were light-skinned folk trying to ape third rate white productions and making fools of themselves in the process. Having said all that, he then strangely praised Charles Gilpin's role in Eugene O'Neill's "Emperor Jones," a role which many Garveyites considered demeaning.*

Ali was pleased, however, with "The Flat Below," produced by Clarence Muse, a well-known Black actor. It was a Black play in every respect, performed in the Black community and a creditable effort.

The Dunbar Players,
Where Black is White

Dusé Mohamed Ali (1922)

Did I see the Dunbar Players?

Yes, I saw them at Washington.

My opinion? Well, I don't think my opinion will be appreciated by them.

Naturally I believe in drama as an adjunct to higher education and culture, and of course, it obviously follows that in proportion to the class of drama enacted so we estimate the intelligence not only of the actors but of the audience.

I cannot say that the Dunbar Players have quickened Negro intellect; that is, if the samples of third-rate white melodrama which they are producing at present is any criterion of their ability. As a matter of fact, I think that they are misusing the name of Dunbar. If Dunbar stood for anything he stood for all that was best in the Negro, and it must not be forgotten that Dunbar was black, whereas the Dunbar Players are colored men and women who try to look as white as they possibly can on the stage. As a matter of fact it was difficult to tell that they were colored people when I saw them in December last at Washington. I repeat, this is not art; at any rate, not Negro art.

Of course, I agree that the black actor, when impersonating a white character, should whiten his face, even as the white actor performing a black part will be forced ot blacken his face in the interests of artistic proportion. And here the comparison ends.

White men performing a Negro drama where the characters are all black is ludicrous. In like manner where the black—I beg your pardon, I mean colored—man attempts a drama of a third-rate quality that is white and whitens his face in order to appear white is also incongruous.

Oh, no. Do not think for a moment that I underrate the ability of the Dunbar Players. Quite the contrary. My main contention is that they are prostituting their artistry. The white man claims that the Negro and Negroids are apes— aping the white men—and the Dunbar Players are simply aping the third-rate white actor by performing a third-rate white drama.

What about Shakespeare? That is just it. Were these actors performing Shakespeare or any other brand of classic drama it would be necessary for them to whiten their faces. But then Shakespeare has some educational value and there would be legitimate reason for their doing so, which does not apply to the very mediocre plays they are performing at present.

While in England I heard about these players; in fact, the late Tom Brown, whom I knew very well, wrote me on more than one occasion about the work they were doing, but it never occurred to me that they were performing white melodramas.

There are many plays extant that are purely colored, dealing with the various phases of Negro life, either historically or otherwise, which might be used with advantage by these players. Moreover, there are a small number of playwrights of the Negro race who would be delighted to write Negro plays for Negro players.

Negro history bristles with drama, whether we take ancient Egypt or the affairs of the present day. There is ample material for the construction of Negro plays apart from those that already exist.

Oh, no! I am not opposed to these players, although I must say in passing that they are as amusing in their way as the people who straighten their hair and bleach their complexions, because, although colored, their outlook is white, and until the Negro shall realize that he has been somebody and will be somebody again, maintaining a separate entity, he is likely to remain in his present condition of semi-serfdom, dependence and spinelessness.

I am sorry you do not see my point of view. I suppose it is because you also think white. I will try to qualify the position I take up in a few words: Mr. Gilpin's performance of "Emperor Jones"—although the play does not meet with the approval of the average "high-brow" Negro—has done more in the interests of serious Negro dramatic art than all of the efforts of the Dunbar Players. Again, the dramatic society at Howard University, Washington, has helped along these lines, because it has produced colored plays possessing some historical and dramatic value.

In conclusion, the play, "Taboo," which has been recently produced at the Sam Harris Theatre, New York, although dealing with a phase of Negro life which is perhaps not wholly acceptable to the American Negro, has given the Negro players an opportunity to show what they can do in the way of serious work, for the *New York Herald,* in commenting upon this production, claimed that "the Negro players had covered themselves with glory."

"The Flat Below"

Dusé Mohamed Ali (1922)

Mr. Miller of Miller and Lyles has given us a rather good drama in "The Flat Below," even when measured by European standards. That this drama in a Negro community should be all Negro in conception, construction and production is as it should be, and I am pleased to note that my recent criticism of the Dunbar Players' white dramatic productions has borne fruit of an exceptionally high order.

"The Flat Below," which owes as much to Clarence Muse, the producer, as it does to the author, deals with a phase of life which is not particularly Negro, but which is common to all humanity dwelling in the Western Hemisphere or within the shadow of so-called Western civilization.

Briefly, a young woman has been seduced by a church deacon. The mother leaves home to avoid disgrace. There is a girl child. The mother in trying to support and educate her child by her own efforts dies from overwork and on her deathbed commits her infant to the care of her late pastor (Mr. Fred Miller). The dying mother supplies the minister with a letter which contains the name of the child's father, which is to be opened only in the event of some crisis arising that might affect the moral position of the pastor in his relation to the girl. In due course the girl leaves college and the reverend guardian places her in charge of a female member of his church (Elizabeth Williams). The deacon (Mr. Clarence Muse) calls, finds that the child is an orphan who has been educated by the pastor of his church, and he at once insinuates that the aspect of the case is not good morals. The sister of the church at once ejects the innocent girl, who is hospitably received by the lady of easy virtue (Ophelia Muse), who is responsbile for the conduct of "The Flat Below." Here the girl (Miss Marion Taylor) has to run the gauntlet of threatened seduction, first, by her own father, the deacon, and then by Big Jim (George Randolph). The lover (Jack Carter) comes to the Flat Below in search of his fiancee and finds her in the arms of Big Jim, who, the better to further his own immoral ends, has tendered his protection to the girl against the advances of her deacon father. Royster, the lover, turns from his sweetheart in disgust and decides to join the merry throng in "The Flat Below" as the pastor enters to receive his ward, whom he takes to the parsonage. The deacon subsequently heads a deputation which calls upon the pastor to request his resignation, and in self-defense as well as in the interest of the girl's good name, the pastor reads the letter her dying mother gave him for such an emergency. The tables are turned, the deacon is discomfited, the hero obtains the forgiveness of the girl and all ends happily.

There is a good moral lesson in this drama, which is not without touches of genuine humor. Clarence Muse played the hypocritical deacon with an ease and a suavity which would have enhanced the reputation of any Broadway actor. That conscientious and painstaking actress, Elizabeth Williams, was good, as she always is, as "Sister Knox," as were the heroine, the "Ruth" of Marion Taylor, and the "Cleo Young" of Ophelia Muse. But the gem of the production was the character study of "Mr. Coffee" by Richard Gregg. It was worth waiting to the end of the play to witness this excellent piece of artistry. Every credit is due to Clarence Muse, not only for his superlative acting, but also for the production and the training of the artists to a high condition of efficiency from material which was both raw and unpromising. By all means let us have more dramas of this character, which is Negro for Negro people—and white people, too, who know how to appreciate true art.

31

Blacks and the Cinema

Here, as in the case of novels, poems, drama and everything else, the essential message is the same—the place of the African race in the arts must be a dignified one. The Garvey aesthetic must prevail.

The Daily Negro Times *(companion to the weekly* Negro World*) congratulates a Black movie company for progressing beyond buffoonery. It goes a step further and postulates the need for a strong Black literature to underpin a viable movie industry. It laments the absence of a very strong literary journal. The* Negro World *itself went a long way towards filling the need expressed here. But what this writer had in mind was something more—a purely literary journal.*

Ferris' piece on "Chinese Manliness" (1922) hits at a very sensitive point, namely the frequent inability of the oppressed to place dignity before money. He contrasts the principled stand of New Bedford Chinese with the Black bit actors who sold their dignity for a mess of pottage in the "Birth of a Nation" perhaps the most successfully libellous film ever made against the Afro-American.

For Ernest E. Mair the film "Pink Gods" was a traumatic experience. So vividly did it depict the horrors of Black life in South Africa that Mair was cast into a mood of brooding introspection. Garvey's program seemed the only way out and "white people in black skins," such as the anti-Garvey Friends of Negro Freedom, had better take note.

Negro Moving Picture

Editorial, Daily Negro Times (1923)

In the February number of *Classic,* a motion-picture magazine, Eric D. Walrond of the editorial staff of *The Negro World* gives an interesting account of the Reol Motion Picture Company, which produces Negro photoplays by Negro authors and with Negro actors. The Reol company has done a great service in raising the Negro screen play from buffoonery to a higher level, and the response of the public has been very encouraging. The company should go on to greater success.

To insure that success, however, we must have a Negro literature to support it. It is a well-known fact that practically all the best motion pictures are based upon novels which were written without thought of the screen. Only the common run of motion picture stories were written directly for the screen and none of them has the vitality of a book. Therefore the screen must depend on novelists instead of scenario writers.

For the dearth of Negro literature there is a good reason. On the whole, we are not a reading people, though we have improved in the last twenty years. Our reading public is not welded together by any great literary publication. If we had such a magazine, able and willing to pay its contributors, we should soon have a worthy body of literature. It is somehow hard to convince our present journalists that it pays to use fiction and that story-writing is hard work and should be paid for. Our Negro literary talent is languishing for lack of a medium, and whoever endows or finances one will have done our race a signal service.

Chinese Manliness

William H. Ferris (1922)

They are taking films for the movies in New Bedford, Mass. These films will illustrate the hazardous adventure of catching whales. It will probably be the first time that the whaling industry will be exhibited on the screen. A fabulous sum has been offered for the picture. High wages are paid the movie actors.

Some Chinamen living in New Bedford were offered a large sum of money to represent Chinamen smuggling opium ashore. They refused both the job and the money, as they did not desire to desecrate their race by representing them in questionable ventures and occupations, even if it was for dramatic effect.

They had no objection per se to posing for the movies. And they had no objection to posing in scenes which represented the dignity and nobility of the Chinaman. But they strenuously objected to being a part to Caucasian propaganda which represented the Chinaman in an unenviable light.

Negro blackface comedians, singers of coon songs and those men of ebony hue who posed for some of the scenes in the *Birth of a Nation,* which represented the Negro as a brute and vagabond, and those Negro actors who on the stage represent the Negro in a humiliating manner might take a hint from the innate dignity and self-respect of the New Bedford Chinamen.

Of course some will say "It is only an artistic interpretation of a type." Quite true. But the Negro has been pictured so long on the stage, in the daily press, in school geographies and histories and by Southern orators and writers in his degrading aspects that it is now time for the black man to be represented in literature and history and on the stage in his higher and nobler aspects. The type of Negro represented by Toussaint L'Ouverture, Frederick Douglass, Sir Wm. Conrad Reeves and Dr. Alexander Crummell is as worthy of being interpreted artistically on the stage as is the type of Negro portrayed in "Emperor Jones."

Pink Gods Depicts Horrors of White Imperialist Rule in West Africa

Ernest E. Mair (1922)

I went last week to a theatre in the Times Square district, where a picture entitled "Pink Gods" was being shown. It depicted clearly and brutally the attitude of the white man toward the native African in his own home. Every black that talks of the impossibility of freeing Africa should see it. The producers of this picture have been horribly realistic in their reproduction of the life of Africa's great diamond fields. Pictures are shown of blacks being X-rayed to find out if they had swallowed diamonds, and in the case of one that had, was taken on to the operating room scene, where his fellow laborers having first been called to witness his misery, the victim is laid out and given ether preparatory to cutting into his abdomen for the "stolen" diamond. The phraseology of the title smacks strongly of Dixieland, such complimentary epithets as "black swine," "black beast" and others equally praiseworthy, being scattered throughout the picture. Altogether it is enough to make any self-respecting and race-conscious Negro squirm with rage. The thought is more and more forcibly being brought home to us that such a thing as justice for black people under a white government is as hopeless a dream as plaiting ropes of sand. That the whites look upon the entire earth as theirs, and all the nonwhite people in it as their God-given slaves, is as evident to the thinking man as the nose on his face, the opinion of white people in black skins to the contrary notwithstanding.

Right after clenching my fists and gritting my teeth at the sights portrayed in "Pink Gods," and while on the home-bound train, I read an article in the *Negro World,* reproduced from the *Buffalo (N.Y.) American,* entitled "America's Need for the Negro." The effect that it had on me was the same as a lighted match has on gasoline—I fairly boiled over with indignation. The writer (white of course) was kind enough to accord us the place in his opinion of being an asset to the United States, and even a potential necessity. "Some well-meaning people," he said, "of both the white and colored races have advocated the idea of the Negroes' return to Africa—that with the advantage gained from his experiences in America he is well equipped to build a civilization in his native land, and that it would be better both for this country and for Africa that he did so. But the consensus of opinion is that this is not possible, and that were it possible it would not be best, especially for the United States. From the economic viewpoint, especially that of manual labor, America needs the Negro. If Negro labor was a good thing for this country, economically speaking during slavery, it is better with his freedom. Negro labor made possible the swift reconstruction of the South after the Civil War." And then he goes on to say that, "In the absence of comparatively much foreign labor, the Negro as a worker is practically necessary to economic success in the South, and is a valuable asset to any part of the country."

When will the blathering idiots such as the "Friends of Negro Freedom," realize that our status as a race is already absolutely fixed in the white man's mind? Will they never understand that we are swiftly and effectively being eliminated from all but the very lowest lines of endeavor? Think again over those words and assimilate their meaning—"In the absence of comparatively much foreign (white) labor the Negro as a worker is practically necessary." Now this entire country had been terribly set back by the Civil War, and our labor made possible its rapid reconstruction. Can you think good reader, what it would have meant to us if all the labor wasted on a thankless and cruel people had been utilized in furthering our own advancement?

I do not believe, as many do, that these wise birds that fight the Universal Negro Improvement Association do so from a sense of what they think is best for the race at large. I think they are opportunists of the meanest kind; that they are seizing on the horse of the Universal's popularity to ride into the limelight of public notice for their own selfish ends. They would turn the Negro from following the road to nationhood by showing him how impossible it all is to succeed in the big venture. What then? Must we remain and with our blood and sweat continue to strengthen the already powerful nations of the Western world, thus making them more able to oppress us? We, the Negroes of the world, are the people whose bleeding backs have been used as the gory rungs of the ladder on which white civilization climbs upward, a ladder that will be thrown away as useless when once it has served its purpose. To try to convince me that a people that can be as frank as the whites have been in their public expressions regarding us will one day become humane and give us men's treatment is trying to convince a rat that he runs no danger attending a convention of cats. Most white people think, as one Southern writer said not long ago, that we are too busy "good-timing" to notice what they are doing; and that this is true of the mass of Negroes is painful, BUT HISTORY SHOWS THAT THE MASSES ARE BUT AS DRIED FAGGOTS WAITING TO BE SET ON FIRE BY THE FEW WHO THINK; and even as the Anglo-Saxon today dominates the very people whose ancestors thought him too dull and brutish to be even a good slave, even so am I convinced that the time is coming in the not too distant future when men of African descent will tell their children of a mighty Anglo-Saxon civilization THAT ONCE EXISTED. No, we are not all good-timing; some of us are keeping tab on every dirty move made by our overlords, and are telling it to the black children of today, "lest (as a race) we forget." I honestly believe my race to be, potentially at any rate; superior to any other race extant in that we have, in addition to the aptitude for modern progresssiveness, those qualities of humility and forgiveness which among others, and more especially the white races, are conspicuous by their absence.

The turn of the tide is here, and in a feeble attempt at poetry I call to the scattered members of my downtrodden race:

Sons of Africa, arise!
    Lo, your freedom's day is dawning
And the war-flare in the skies
    But precedes a better morning.
Do your souls not burn within you?
    (Ugh! That smell of black flesh toasting)
Not my brother's body only,
    But my spirit, too, is roasting.

Sons of Africa, arise!
    God himself doth call—awaken!
High against the empyrean skies
    Write the name of Ethiopian
Death alone can buy redemption;
    Blood must purchase sin's remission;
Fighting Wrong, he lives who dies—
    Sons of Africa, arise!

PART VI

SHORT STORIES AND VIGNETTES

32

Eric D. Walrond,
Amy Jacques Garvey
and Zora Neale Hurston

The three authors represented here are all well-known. Eric D. Walrond is remembered for his collection of short stories, Tropic Death *(1926) and for his association with* Opportunity *magazine. Much of his apprentice writing, however, appeared earlier in the* Negro World. *Amy Jacques Garvey was a most remarkable woman in her own right. She held a variety of important posts within the U.N.I.A. and shared her husband's interest in journalism and literature. She edited the two-volume* Philosophy and Opinions of Marcus Garvey *(1923 and 1925), and two volumes of Garvey's poetry—*Selections from the Poetic Meditations of Marcus Garvey *(1927) and* The Tragedy of White Injustice *(1927). She also edited the women's page of the* Negro World. *Zora Neale Hurston was, of course, one of the bigger names of the Harlem Renaissance. Her early association with Garvey's newspaper is for all practical purposes unknown. Yet the* Negro World *provided her with her first significant national and international exposure. She published prose as well as poetry, fiction as well as non-fiction in the Garveyite organ.*

Walrond's first three pieces are selected from a number of fanciful short sketches revolving around women of varying racial backgrounds. They were a strange amalgam of voyeurism, restrained sensuality and, in the case of "A Vision," pastoral serenity. In each case the startling beauty of the female subject was set off against the unkempt and uncouth figure of Walrond himself, as he lurked Quasimodo-like around the unattainable object of his affection.

Walrond gave free reign to his fancy here, as he frolicked in a region "miles and miles past the horizon of realities." Here was a region of art purely and unabashedly for its own sake, wherein he could "clearly [separate] my art from my propaganda." This anti-propaganda attitude made him an odd man out in the Negro World and he inevitably parted company with the paper in due course.

Walrond's last two selections, "Ambassadors" (1923) and "I Am An American" (1923) are clearly drawn from his own wanderings around the ports of the greater Caribbean area. Both have, as a sort of semi-hidden agenda, an attack on racism in the United States.

Amy Jacques Garvey's "Whither Goest Thou?" is as unashamedly propagandist as Walrond's female sketches are unabashedly the opposite. Her message is as clear as it is unstated. There is no justice for the Black race in the United States, whether it be North or South. "Fall in behind Mr. Garvey's program or perish," she seems to say. Nor does she need to say it, for the message could not be clearer.

Zora Neale Hurston's three-part "Bits of Our Harlem" (1922) provide a fascinating fictionalized documentary of some mundane aspects of that great community. She brings to the documentary an elegance and flourish born of keen observation and a consummate artistry. It is clear that even here, in these apprentice efforts, her literary skills are already immense. There is a biting wit here which, despite its ability to sympathize with the downtrodden, nevertheless teeters uncomfortably on the brink of cynicism and scorn. We obtain a glimpse here of a bright and impatient young woman, eager to progress, perhaps at any cost.

A Black Virgin

Eric D. Walrond (1922)

Yesterday I strode into the library and had a glimpse of her. I cross over to the table next to the paper rack so as to be able to get a good look at her. She sat simply at her task, not ten yards from me, her eyes fixed on the writing she was doing. Her eyelids are long—and fluttering. Entranced, I gaze, not impudently, as becomes a street urchin, but penetratingly, studying the features of this exquisite black virgin. Her hair is black—a mass of shining curls. Bobbed. She is not what F. Scott Fitzgerald or the editors of Mr. Hearst's *American* would call a flapper. The pink in the pigment of her velvety black skin is evident. I can see it boring its way to the front. My inquisitive mind sends me farther. I look at her throat. It is long and slender and beautiful. It is not confusing in the color, as are her eyes. It brings about a sort of equilibrium of her entire exotic being. What shall I call it? Olive? Too misleading a word. Or ripe star-apple? That's more like it. . . . For a long time I sit there dreaming—dreaming—dreaming. Of what? Of the fortunes of the flower of youth? Of the curse of bringing a girl of her color into the world? Of fight, of agitation, of propaganda? No. Clearly separating my art from my propaganda, I sit and prop my chin on my palm and wish I were an artist. On my canvas I'd etch the lines of her fleeting figure, I'd know to a T the right shades of color to use to transform her madonna-like face for the world to look and sigh at. Her eyes, her hair, her teeth, her lips—God, those lips! . . . The place is close and I start to go. But before I do that a strange temptation seizes me. Her voice. I wonder what it is like? I go to her. "Will—will—you please tell me where I can find a copy of *Who's Who in America?*" I startle her. Like a hounded hare she glances at me. Shy. Self-conscious, I think of my unshaved neck and my baggy trouser knees. I fumble at the buckles of my portfolio. Those eyes! I never saw anything so intensely mystical, so appealing, so full of pathos and the emotions of a soul. "Why, yes, I think there is one over there." Her voice falls on my ear as the ripple of a running stream. Her face I love—her voice I adore. It is so young, so burdened with life and feeling. I follow the swish-swish of her skirt, I get the book and she is gone—gone out of my life!

A Vision

Eric D. Walrond (1922)

I am on a high precipice at the edge of the sea. At my feet its gushing waves splash up against the mouth of a medieval cave. Out on the pearl-like waters of the Caribbean a brigantine drops anchor. It is night. A light tropical breeze tickles my lungs. The sky is scarlet. There is a fire on a sugar plantation five miles away. It does not disturb me. It only adds lustre to the night. I fall asleep. . . . Awaking, I am amazed at what I see. there is a sort of round-table a few steps below me—a ledge-like thing with a flat marble top. On it, garbed in a gown of flimsy silk, is a girl. She is dark. Her hair is long and flowing. There are chrysanthemum buds in it. Her form is perfect, her feet are bare, her arms soft and beautiful. She starts to dance—a wild, barbaric kind of dance— baile libre! A dance that whips up my failing hopes, that sends me miles and miles past the horizon of realities. It is not the sort of dance that is advertised in the catalogues of New England preparatory schools. Nor what connoisseurs of the art call "aesthetic" (hateful word!). It defies description. Safe in the darkness I watch her. Memories of boyhood days, of love affairs, of the joy and charm of youth come back to me. It is life. Entirely unaware of me she goes on, and on, until, like a panting deer, she falls—falls at my feet. I rush to her and lift her in my arms. She faints. I do not try to revive her. I gaze at her lovely form long and longingly. Then, all of a sudden, her eyes fly open. She sees my terrible face, and is afraid. Trembling she draws the muslin about her—Eve-like. Without saying a word she gets up, turns up her lips in scorn, tosses here head proudly at me, and vanishes! My face wet, I start to go, then lo! at my feet I stumble—yes, stumble—upon a red chrysanthemum! I take it, squeeze it to my lips, and all is night!

Regrets

Eric D. Walrond (1923)

Hours I sat, unhungered, in the cafeteria, and watched, and enjoyed them as they came in. Buried in a bouquet of feminine roses she blew in, and, metaphorically, threw a dash of icy water in the cold sphinx-like face of the untemperamental. To get a good picture of her one must be drunk with the wine of the South, and have known New Orleans nights, and Florida springs, and idolized Botticelli, and taken a plunge in an amethyst sea. And bummed around seaports, and spent nights in Bohemia, and loved and lost.

I am lost in the depths of her sapphire eyes. Of everything else I am oblivious. I drop my fork, and, wide-eyed, feast on her, and sighingly droop my eyes. And my soul tugs at its moorings, and tugs, and tugs, and keeps on tugging. Soon it is out of my control, and goes galloping away on the horizon of a far-off sun-swept prairieland; and I dream, and dream—the usual heroic bourgeois twaddle.

Again I lift my eyes. She is looking at me, and I smile, and she smiles beautifully, and I, boy that I am, lower my eyes, and nervously finger my cravat. She looks at me wonderingly, and I get black in the face, and she lifts her eyebrows questioningly, invitingly, and I sigh and half-moan, and get up, nut that I am, and walk out.

Ambassadors

Eric D. Walrond (1923)

Abashed, the German sailors slunk into the corner. Brazenly, outlandishly, she had said it.

"I am Santiago's woman! Soy la mujer de Santiago!"

One of them, a stern, darkly sunburned youth, with a pipe between his lips, timidly edged to the door. In Cartagena a week before he had had an adventure—a very salutary adventure—in which he had emerged with a stiletto jab on the bridge of his nose. Just between the eyes. There, too, it was on account of a native woman. But then he was drunk and wild and half mad. Tonight, however, he was given to temperate action. And the five of them in a cantine of dockmen—Guatemalans, West Indians, Americans, Negroes—formed an exceedingly picturesque lot.

"Soy la mujer de Santiago!"

Again she had to say it. For the eighth time now. It did not tire her. Indeed, one might say she enjoyed saying it. She smilingly lifted her head from the purple pages of the *Mercurio*—a raw Chamarrudo girl like that—published at New Orleans, La., and, putting her fingers between its leaves to mark the Benavente *novelita,* informed a ninth newcomer:

"Yo no hago negocio. Soy la mujer de Santiago!"

Back to the lure of Benavente she went.

Across, on the other side of the bar, Santiago, a Latinized Jamaican Negro, his yellow teeth dropping one by one out of his mouth, a Stetson hat on his squirrel-like head, fire in his Oriental eyes, gazed entranced at the ribald cajoleries of an outcast from Belize—at the moment seriously relating for the millionth time an uproariously funny story about Nebuchadnezzar and God. Not once did Santiago throw an eye at his pretty esposa across the way.

"Drink, fellows, drink!"

It was not that. In reality she was the bar man's woman. It was not a question of disliking their kind. So they'd drink. Santiago put five glasses of white rum on the table. The German youths, like a set of hairy-chested kings from the North, grouped about the bar and began to sing—to sing the *Schleswig-Holstein* and *meerumschlungen.* After that they drank.

After a drink a man is inclined to "loosen up." One of the Germans, stoic, a tropical tan, militarily built, golden eye-browed, came up to me.

"Come over here," he said, "and have a drink."

Instead we went over to the other side of the bar, near to where Santiago's woman was reading the Benavente *novelita.*

"You know," he said, "I often think of your people in the States. I have lived in America—in the Southern part of America—and now I know how they treat your people there. Years ago I lived in Charleston, S.C.; Savannah, Ga., and later Tampa, Fla.

"Why don't you come to Germany? With $500 American money you could live like a lord in Germany. You wouldn't have to bother for the rest of your life. See that fellow over there?"

He pointed to the youth with the scar on his nose.

"Before the war he was a big business man in Bremen. That other fellow—the oldish one there—that's Herr—. Used to be at Munheim, in Austria. Very brilliant fellow. Well, we are out here on this ship making all kinds of money. The captain he gets $9 a month. The chief steward he gets $7. How much we get? $1.75 a month, American money. Or 56,000 marks. Today I sent $1 to my wife; I have a wife and two kids in Bremen. There's the receipt for it. One dollar will last her two months in Germany—until I get back.

"Of course, we do a little trading—cigarettes, razors, perfumes. German goods. Come aboard tomorrow if you like and I'll show you some of the stuff. It's too late now; the steward's already asleep."

"The steward?"

"Yes; he's got the key. Ah, you don't understand. All the German ships trading to the West Indies and Central America carry stores for sale. It belongs to the company, and the crew gets a commission on all the goods they manage to sell.

"Yes, come to Germany. In Germany a man's a man. What's the difference, black or white? I tell you, these two fellows over there go to the university. In 1914 I got my doctor's degree. But I've got to make a living, and I'm out here. You'd like it in Germany. With $500 American money you could live like a lord.

"About the new Germany? I tell you, Germany is like a big wheel that needs turning. High and low, everybody is helping to turn it. That is the Germany of today."

Far into the night these German sailors drank and sang—out there in that black, dirty hole they call Porto Barrios. And as the dawn broke through the sky I staggered down the railroad track, thinking of these apostles of normalcy, who go about the world "niggering" nobody, Gawd-damning nobody, making friends (didn't I hear wherever I want in Central America, a good word for the Germans?), cheerful, happy, hard-working, coming back! Could a nation wish for better ambassadors?

I Am An American

Eric D. Walrond (1923)

I had deserted the languor of the prado to explore the depths of those labyrinthian callecitas one associates instinctively with the mystic lore of brujeria. It was two o'clock in the morning. Along el Avenida Italia old ragged brown women smoking Ghanga weed—"It mek you smaht lek a flea"—huddled up against the picturesque dwellings. Taxis filled with carnivalling crowds sped by. Foreign seamen staggered half-drunk out of Casas Francesas. Doggoning the heat Babbitt and silk-sweatered Myra clung desperately to flasks of honest-to-goodness Bacardi. Bewitching senoritas in opera wraps of white and orange and scintillating brown stept out of gorgeous limousines.

Nostalgically I dug into the bowels of the dingy callecitas. Something, I don't know what drew me, led me on. Was it the glamor of the tropical sky, the hot, voluptuous night, the nectar of Felipe's cebada? Or, maybe, the intriguing echo of Mademoiselle's "Martinique! Hola, Martinique!" as the taxi skiddadled around the corner? It was all of these and more. Yonder, in those open cafes (doesn't it ever rain in Habana?) scores of youths tranquilly sipt rum and wine and anisette. In the parque scores more sat on benches and softly talked—not of the overwhelming cares of this world, not of the relative fitness of Ambassador Crowder, but talk, talk, for the sheer beauty of it.

On I drifted. In the middle of every block I saw native laborers sleeping on the piazzas. In dark shadowy halls, black folk, ulcered, leprous, unwashed, victims of the hideous wiles of brujeria, sang and crooned and rocked their knees while they fondled statuettes of the Virgin. Half an hour later I emerged on a boulevard of Andalusian architecture—El Paseo Malecon. It overlooked the sea. For miles a wall fringed it. On the wall I sat and dreamt and gazed across the bay at the dark outlines of Morro Castle. Violet-like was the blueness of the Caribbean. It licked the black rocks at my feet. Above stars of silver glittered in an ebony sky. It was an ideal night.

Not a soul was in sight. The paseo was deserted. Reluctantly I tore myself away and started back. I walked as in a nightmare up the silent paseo. In the distance I espied a figure. No, the paseo was not deserted, after all. There was a man coming towards me. He had on sandals and dragged his feet after him as he walked, as if they were swollen. Nearer I closely examined him. He had on a sailor jacket, crocus bag trousers, and a woolen cap pulled over his eyes. I stopped him and asked him to show me the way back. He threw back his head—he had to—to answer me. I could not see his eyes. I saw, or thought I saw, two bits of coal blazing at me. No mistake about his cheeks, however. They were round as apples and black as jet. But the amazing thing about my derelict friend was the first words that came out of his mouth, "I am an American, I am. I came from—." He mentioned a rural town in Georgia.

On down the boulevard we tramped in silence. He piloted me down to the prado, where, at the edge of a fountain, he rhythmically talked to me.

"How long have you been in Cuba?" I asked him.

"Oh," he replied, "On to eight years. I left my home town in Georgia about eight years ago. Just eight. I hit it for Florida where I worked in a grease factory. Then I came on here. That was before the war, you know."

"In the first place, I like Cuba," he vouchsafed, "it aint' like the States. You ain't got to do no hustling. Of course a lot of people say niggers are shiftless anyhow and all that, but that isn't all. A man who slaves from six to six—what time has he got to look about himself? Now look at me. I ain't got a hell of a lot, but I live just the same. What more do I want? I am happy. I and three other fellows—all of us from back home—the four of us live in a house down by the railroad station and we get along pretty good. Of course, if I had a family, maybe things would be different, but I haven't. Yes, I get a little to do now and then—working on buildings and in factories. I am a plasterer. But there ain't much money in Habana. Six dollars a week. No, there ain't much money in Habana."

"But the Spaniards treat you all right, don't they?"

"Oh, so-so. I tell you. When I came here first I had a hell of a time. New, green—you know. Called me 'Negro Jamaicano.' Sure got it in for the Jamaicans here. Say they bring things down—make labor cheap. But them black folks from Kingston ain't to be blamed. The English government is at fault. Jamaica's got as much chance as Cuba—but it ain't developed.

"Yes, now I can jabber the language and I get on all right. I am treated like a regular native. For instance, if I went in to the Hotel Inglaterra or the

Hotel Plaza or the Centro Gallego—they wouldn't just let me stand there without asking me what I want and freeze me out, like they do in the States. They'd come to me and I'd get everything I want, like a white man.

"I tell you. I meet a lot of fellows and they try to get me on ships to work my way back to the States, but the way I figure it out, I can't see it. I tell 'em nothing doing. Nothing doing. I ain't going to leave Habana. I am not going back to the States. You don't hear of any niggers getting lynched in Habana. Nor any black and white laws—laws for the white folks and laws for the black folks. All look alike in Habana.

"Well, there you are! That's how it is in a nut-shell. I ain't got no kick coming. If I am a bum they treat me like a bum. If I am a man they treat me like a man. It's up to me entirely. It is up to me. . . . That's the way it is in Habana."

And, quite sepulchrally, I said, yes, yes, yes.

Whither Goest Thou

Amy Jacques Garvey (1923)

"I stole these things. For God's sake, send me away where I can get food to eat and a warm place to rest my head. Send me to Atlanta—anywhere," cried a Negro to the police lieutenant at a West Side precinct in New York City, at the same time depositing two packages on the lieutenant's desk.

Bill Jones, formerly of the South, now of nowhere, stood shivering in a suit of homespun tweed, a cap drawn tightly over his head. Surely Shakespeare must have pictured such a man when he penned these lines:

Famine is in thy cheeks,
Need and oppression stareth in thy eyes,
Contempt and beggary hangeth upon thy back;
The world is not thy friend, nor the world's law.

But let us hear his tale. It runs thus:

"Two years ago I was a care-free and happy young man, working on a farm in Winona, Miss., where I was born. One Sunday night my pal and I, on leaving church, were attacked by a white mob. A white man pointed my pal out as having been seen with a white woman, and we were taken into the woods. My pal was lynched and burned and I was beaten into unconsciousness.

"When I regained consciousness I found myself on a train and a colored man bending over me. He read aloud a note pinned to my coat: 'Nigger, don't set foot back in Mississippi or you'll be a dead man.'

" 'Never mind,' said the man, 'I will help you all I can,' He did. He took me to his home in Eldorado, Ark., and cared for me.

"After I got well I found work and for more than a year I tried to forget that horrible night.

"Passing through the main street of the town one night I saw quite a few colored folks gathered together; some crying, some talking excitedly. One old woman was on her knees praying aloud. 'What's the matter?' I asked, and someone said: 'Read,' pointing to a notice stuck up on the outer wall of a little shop: 'Niggers, clear out of town in 24 hours or else you will be as good as dead.'

"Not one of our group had expected such a thing. No trouble had ever occurred between the whites and the blacks in that town. Of course, quite a number of whites had come in and Negroes had become more prosperous since the war. I myself had hoped to be able to buy a home and settle down. What now? Stay and be tortured to death? A thousand times no! Whither, then? Anywhere.

"Next evening found me on a train bound for an Eastern city. Arriving in New York City with a little money I soon found lodgings, after which I set out to find work. I scanned the 'want' columns of the newspapers daily, made several applications for positions, but I was always greeted with the same answers: 'No colored help wanted,' or 'you must have experience.'

"One week passed without success and the second week I tried the employment agencies, but I was asked for recommendations. Should I have waited in Eldorado for recommendations? I tried to explain to an agency clerk why I had no recommendation. 'Why didn't you stay South from the start?' the impatient clerk asked.

" 'Man,' I cried, unable to bear it any longer, 'have you ever seen one of your kind being roasted alive by a white mob? Have you ever smelled burning human flesh and heard the dying groans of your best pal? Have you ever been beaten almost to death and thrown into a dirty Jim Crow car? Man, go South!'

"Out in the street again. Back to my lodgings, only to meet an irate landlady at the door demanding either her rent or her room. She wanted rent and I wanted food.

"I retraced my steps downstairs to the street and as the keen winter air struck my cheeks, I buttoned up my overcoat and plunged my bare hands deep down in my pockets. My right hand touched something cold. I pulled it out—a nickel! My last nickel.

"I walked on for blocks until I came to the subway. I could at least think if I were warm, so I purchased my ticket and boarded the first train.

"Thoughts, countless thoughts, chased through my brain, but at the terminal I was in the same position, penniless and hungry. All my possessions—a couple of suits of underwear, shirts and socks—were in my suitcase at the room; the balance was on my back.

"I changed my coach for the return trip, and kept riding up and down for about two hours until a conductor found me out and ordered me off the train and a guard saw me to the street.

"My mouth felt hot and dry inside; my stomach almost kissed my back. Unable to bear it any longer, I went into the nearest pawn shop and left my overcoat. I came out, fifty cents in hand, and darted into a restaurant.

"Satisfying my hunger to the extent of fifty cents, I was again on the street. It was eight p.m. by the nearest clock; the snow commenced to fall. I dodged in and out of hallways until 12 o'clock, when they were all closed.

"I walked up and down for a couple of hours until my body was almost rigid with cold; my brain was on fire. I backed up against a shop door—visions of that last night in Winona, Mississippi, came before me. At intervals I heard the haunting cry of my dying pal—a mail wagon came—I felt the heavy lash of the whip—my stiff hands felt something—two mail bags."

The police lieutenant looked at Jones. "Hem," he said, "this is a federal case," and instructed his assistant to lock him up and trace the owners of the bags.

The owners of the bags were found, but refused to prosecute Jones once their property was returned. A detective at the station finally made a charge against him, and he was taken before a magistrate, who promptly dismissed the case.

Jones, summoning what little strength he had, appealed to the magistrate to send him to prison, but the police with a "This way out" led him toward the door. "Officer," said Jones, "you are sending me out into the streets again hungry and cold. I am going to commit one of the most fiendish robberies, for by hook or by crook I must have food and warm clothes."

The door closed behind him and the blizzard raged before him.

Negro, whither goest thou?

Bits of Our Harlem (1)

Zora Neale Hurston (1922)

He came into the shop with a pitifully small amount of cheap candy to sell. The men gruffly refused to buy or even to look at his wares, and he shuffled toward the door with such a forlorn air that the young lady called him back. She was smiling partly because she liked to smile, and did so whenever fate gave her a chance, and partly to put the tattered little hunch-back at his ease.

The boy approached the table where the girl sat with the air of a homeless dog who hopes that he has found a friend.

"Let me see your candy, little boy." She toyed with the paper wrapped packages for a while. She knew that she would buy one even though she had but fifteen cents in her pocket-book and a very vague notion as to where her next week's rent would come from. The hunched-back boy looked too dejected to turn away, however. She handed him a nickel.

"Thank yuh ma'am." said the boy. "You certainly is a nice lady. You ain't mean lak some folks."

"Thank you," rejoined the girl, "and where do you live?"

"I lives down on Fifty-third street. My mama, she dead when I wuz a baby an' my fadder, too, he dead."

"Who takes care of you?"

"My grand'ma, an' she teached me th' Lawd's prayer an' I goes tuh Sunday school when I got shoes. See this coat? Aint it nice? A lady give it to me."

"It is a pretty coat," agreed the young woman, "and do you belong to the church yet?"

"Naw, not yet, but I guess I will some day. A lady that used to live wid us she got religion, but after a while her sins came back on her. Do you know my teacher?"

"No, I don't. What does she teach you?" "She, she teach me how to read and count a hundred, but I forgot what comes after 97. Do you know? Let's see, 95, 96, 97—gee, I can't learn that."

"Of course," laughed the girl, "98, 99, 100. What else does she teach you?"

"She say when I go to Heben I be white as snow an' the angels goin' to take this lump out of my back an' make me tall. I guess maybe they roll something over my back like dat machine, what dey rolls out the street wid."

The girl felt very much like laughing at this original idea but seeing his serious face she resisted and asked him very kindly how old he was.

"Let's see," answered the boy. "Gran'ma she say I'm fifteen, teacher she say I'm sixteen, I guess I'm sixteen cause once, long time ago, I wuz fifteen before."

The young lady exhibited signs of flagging interest and asked no more questions but the boy showed no inclination to go. His eyes never left her face and at last he asked, "Where is yo' mama and papa?"

"Both dead."

"Who takes kear of you, then?"

"Why, I do, myself."

"Nobody buys you nothin' to eat, neither?"

"No."

The hunch-back looked pitying at the girl, at himself, at the floor and at last said in a voice full of pity, "I guess maybe I can put on some long pants an' marry you an' then I'll buy you something to eat."

The girl would have laughed but the world of sympathy, understanding and fellowship that showed in the boy's face and choked the voice, restrained her. How often had she sought that same understanding fellowship within her own class, but how seldom had she found it!

"Well, lady, I'm goin' now cause I got to make a fire in the stove for grand'ma. But I come back agin some time cause youse a nice lady. Maybe I bring you some Easter candy if I have some nickels—that's the day the Jews nailed Jesus in a box an' put rocks on it, but he got out—ask the Bible, he knows."

Bits of Our Harlem (2)

Zora Neale Hurston (1922)

We looked up from our desk and he was standing before us, tall, gaunt and middle-aged. In his hand was one of those tin receptacles for charity-begging. Like all other long-suffering Harlemites we shuddered. Beggars with the tin cups are so numerous. He smiled and stood there. We tried to look austere— some money-seekers may be easily intimidated—but not so our hero.

"Well, what can I do for you?" we asked, looking the visitor in the face for the first time.

"A few pennies for homeless children," he answered.

We felt that it was useless to struggle, so we donated a dime. No sooner had the coin rattled to the bottom of the cup than we received a hearty "Thank yuh. God will shorely bless yuh."

We looked closely at his face this time and saw fanatic fires burning in the small eyes set in a thin freckled face. But our eyes rested longest on the mouth and environs.

The short, thin upper-lip showed his Caucasian admixture, but a full drooping under-lip spoke for the Negro blood in him. A fringe of scrubby rusty-red hair completely encircled the whole. When he spoke, four teeth showed forlornly in the bottom jaw. We are still wondering if there were any others scattered about in his aging gums.

"You don't know me, do you?" he asked.

"I am afraid I haven't had the pleasure," we answered.

"Well, they calls me th' black Longfellow."

We brightened. "These be gray days, and a sweet singer in Israel is to be highly honored. Would you favor us with a selection or two?"

"Shorely, shorely; but drop a few mo' pennies, please."

What are a few pennies against the songs of an immortal bard? We dropped in six cents.

The poet cleared his throat and sang:

"God Shall Without a Doubt Heal Every Nation

"There shall be no sickness, no sorrow after while,
There shall be no sickness, no sorrow, after while,
There wil' be no more horror,
Watch for joy and not for sorrow,
God shall heal up every nation tomorrow, after while.

"God will bring good things to view after while,
God shall make all things new,
Every child of God will without a doubt be called a Jew.
God will make us all one nation, after while."

"Ain't that beautiful, now?" the poet asked. "I'll recite yuh another one."

Before we could protest he was in the midst of

"The Automobiles

"Once horses and camels was the style,
Now they fly 'round in automobile,
They don't look at a policeman's sign,
Sometimes they run over chillun,
Sometimes over a divine,

When they are drunk with devils' wine,
They scoots—"

But we had fled into the inner office with out fingers in our ears.

Bits of Our Harlem (3)

Zora Neale Hurston (1922)

The hurly-burly of Lenox Avenue fretted our soul. The dirty corpses of yesterday's newspapers, flapping upon the pavement or lying supine in the gutter, together with the host of the unwashed and washed but glaringly painted, was too unlovely and we fled up 131st street. We were not really hungry but we longed for rest.

A little sign caught our eyes. "Odds and Ends," it read. A yellowish teapot was depicted in the midst of the inscription. A little hunger, a great weariness of spirit, and a sufficient amount of curiosity drew us into the basement dining room.

A raucous bell rang when we opened the door and a soft-footed attendant instantly appeared to take charge of our wraps.

Back of a green screen was a snug room full of odds and ends. Chairs from Colonial New England, bits of pottery from France and Spain, candlesticks from China, bric-a-brac from Nippon, samplers from England—the ends of the world brought together in a basement! The effect was pleasing, very pleasing.

And the guests. At one table was a woman writer of some ability in company with a wealthy realtor. In a corner, dining alone, a lawyer of national fame slowly sipped his coffee behind a red candle and nodded to a world-famous baritone and composer. A widely discussed editor was dining with a young woman who hopes to be an editor some day.

But the atmosphere is the most attractive thing about "Odds and Ends." We do not know whether it is the subtle lighting, the ingenious arrangement of the furnishings, or the spirit of the great number of celebrities that frequent the place. There IS a peace, a calm that falls like a benediction upon the guest who enters there. The food was delicious, but mere food does not create atmosphere. Perhaps it is the kindly spirit of the proprietor—we do not know him yet—that bids the weary rest.

PART VII

MUSIC AND ART

33

Jubilee and Other Music; Augusta Savage

The musical concerns of the Negro World *writers matched their concerns in the other branches of the arts. Here too they felt that the Black role should be a dignified one. It should also be a racially responsible role. For great music, as for great poetry or a great novel, a primary sectional appeal would not preclude universal acceptance.*

Traditional Black music, like Black folktales and dialect verse, was in danger of being bastardized by cheap contemporary imitations. Afro-American artistic endeavor seemed perpetually to live under the shadow of this threat. White America seemed to insist on robbing Black art of its dignity as a condition precedent for acceptance. Thus Black folktales had first to be reinterpreted by a Joel Chandler Harris; a Bert Williams had to bury his aspirations for serious roles and settle for comedy in blackface; and the moving songs of the slaves were in danger of replacement by latter day "darkey melodies."

It is for these reasons that Robert L. Poston, William Isles and William H. Ferris all expressed dismay at the then current trends in jubilee music. And although the U.N.I.A. fostered the developing jazz music (as witness Garvey's Universal Jazz Hounds of the 1930s), these writers all hoped that Black musicians would master all music, classical music included.

The Black Star Line Band, led by William Isles, was already experimenting with classical music, and with telling effect, according to the testimony of William H. Ferris. Isles himself was a gifted musician. His knowledge of the history of music, both Black and universal, was also very vast. His "The Negro and Music," reproduced here, is excerpted from a six part series which he published in 1922. He hoped to expand it later into a book.

Robert L. Poston, author of "A Sin Against Jubilee Music" (1921), later married sculptor Augusta Savage, the subject of Eric D. Walrond's article. It was in the nature of the U.N.I.A. to be among the first to seek out and highlight new Black talent. The multi-talented Savage became a well-known and important figure in the history of Afro-American art. Some of her poetry has already been quoted in this volume.

A Sin Against Jubilee Music

Robert L. Poston (1921)

We very often hear sung these days jubilee music by colored audiences. Some colored people take the position that we should not sing it; others say that it is the proper thing to do, and thus we have an argument, with a good many supporters on both sides. And this is as it should be. There are good reasons why we should sing jubilee music. There are equally good reasons why we should not. And the latter view is growing in popularity in proportion as the brand of jubilee music issued to us these days opens doubt regarding its genuineness, its authenticity. There were songs born out of the hearts of the suffering slave which come down to us today pure in the sublime and the good. No person can hate such music without proclaiming himself lacking in some of the nobler characteristics of man. Jubilee music had its origin in a heart of love, and it very often moved the enemy to acts of charity where force seemed impotent to overcome. Jubilee music is one of the seven wonders of the age. We mean real jubilee music.

But there is a brand of jubilee music which professional song writers offer today which gives us reason to doubt its authenticity. It is real funny, yet it is not all fun. It makes us laugh when we should be crying and it makes us cry when we should be laughing.

Not long ago we attended an affair when one of the late jubilee numbers was to be sung by a male quartette. Four very intelligent looking young men came forward, said something in unison real fast and then stopped short. The lady accompanist at the piano then filled three brief moments with some of the most beautiful strains imaginable, when she was suddenly interrupted by the four impatient voices breaking in at the most unexpected time. They sang on a little while, when they again stopped as suddenly as they had begun.

The peculiar words of the song, together with the peculiar way in which it was rendered, caused us to laugh. A gentleman sitting behind us touched us in the back and said: "Sonny, you should not laugh at that song. It is one of the songs of our foreparents, and you should not be ashamed of our foreparents." Oh, how we felt like telling him that we were not ashamed of our foreparents, for they sang no such song as that; but we were ashamed of the fellow who wrote that song and blamed it on them.

It is a fact that our foreparents were simplicity personified, but they never were ridiculous. There is a limit we must set for these wild writers of jubilee music or else there will be justification in the position of those who say we should not sing it.

We must consider that even where there is no doubt of the authenticity of the music there is slight reluctance on the part of many to sing it, because we are not far enough removed from the conditions which brought it forth to be entirely free from certain unpleasant emotions when we hear it sung. But when the genuineness of the music is questioned the tendency always is toward disgust, and that men laugh sometimes when they hear it sung is not difficult to explain.

Were we asked to answer in a sentence the query, "Whether or not we should sing jubilee music?" we would answer: "Yes, when it is genuine."

The Negro and Music

William Isles (1922)

In studying comments, past and present, on the Negro and music, I observe that there has been a tendency to advocate and encourage as much as possible, and in various forms, the songs of the days of slavery. We cannot afford to overlook so important a matter, which is of vital importance to the race; therefore, I will throw some light on the subject which I hope will be of future guidance, especially to those members of my race in this branch of science and art.

It is an acknowledged fact that the Negro is foremost in producing original music. Music is one of his natural gifts. Music is his soul life itself. Further comment here is unnecessary, as we can follow the pages of history and even back to prehistoric periods. Then, surely, our good friends, when writing about us, can find other works of high art worth mentioning, rather than the songs we used to sing while in slavery on the cotton plantations, as though they were the highest musical attainments of the Negro. Not that I detest these songs. God forbid! They were born out of the suffering souls of our foreparents. That we should forget them? No! I can hear those chants as they rose from their bruised and beaten bodies. That the melody of the work songs should be discarded? No! I can again hear the syncopated rhythms as they flow from the banjo. Yes, it would get you a-going. Under the sweltering heat and burdensome toil it has kept their spirits alive.

Yet there are many reasons why we should object to any attempt on the part of anyone to hold us to this standard, whether by encouraging the singing of these songs daily in our institutions or by having them thrust wholesale upon us in the form of jubilee singers, etc. . . .

Be it distinctly understood that I am not advocating a wholesale condemnation of Negro folksongs, for I know too well the wondrous virtues in many of them, spiritual and otherwise; but let me begin to sing the following Negro slave song, which was given much publicity and encouragement in some of our papers:

I kin fill dis baskit if I choose,
Den Massa gwine give me Christmas shoes,
Two red han'k'chief an' a walking cane.
Den I'se gwine strut down de Big house Lane.

And immediately there will be a battle between the spirit of freedom within and the spirit of slavery trying to enter. The soul of this new Manhood Race of ours rebels against such utterances. They are far from being in keeping with the spirit of the Negro of today, and these are the kind of songs of which I speak. . . .

It is somewhat discouraging to state that although the time is ripe for the Negro to display his skill and ability in the field of fine art and higher learning, there should be an unwillingness on his part to advance into a higher musical development.

This may be attributed to many causes. First, for years and years he has imbibed the teachings that ragtime was his, and there he stayed and worked and worked until he was crowned king of "rags," and now he is told that jazz is his, and he seems willing to stay here and work and work to be crowned king of jazz. Second, as a musician he is chiefly employed in the lower standard of music, and consequently he not only lacks inspiration for higher development of the art, but seldom educates himself beyond the field in which he is employed. Third, many a Negro has gone through arduous training and after being prepared, launched out full of hope, only to be disappointed by finding the world cold to him. He does not get that support and encouragement from his own, which is so characteristic of other races, and in this way many a virtuoso has been lost to the race. We also find that for nearly two hundred years many of our great stars have found themselves at times wholly dependent upon the white race for their success. With such rare talent among us, what a different story we would have to tell were we a nation with our own opera houses, music halls and theatres!

Is not such an objective worth while striving for? This is but one of the many joys missing in the life of the Negro, and should be the longing in the soul of every musician. It is true that despite these handicaps many a Negro has long since broken away from the shackles of slave songs and that we can point with pride to many musicians of the race who have risen to heights of fame in musical achievements; but, as I have stated, on account of their dependence upon another race for success, they have at times met set boundaries beyond which they could not pass.

A Great Negro Artist

One of the many musicians who have met with this setback was Joseph Boulogne, a French Negro, and one of the greatest musicians and swordsmen of the eighteenth century. He was born in the island of Guadeloupe December 25, 1745, but spent most of his life in France, where he was educated. He had a conspicuous career and was accepted in the highest society of France. As a swordsman he defeated some of the best blades of Europe. As a musician, at the age of twenty-one, he had inscribed to him his Opus LX, six trios for two violins and bass. He was one of the first French musicians who wrote string quartets and preceded such great composers as Toeschi (1765), Cannabich (1766), Boecherini (1767), Talou and Missiwecek (1767), Haydn (1768), Seemans, Gasman, Regel and Aspelmayer (1769), Vanhall, Gossec and Carlo Stamitz (1770), de Mochi (1771) and J. Ch. Bach (1774).

So brilliant a musician was he that his appointment as director of the opera at the Royal Academy of Music was seriously considered. This appointment was bitterly opposed by some of the famous singers and dancers headed by Mlles. Arnould, Guimard and Rosalie, who petitioned to the Queen stating that their honor and the delicacy of their conscience would not allow them to take orders from a Negro. Once again the curse of race prejudice seemed to say "Thus far shalt thou go and no further." This state of affairs exists today in a more systematic form, and but for a few scattered exceptions the Negro will not be able to attain the height of his musical ambition until he has created for himself institutions which are so essential to his progress in this line of endeavor.

Although I have clearly explained in my previous articles, also citing many facts why the Negro should not hold himself to the slave song standard in the field of musical art, and although I have pointed out his drawbacks and the way for greater musical development, there yet remains another substantial fact which I could not refrain from mentioning in brief in these, my closing remarks, and that is the opinion of S. Coleridge Taylor upon the question. (I say in brief, as it is my intention to write in detail the achievements of great musicians of the Negro race, at which time I will comment more fully upon this gentleman.)

Samuel Coleridge Taylor, though dead, holds the distinction of being the most cultured musician of his race. He was a man of the highest aesthetic ideals, who sought to give permanence to the folksongs of his people by giving them a new interpretation and added dignity. In compiling his book, *Twenty-Four Negro Melodies,* he has this to say:

"The Negro melodies in this volume are not merely arranged; on the contrary they have been amplified, harmonized and altered to suit the purpose of the book. I do not think any apology for the system adopted is necessary. What Brahms has done for the Hungarian folk music, Dvorak for the Bohemian and Grieg for the Norwegian, I have tried to do for these Negro melodies. The plan adopted has been almost without exception that of a *tema con variazioni.* The actual melody has in every case been inserted at the head of each piece as a motto. The music which follows is nothing more or less than a series of variations built on the said motto. Therefore, my share in the matter can be clearly traced and must not be confounded with any idea of 'improving' the original material any more than Brahms' variations on the Hayden theme 'improve' that."

Mr. S. Coleridge Taylor's selections of Negro melodies which by the way are taken from Africa, America and the West Indies, are extremely gratifying and are not only in keeping with the Negro of today, but mark that higher intelligence accumulated by the Negro during years of progress. It is said of one of these songs, which was gathered from the Ba-Ronga district on the borders of Delagoa Bay, South Africa, that it is certainly not unworthy of any composer from Beethoven downward.

In the onward march of progress, the Negro has evolved upon a new and higher plane of human affairs, whether they be science, art, literature or music. His eyes are open to behold the dawn of a new era pregnant with possibilities and full of hope. He is determined that nothing shall deter him from his objective. He shall not be dragged backwards, and the vicissitudes of life through which he has passed shall not only be history but be regarded as milestones in the march towards his goal. The old adage of "Servants, obey your masters," will make of you nothing more than a servant. Therefore, in conclusion I say, let us march on. On to the highest heights of human development. We have had the experiences of a hundred battlefields. Let us convert them into grand martial strains which shall ring from a thousand

bands and fire us to do or die. We have seen life and all its tragedies. Let us
convert them into operas and draw out of our men and women that genius
which is so latent within them. Our souls are receptive to nature and all its
beauties. The singing of birds, the trickling of the brook, the blooming of
flowers and the grandeur of the landscape—Let it give outburst in music, a
new music born of a free being, free in mind, free in body and free in soul.

Negro Music

William H. Ferris (1921)

The New York press spoke favorably of the plantation melodies and jubilee
songs which were sung by Negroes at "America's Making" on Negro Night,
November 10, at the Seventy-first regiment Armory, New York. Dvorak, the
Bohemian composer, said that the songs of Negro slaves was America's only
real contribution to music, and we are proud of that fact.

But we also aspire for greater things. In the early spring of 1916 a colored
quartet sang the Negro melodies acceptably in a Congregational church in
Illinois. After the affair was over one of the singers overheard the wife of the
pastor ask the white clergyman who was in charge of the singers, "Have you
any real Negro musicians in Chicago, I mean musicians who count?"

Well the Negro is now developing real musicians, musicians who can
master melody and harmony as well as rhythm, syncopation and jazz. The
Black Star Line Band is now interpreting in an artistic manner the "Overture
to William Tell" and Verdi's "Rigoletto." We have already described Miss
Helen Hagan's superb recital in Aeolian Hall, New York. We heard the same
kind of playing, the same blending of temperament and technique, the same
mastery of phrasing and expression when Miss Andrades Lindsay of the
Martin Smith Musical School interpreted the works of Beethoven, Schubert,
Schumann, Strauss, DeBussey and Brahms, as well as the works of Coleridge
Taylor and Dett.

And on armistice night, in Liberty Hall, New York City, over two thousand
persons applauded the singers and the Black Star Line Band until the rafters
of the roof echoed back the sound. One of the numbers that made a hit and
called for an encore was Verdi's "Il Trovatore," sung by two colored singers
in a manner worthy of grand opera stars. All these things indicate that the

Negro cannot only master and appreciate his own folk songs, but also the world's masterpieces. And he will undoubtedly accomplish greater things in the future.

Negro Composers and Negro Music— Is There Race in Music? Is There Race in Art?

William H. Ferris (1922)

At no period in the Negro's history has he been subjected to so close a scrutiny as at present. During the ante-bellum days, he was regarded with mingled feelings of pity and contempt. From the close of the war to 1895, he was regarded as a mascot and ward of the nation. From 1895 to 1915, he faced a spirit of growing hostility in the North and in the South. In 1915 we entered upon the fourth phase, the age of critical study, observation and dissection of the Negro. The microscope, the magnifying glass and the X-Ray have been turned upon him. He has been poured into the crucible and subjected to the fire and acid test. The analysis has disclosed some favorable and some unfavorable things. Among the favorable things disclosed is that the Negro race has made a real distinct contribution to the world's music.

Madame E. Azalia Hackley is writing a book on this same theme. Mr. J. Rosamond Johnson, of New York, who has attained fame as a musician and composer, and Mrs. Maud Cuney Hare, of Boston, who has won an enviable reputation as a musician and musical writer brought to the knowledge of the Chicago public in the winter of 1917, the tribute which the world's masters of song have paid to Negro music. Mr. Johnson in his recital surprised the audience by stating that the motif of "Walk Together, Children," was developed by Antoine Dvorak in the Symphony to the New World, which is played every year. He also stated that Dvorak said that the Negro melodies were the only original American music, and that the motive in "Go Down, Moses," was as strong as the motif in "Siegfried."

Mrs. Hare's talks on the "Influence of Afro-American Folk Song and Musicians" of color were a revelation to the audience in Quinn Chapel. She told of the tributes that Dvorak, Percy Grainger, and Walter Damroach paid to Negro music and showed how Grainger, Cadman, Walter Damroach, Powell Scott, Fisher and Homer have developed Negro themes.

She also spoke of the careers of Joseph White, H. T. Burleigh, Will Marion Cook and James Weldon Johnson. She said that J. Rosamond Johnson has written songs for Anna Held, William Russell and other operatic stars, and that Beethoven contemplated dedicating one of his masterpieces to Bridgetower, the colored violinist. She said that Beethoven may have had Negro blood coursing in his veins, and that a book in the Royal Library of Berlin describes his grandfather as a man of brown complexion with heavy Negro features.

Mrs. Hare developed the ideas which she had so brilliantly sketched in her recital more elaborately in her article in the *Musical Observer* for February. She said in her article: "Modern ragtime is supposed to have originated in the South and West, later becoming popular in New York and the country at large. However, according to Ernest Newman, it has been made use of from time 'immemorial.' He gives many examples of its use in works of classical composers. The passage, 'How Vain is Man' in Handel's 'Judas Maccabeus'; Schuman's 'Promenade'; Beethoven's 'Pianoforte Sonata, Op. 28' (first movement), 'Waltz'; and Tschaikowsky's fourth and fifth symphonies. One might add the fourth movement of Glayonnoff's 'Symphony in B.'"

The odd progression of Negro folk songs, including the raised sixth in the minor key, which occurs in "Weeping Mary" and "Ain't I Glad I Got Out of the Wilderness," has been used by no less a composer than Beethoven.

But by claiming that there is something in the rhythm of the Negro melodies that is basal and fundamental and worthy not only of preservation, but also of cultivation and development, Mrs. Hare is not defending what she terms "the ordinary songs of today, the so-called popular songs, written in ragtime set in execrable rhymes."

Mrs. Hare closed her illuminating article by referring to the wonderful tributes which Dvorak and Mrs. Kemble paid to Negro music. Dvorak said: "There is nothing in the whole range of composition that cannot be supplied with themes from this source." But Mrs. Kemble in her *Life on a Georgia Plantation*, went a step further. She said: "With a little adaptation and instrumentation one or two barbaric chants and choruses might be evoked from the songs that would make the fortune of an opera."

At a time when the Negro's possibilities and capabilities are discussed it is of interest to know that the Negro has evolved a form of music which when pruned of its corruptions and developed, contains wonderful possibilities. The Negro melodies and plantation songs were first called to the attention of the cultured people of the country by Col. T. W. Higginson, in an article in the *Atlanta Monthly* in 1867. They became popular when the Fisk Jubilee Singers began their tour of America and Great Britain in 1871. But, before that time, individual colored musicians attracted attention. Bridgetower, a colored European violinist, was a contemporary and friend of Beethoven; Brindid de Salas, another colored violinist, played before and was decorated by the crowned heads of Europe. Chevalier Sainte Georges, a man of color, was called the Voltaire of equitation, fencing and instrumental music, and was knighted by Louis XVI of France. Abbé Gregoire says of him: "Some of his concertos are still held inestimable. . . . His bow and his boil set all Paris in motion."

Will Marion Cook and Cole and Johnson have done some clever composing in the lighter vein. Dr. W. E. B. DuBois has eloquently said: "In later days Cole and Johnson, and Williams and Walker lifted minstrelsy by sheer force of genius into the beginnings of a new Drama. The next step will undoubtedly be the slow growth of a new folk drama built around the actual experience of Negro American life."

Is There Race in Music?

But, we must not let this talk about developing Negro music, Negro drama and Negro art draw us too far afield. There is something in art that makes a universal appeal to the human mind, and we may well ask the questions, "Is there race in music?" "Is there race in art?" Have not Americans, colored and white, crowded the Boston Theatre, in Boston, Mass., to hear Wagner's Trilogy, "Lohengrin," "Tannhauser," and "Tristan and Isolde," Gounods's "Faust" and "Romeo and Juliet," and Verdi's "Aida," which were the production of German, French and Italian composers?

And did not a colored chorus in Boston under the direction of Prof. Theo. Drury creditably render Verdi's "Aida" in 1907 and "Faust" in 1908? Did not the same Prof. Drury stage "Carmen" in New York in 1900? Is it not true of great music, as of great poetry, great painting, great sculpture and great architecture, that it makes a fundamental appeal to the soul of man, and that this accounts for the universality of Homer, who has sent his name down the ages for twenty-five centuries so that he has appealed to lovers of poetry of all races? Is it not the fact that Shakespeare's poetry appeals to Germans, Frenchmen, Jews, Italians, and Negroes, as well as to Englishmen, that stamps him as the world's greatest poet?

The great musician, poet, dramatist, painter, sculptor and architect gets his inspiration at first from the native soil and makes his first appeals to men of his own race, as did Robert Burns. But, if he is to live in literature, art or music, there must be something about his poetry, art or music that makes a universal appeal to the human heart, as Burns did in his "The Cotter's Saturday Night" and "A Man's a Man for A' That," and Handel in his "Hallelujah Chorus."

The Negro in slavery, untutored as he was, could only pour forth the longings of his soul in simple melodies. Must we say then that Negro musicians trained under German, French or Italian masters cannot produce masterpieces? May we not hope that other men of Negro blood will do in music, poetry and drama what Pushkin did in poetry, what Dumas did in fiction, what Tanner did in art, and what Coleridge-Taylor did in music? We further hope that within the next twenty-five years a colored dramatist will arise in America who will so interpret the Negro's experiences that he will make an appeal not only to men of his race, but to the world at large; not only to men of his own day and generation, but to men of all time.

The world of literature, art and music knows no color line. William Stanley Braithwaite of Boston became an authority upon magazine verse by his sympathetic interpretation and criticism of current poetry in America.

Genius will ultimately win recognition, even though it shines through a dark complexion. Let the ebony-hued painter paint a picture that the world wants to see. Let the ebony-hued poet sing a song that the world wants to hear, and let the ebony-hued musician by his rhythmic cadences, in the striking words of Carlyle, "Lead us to the end of the infinite and let us for moments gaze upon it," and mankind will forget the color, hair and features of the genius who lifted it to the Mount of Transfiguration. Now, to the toiling, struggling, striving colored artist, poet and musician, I would say, "Light the torch of your inspiration upon the heights of Mt. Parnassus," and through you the world soul will speak a message to all mankind.

Augusta Savage Shows Amazing Gift for Sculpture

Eric D. Walrond (1922)

In sculpture the Negro is just beginning to find expression. Meta Warwick Fuller of Boston, a former pupil of Rodin, is the only sculptress of whom the race can justly be proud. This was up to a few weeks ago, before the discovery of Augusta Savage, a twenty-year-old colored girl of Green Cove Springs, Florida.

Augusta is a student in the "life" class of Cooper Union and has a very interesting story to tell. Interesting not only because she is the first girl of any race to complete three years' work at this famous institute in six weeks, but because she is a mixture—a primitively sensitive one—of poetess, sculptress, portrait artist.

She lives in a poorly lighted room in Upper Harlem, and while putting the finishing touches to a bust she is making of Marcus Garvey, told me the story of her life.

Just three years ago, while on a visit to Palm Beach, Augusta was driving on a wagon with Prof. Mickens, principal of the public school which she was attending. They were passing a pottery. In front of it were heaps and heaps of soft clay. As soon as the girl saw it she became excited and jumped off the wagon. She asked the potter, a Mr. Chase, for some of it, and after a little persuasion and Prof. Mickens' intervention twenty-five pounds were given her.

Augusta went home and with agitated fingers modeled a statue of the Virgin eighteen inches high. She took it to Prof. Mickens, who was amazed at the delicacy with which it was executed. Prof. Mickens showed it to Mr. Chase, the potter. A consultation followed. The upshot of the matter was Prof. Mickens persuaded the girl to instruct a class in modeling at his school. Mr. Chase donated the clay for the work. Augusta taught modeling at $1 a day for six months.

At the West Palm Beach County Fair a year ago last March Miss Savage asked permission to exhibit some of her work. This was an unusual request. The committee had made provision for everything one expects to find at a county fair, but certainly not for the work of an untutored sculptress. However, Mr. George Graham Currie, superintendent of the fair, of whom we shall hear more later on in the story, granted permission to her.

At the fair Augusta's sculpture elicited enthusiastic praise. A number of "Yankees" had come down to Palm Beach and quite a number of them commented on her work. Her statuettes sold for from 25 cents to $5. Through Mr. Currie's kindness the County Fair voted her $25 in prizes and an honor ribbon. United States Senator Tom Campbell of Florida was among those who came forward, shook her hand and urged her to come to New York to study.

In New York Augusta was like a lamb astray in a barren wilderness. Fortunately, Mr. Currie while on a trip to New York had met the late Solon Hannibal Borglum, America's famous sculptor and founder of the School of American Sculpture. He gave the girl a letter to Mr. Borglum.

One day, very reluctantly, she tiptoed into the great man's office. Mr. Borglum's secretary greeted her. She told him her mission. The secretary went back and told Mr. Borglum "There is a Negro girl outside who wants to study sculpture." Mr. Borglum invited her in. As she entered he rose and offered her his chair and told her to tell him just what made her think she could ever become a sculptress. She sat down and told him the simple story of her life. While the girl talked uninterruptedly Mr. Borglum half closed his hawklike eyes and fixed his steady gaze on her. When she finished he said: "Young lady, I am very pleased to hear your story, but from what you say you haven't any money, and the young ladies who come here are the children of the rich and pay immense fees." However, Mr. Borglum offered to help her to get in Pratt's or Cooper Union, and gave her a letter to Miss Kate L. Reynolds, principal of Cooper Union, with the consoling remark, "and if she can't get you in, come back to me."

At Cooper Union Augusta found 142 girls on the waiting list. But she was in company with a young colored man who, undaunted, "spoke up for her." The result was Miss Reynolds asked to see some of her work. A few days later she took down a bust of a Negro minister she had made. Miss Reynolds liked it and said she would let the girl hear from her in a few days. Promptly the next morning Augusta received a card notifying her that she would be admitted. That was the second week in October, 1921.

In February, 1922, Augusta's funds began to run out. She went to Miss Reynolds and told her she would have to discontinue her studies. Miss Reynolds nearly wept. She gave the girl a letter to a friend on Fifth Avenue, who gave her temporary employment. In the meantime Miss Reynolds promised to do everything she could for her.

A special session of the Advisory Council of Cooper Union was called to consider Augusta's case. It adopted a resolution to give financial aid to the girl. The circumstances, as Miss Reynolds pointed out to the writer, warranted it. Ordinarily it takes four years to complete a sculpture course at Cooper Union. When Augusta went to Cooper Union she was put in the first year class. She stayed in it two weeks. In the second year class she stayed one month. Now she is in the "life" class, which is the fourth year.

George Graham Currie in his "Songs of Florida" dedicates the following poem to Augusta, "a young sculptress, in acknowledgment of her effort to make a bust of the author":

Recreated

Augusta is a sculptress fine—
    A poetess as well;
Her coal black hair and eyes that shine
    A soulful story tell.

Her agile step, her lissome grace,
    Her happy, carefree mien,
Proclaim her o'er her swarthy race
    A veritable queen.

But other maid such attributes
>   Might boast as well as her;
And that she is common, Heaven refutes,
>   Or else my muse must err.

For out the fair Augusta stands,
>   A mother though a maid;
And subject to her art's commands
>   Is pure and unafraid.

With steady eye she looks on me
>   Then takes a lump of clay—
When lo! another self I see,
>   With all my faults away.

As a sample of Augusta's own poetry the writer quotes the following and leaves it to the critical judgment of the reader to determine whether it is good poetry or not. . . .

My Soul's Gethsemane

At the forks of life's high road alone I stand
>   And the hour of my temptation is at hand.
In my soul's Gethsemane
>   I have still your faith in me,
And it strengthens me to know you understand.

Certainly we have another sculptress we can gloriously be proud of. Miss Savage plans, in her efforts to get a larger scope of training, to "do" busts of distinguished Negro citizens, including Mme. Lelia Walker Wilson, Harry T. Burleigh and the late Bert Williams. Through the efforts of Miss Sadie Peterson, the librarian, she has done an excellent bust of W. E. B. DuBois, which will be presented to the 135th Street branch of the Public Library at a special function shortly after the Christmas holidays.

PART VIII

SIDELIGHTS ON THE LITERARY SCENE

34

Quarrels With Claude McKay

The leading literary lights of the Garvey movement were very much a part of the mainstream of the Harlem scene. The Negro World *is therefore an interesting source for some of the important and no-so-important events that served as a backdrop to the emerging Harlem Renaissance.*

Claude McKay is considered by many to have been the best poet of the renaissance. With Marcus Garvey and the U.N.I.A. he kept up a running love/hate relationship for many years. McKay published in the Negro World *in 1919. When he journeyed to England late that year he continued to remit articles from there. He also introduced Blacks in England to the* Negro World *and other Afro-American journals.*

McKay at this time, however, was deepening his involvement with socialist organizations, both in the United States and Europe. This inevitably led him into a hostile attitude towards the U.N.I.A. The Garvey organization replied in kind, while simultaneously praising his abilities as a poet.

The three Negro World *articles reproduced here all address themselves to this ideological quarrel with McKay. The first is a commentary on a notorious incident, wherein a* Liberator *ball in New York was raided by the police, allegedly on account of McKay's interracial dancing. In the second, "Black and White Labor" (1922) the* Negro World *quotes a McKay editorial from the left-wing* Liberator. *Here McKay expresses reservations about his white comrades' position on the race question. He nevertheless pledges continued allegiance to socialism. As far as the Garveyites are concerned, this proves that McKay has arrived on the brink of Garvey's race first ideology. Yet McKay hesitates to follow the logic of his argument into Garvey's camp.*

McKay's lingering doubts on the racial question nevertheless led to his break, shortly afterwards, with the Liberator. *This time the* Negro World *supported McKay. In its view he had fallen foul of the* Liberator's *co-editor, Michael Gold, a racially intolerant example of "hypocritical radical trash."*

Claude M'Kay, Negro "Constab" Editor, Cause Of A Disturbance

Whites Object to His Dancing with White Woman at a Ball—Advocate of Social Equality

Anonymous (1922)

Claude McKay, Negro protege of Sir Sidney Olivier of England, who was discovered by the Ex-Colonial Governor as a Negro Constable or "Constab" of exceptional ability, and who has since won a name as a poet, is alleged to have been the cause of a terrible mix-up at a recent ball given by the *Liberator Magazine* of New York.

The *Liberator* is a radical paper published in the interest of Socialism, and McKay is one of its editors, being the only Negro on the staff—the other editors are white.

At the ball there were white guests, and it is alleged that Claude McKay delighted himself in dancing with one of the white women, to which Police Captain Howard objected. Claude McKay is an advocate of social equality, and it is alleged that he delights to be in the company of white ladies.

We are very sorry to note the occurrence, but happenings of this kind tend to show the impossibility of Negroes ever gaining social recognition among the whites. Such Negroes who preach the idea of social equality may well throw up their hands at the experience of McKay, who has, for some time, been nursed by white philanthropists as an exceptional Negro genius.

Black And White Labor

Unsigned Editorial (1922)

In the *Liberator* for August Claude McKay points out to white radicals their duty towards the Negro.

> Some friendly critics think that my attitude towards the social status of the Negro should be more broadly socialistic and less chauvinistically racial as it seems to them. These persons seem to believe that the pretty parlor talk of international brotherhood or the radical shibboleth of "class struggle" is sufficient to cure the Negro cancer along with all the other social ills of modern civilization. Apparently they are content with an intellectual recognition of the Negro's place in the class struggle, meanwhile ignoring the ugly fact that his disabilities as a worker are relatively heavier than those of the white worker.
>
> Being a Negro, I think it is my proud birthright to put the case of the Negro proletarian, to the best of my ability, before the white members of the movement to which I belong. For the problem of the darker races is a rigid test of radicalism. To some radicals it might seem more terrible to face than the barricades. But this racial question may be eventually the monkey wrench thrown into the machinery of American revolutionary struggle.

McKay is of the opinion that the Negro radical should not desert the Socialist party, but remain in it and act as a sort of "check" on the doings of the white radicals.

This is the crux of the whole difficulty between black radicals and white radicals. McKay and the rest of the Negro "proletarians" who cling to radicalism as the only "way out," in making this admission that there IS friction, due to race prejudice, between black and white working men, are playing directly into Marcus Garvey's hands. That it is hopeless to dream of white and black men working together, due to the white man's arrogance and racial superiority complex, is a point conceded by the harshest critics of Marcus Garvey. In pleading for sympathy and understanding of the black radical McKay is acknowledging one of the chief weaknesses of the Socialists. In order to get the fruits of their upward struggle, black working men must think and act racially, and forget all this anti-"bourgeois" twaddle about the "solidity" of the laboring class.

The McKay Incident

Unsigned Editorial (1922)

In the resignation of Claude McKay from the position of Executive Editor of *the Liberator* we have an example of the "breadth" of white radicalism. Michael Gold, who objected to the "Negroizing" of *The Liberator,* will be remembered by readers of *The Negro World* as the writer of that illuminating article on the Garvey movement which appeared in the *New York World* in 1920. Gold is a radical with a bourgeois complex. Like a majority of his fellow radicals, he is a violent Socialist, Communist, Unionist, Social Communist, Communist Unionist and Internationalist. Following the anti-capitalist fad, he is interested in Russia, China and Korea, Africa, Asia and the Negro. In the ills of all these groups he takes a solid interest. Over sex and psycho-analysis, poetry and pragmatism, psychology and the future of society—over all these things he'd sit and talk. A don't-give-a-damner, he is a trust hater, an open shop advocate, and free of prejudice of any sort.

Yet he objected to working side by side with a Negro; to seeing the Negro get a square deal in America.

And in the McKay incident the lesson to our group is obvious. If we must pal around with a white man, let us do so with a bourgeois white man! No hypocritical radical trash for us!

35

A Gathering Of The Harlem Literati

The Harlem of the 1920s was a place of intense ideological rivalry among nationalists, integrationists, socialists and communists. Literary events seem to have provided a unique setting where a temporary truce might be called. The event described by Eric Walrond in "Junk" (1922) took place in the midst of an acrimonious "Marcus Garvey Must Go" campaign led by liberal and socialist integrationists. Yet indications are that representatives of the Crisis, Messenger *and* New York News, *all of them in the forefront of that campaign, could sit down peaceably enough with the Garveyite editors from the* Negro World *and its sister paper, the* Daily Negro Times.

Junk

Eric D. Walrond (1922)

It was editors', writers' and poets' night at the Carl Van Doren lecture at the 135th Street Library last Wednesday night.

In the front row I saw W. A. Domingo; Floyd J. Calvin, the *Messenger's* satirical windjammer; Thomas Millard Henry, who I am told, is a "poet"; William Pickens, the short story writer.

In our row were Countee P. Cullen, poet; T. Thomas Fortune, editor, *Daily Negro Times;* Miss Ernestine Rose, librarian; Cecil Gaylord, artist; Cleveland Allen, reporter for the *Harlem Home News;* W. A. Stephenson, managing editor *Daily Negro Times,* who looked great in full dress.

Elsewhere in the assembly one espied William H. Ferris, literary editor of *The Negro World;* Alderman George W. Harris, editor, *The New York News;* Walter F. White, literary critic; Augustus Granville Dill, business manager, *The Crisis,* who supported a flaming chrysanthemum in his button-hole; Aubrey Bowser, author of *The Man Who Would Be White;* Miss Sadie Peterson, the poetess.

Mr. Van Doren, who is literary editor of *Century,* and professor of English literature of Columbia University, talked on "The American Novel." He gave a swift kaleidoscopic review of the works of Fenimore Cooper, Herman Melville's *Moby Dick,* Hawthorne's *Scarlet Letter,* and a couple of other books we do not quite remember.

It was a retracing of the ground covered in his two recent books, *The American Novel* and *Contemporary American Novelists.*

After the lecture Mr. Van Doren said he'd be glad to answer any questions the folks had to ask.

"Mr. Van Doren, those two novels, *Birthright* and *White and Black*—don't you think they show a tendency—a kinda opening—"

The intrepid Mr. Cleveland Allen had broken the ice.

"Yes, I think so."

"But, Dr. Van Doren," it was Mr. Allen's exasperating stutter, "don't you think Mr. Stribling made an awful mistake when he made Peter Siner—"

What Mr. Stribling made Peter Siner do evidently was familiar to Mr. Van Doren, so he quickly answered, "As a matter of fact, if I was on the *Century* at the time I would have had Stribling change that ending."

"Now, say that again," said Mr. Dill at the conclusion of the lecture as he curled puppy like on top of the table, boutonniere aglow, "Just say it, it makes my heart boil with joy! Down at Atlanta University I attended a commencement—"

But there were other questions the folks wanted to ask Mr. Van Doren. The Alderman, for exmple, tonsorially Charlie-chapped, had a suggestion to offer.

"Mr. Van Doren: You spoke about a Negro writing a novel showing out his problems and upward struggles. Now don't you think a great epic poem—"

"Yes, I think so," said Mr. Van Doren.

"Something," continued the editor-alderman, a mystic glow in his eyes, "something like Longfellow's 'Evangeline.' Something-oh!-moving-bitter-showing out the struggles—"

"There's a pointer for you," I whispered to Cullen, pinching his leg, "grab it before Mr. Henry runs away with it. He's taking notes! Look out!"

One man wanted to know if the white publishers did not, as a rule, object to featuring ennobling books about the Negro.

"That's the question I had on the tip of my tongue." put in Mr. Aubrey Bowser in the tete-a-tete following the talk, "Octavus Roy Cohen he tells me the only way he can get in the *Saturday Evening Post* is to write that dialectic slush he puts into the mouths of Negro college graduates."

"Dr. Van Doren!" Prof. Ferris' basso profundissimo rang out and nearly lifted the rafters of—Liberty Hall, did I say? "Dr. Van Doren, don't you think the American public is not quite ready to receive a high class novel about the Negro?"

Prof. Ferris ended the question with a dogged characteristic whine. Other questions, chiefly racial, popped up and Mr. Van Doren, who is an outspoken liberal and friend of the Negro race, disposed of them with a great deal of charm and wit and ofttimes humor.

On the whole, we enjoyed it tremendously. One thing we, with our philologic ear to the ground, especially liked was the way Mr. Van Doren pronounced words like "character" and "American." Only those who heard him can appreciate just what I am driving at.

Note—We should have said a word about the other folks in the audience, apart from the celebrities and near-celebrities mentioned. There were at least twelve married women who had books under their arms; eight school teachers, two (the white ones) who slept sonorously when Mr. Van Doren began to point out the fictional possibilities of places like the Great Lakes. Also, six thoroughly "repressed" ladies, a few dusky he-flappers from C.C.N.Y., and one individual who told us confidently, as we bolted to get our overcoat. "Fine lecture, wasn't it? Yes, I liked it very much because I'm studying the novel down at New York University!"

Well, wouldn't that—

36

Arthur Schomburg's Library

As in the case of "Junk," Eric Walrond's "Visit to Arthur Schomburg's Library . . ." (1922) presents us with a rare and precious look beneath the surface of literary Harlem. Schomburg was Afro-America's most famous bibliophile. He and his fellow book collectors provided an important part of the infrastructure upon which a literary movement could be built.

Walrond describes a veritable pilgrimage to Schomburg's Brooklyn home. He captures Schomburg's intense love for his collection and the awe in which younger writers evidently held him. He also records, very interestingly, Schomburg's spontaneous review of James Weldon Johnson's Book of American Negro Poetry. *This is reminiscent of Schomburg's harsh* Negro World *review of Carter G. Woodson's* The Negro in Our History *(reproduced in Chapter 12). Schomburg's intimate knowledge of the sources apparently made of him a stern critic.*

It was more than fitting that the 135th Street library in Harlem, mentioned more than once in these pages, should have become the depository (in 1926) for Schomburg's magnificent collection.

Zora Neale Hurston's "Mr. Schomburg's Library" adds little to Walrond's account. Hurston was a member of Walrond's party and was publishing poetry and prose in the Negro World *at this time. She was already fast becoming a familiar figure in the Harlem literary scene, and this about three years before she has hitherto been thought to have arrived in Harlem.*

Visit To Arthur Schomburg's Library Brings Out Wealth Of Historical Information

Eric D. Walrond (1922)

A visit to Arthur Schomburg's library! It is easy to appreciate why writers and artists, poets and anthologists, of both races, flock to the unpretentious little dusty-brown house on Kosciusko Street. Not only is it famous for its golden treasures, but the man, the mighty human spirit behind it, is the most precious, the most interesting curio of all.

A young lady in our party is a Columbia student who abominates what she calls "form" and "useless ceremony." She has had experience with Negro celebrities. She knows what to expect; therefore, she went armed. Armed to her pearl-white teeth. As we put our feet on the hallowed ground and the warm glitter of Mr. Schomburg's brown-black eyes shone down upon us, she gave way to a characteristic weakness—whispering—whispering out of the corner of her beautiful mouth.

"Well, I declare," stamping a petulant foot. "Why, I am flabbergasted. I expected to find a terribly austere giant who looked at me out of withering eyes. But the man is human, ponderously, overwhelmingly human, a genuine eighteen karat."

We enter a sitting room that exudes a classic odor. On the walls are a mezzotint of St. George, a water color drawing of a Negro drum-major in Queen Anne's army, a sylph-like sketch of an Ethiopian princess, prints and pictures, paintings and daguerreotypes.

"What would you like to do first?" It was Mr. Schomburg's amiable voice. "Here I have a set of books of Hayti. I'd like to show you Baron DeVastey's *Cry of the Fatherland in the Interest of All Haytians,* which is, of course, a very valuable work. Spencer St. John wrote a famous book on the black republic, too. Yes, miss, help yourself. Here is Madison's *History of Hayti,* in three volumes. Oh, yes, Japan vellum is expensive, but I believe in expensive printing.

"Over here is a book I'd like to call your attention to. It is Henry Calloway's personal copy of *Zulu Folk Lore,* bound in morocco. It proves that the Zulus, like the Jews and Russians, had a folk lore of their own, and—How did I get it? Oh, well, that is neither here nor there—"

"But tell us," went up a chorus.

"You see Calloway presented it to Ralston, president of the Folk Lore Society of London; and Ralston, upon his death, willed it to Andrew Long, the celebrated writer. Later it strayed into the library of a famous Lord Somebody in London and I got it at a sale. As you see, it was set up and run off by Negro printers in Springvale, Natal, in 1868. That was the beginning of folk lore in Africa."

"I imagine," breathed one of us, "he must have a lot of money to be able to buy all these books."

But Mr. Schomburg had overheard.

"That is the mistake a lot of people make. Because I buy a lot of books it does not mean that I have a lot of money. I can't spend it and have it too.

"Here is something I'd like you to make note of. Our friend James Weldon Johnson has just got out a *Book of American Negro Poetry,* but it seems as if he has neglected a very important poet, and that is Leo, of British Guiana. Here is his *Poetical Works.*"

Glancing at it, one is at once struck with the beauty and rhythmic passion of "Ruth, a Poet's Poetry," in eighty-one stanzas.

Leo's real name," Mr. Schomburg informed us, "was Egbert Martin. He first attracted the attention of the world when he took first place in a prize poem contest run by *Truth,* a newspaper in England. Oh, that brought the world to his feet, and he became a great friend of—what is the name of that great poet during Queen Victoria's reign? Tennyson; yes, and that is the man our friend Johnson left out. Just listen to this and tell me if it does not remind you of Claude McKay's 'If We Must Die':

Stolen and sold to Africa,
Imported to America,
Like hogs and sheep in market sold,
To stem the heat and brook the cold!

"And this as Mr. Garvey would say:

When will Jehovah hear our cries?
When will the sun of freedom rise?
When will a Moses for us stand
And free us all from Pharaoh's land?

"Why, Leo is one of the greatest Negro poets in history. I can't for the life of me see why Mr. Johnson overlooked him.

"There are two other things I don't like in that *Book of American Negro Poetry,*" continued Mr. Schomburg, "and they are, one, the part about Negro music, and, two, the inclusion of Dr. DuBois as a poet. DuBois is no poet. If Johnson wanted to write on music, he should not mix it up with poetry."

Asked to approximate the total number of books by Negro authors in his possession, and the subjects about which they wrote, Mr. Schomburg replied: "I think I've got about 2,000 books by Negro writers, and they cover every imaginable subject under the sun—science, mathematics, religion, philosophy, psychology, finance—everything.

"Over here I have thirty-four editions of Dunbar and seventeen books by Booker Washington. Didn't think they wrote so much, did you?"

Our Latin was being taxed severely to decipher an inscription at the bottom of an original Van Dyke of Jacobus Capitien. Yes, it is the one engraved by Tange—that much we find out—but as to the other things—

"Say, Miss Hurston, I don't suppose you know who Francis Barker was—"

"Oh, yes, I read Bacon's Essays at Howard."

"Not Bacon. Barker—Francis Barker. Barker was private secretary to Samuel Johnson. Here is a letter I received a few years ago from the author of Barker's Life. Barker was a slave, and Johnson, so impressed was he with his literary and aesthetic sense, made him his amanuensis. Read it."

Before we got halfway another historical phenomenon had broken in on us. With a copy of Gustavus Vassa's *Life* in his hand, Mr. Schomburg again unsettled our universe.

"I don't believe many of you know that Matthew Henson is not the only Negro who went to the North Pole. Back in the eighteenth century Vassa, as he relates in this book, visited it as a member of Lord Mulgrave's expedition. Here is what he says:

"Thus I went on till May, 1773, when I was roused by the sound of fame to seek new adventures and find, toward the North Pole, what our Creator never intended we should—a passage to India. An expedition was fitting out to explore a northeast passage, conducted by the Hon. Constantine John Phipps, since Lord Mulgrave, in his Majesty's sloop of war, the *Race Horse.* On the 4th of June we sailed towards our destined place, the Pole; and on the 15th of the same month we were off Shetland. . . . On the 28th of June, being in lat. 78 deg. we made Greenland, where I was surprised to see the sun did not set."

But all of this was very fine, interesting, and all that. It is certainly heartening to be able to look Gertrude Atherton in the eye and inform her that Alex. Hamilton was unquestionably a Negro. Did we not have our hands on a copy of *The Afro-American Magazine,* published in 1859 at 48 Beekman Street, New York, by a descendant of Hamilton—Thomas Hamilton—and reputed to be the most literary periodical by Negroes in America? Of course. but the motif, the raison d'etre, the whys and wherefores, the philosophy, the spirit of the man—that is the thing I wanted to get at. I communicated my desire to him.

"Ah, my boy, I don't as a rule, submit to interviews. Interviewers are always lying about me. How I started? Oh, I think it was way back in my school days in Porto Rico. I used to attend El Instituto Nacional, and it was a passion for us boys to collect books about poets, and I decided I'd fish out all the books I could by black poets. And I am still doing it. Not so very long ago my lodge, Prince Hall, gave me a beautiful gold medal," and he showed it to us, "for my services to the lodge. I came to America thirty years ago with the intention of studying medicine. But I perished by the wayside. Instead, I became interested in the struggle for independence in Cuba and Porto Rico. I was secretary of one of the revolutionary clubs, Las Dos Antillas, and charter member of the Porto Rico Revolutionary Party until it was dissolved by order of the U.S. government. At present I am employed as chief of the mailing department of the Bankers Trust Company."

Mr. Schomburg's Library

Zora Neale Hurston (1922)

I have been for a visit to Mr. Schomburg's library. It is a marvelous collection when one considers that every volume on his extensive shelves is either by a Negro or about Negroes.

Among other things I came upon a book called "Journal of A Residence in Georgia," by Frances A. Kemble. She was an English lady who married a Southerner and lived on his plantation for a year, 1838-1839. The book is an old one and seldom met with, so I shall quote from its extracts, that Negroes may know her interesting viewpoint:

"I think an improvement might be made upon that interesting caricature published a short time ago (1838), called the 'Chivalry of the South.' I think an elegant young Carolinian or Georgian gentleman, whip in hand, driving a gang of sick colored women would be a pretty version of the 'Chivalry of the South'—a little coarse, you will say. Oh! quite horribly coarse, but then so true—a great matter in works of art, which nowadays appear to be thought excellent only in proportion to their lack of ideal elevation. That would be a subject, and a treatment of it, which could not be accused of imaginative exaggeration, at any rate."

So much for the boasted "chivalry of the South." She then turns her attention to the "poor whites":

"On our drive we passed occasionally a tattered man or woman whose yellow mud complexion, straight features, and singularly sinister countenance bespoke an entirely different race from the Negro population in the midst of which they lived. They are pinelanders or 'poor white trash' of Georgia, I suppose the most degraded race of human beings claiming an Anglo-Saxon origin that can be found on the face of the earth—filthy, lazy, ignorant, brutal, proud, penniless savages, without one of the nobler attributes which have been found occasionally allied to the vices of savage nature. They will not work, for that, as they consider, would reduce them to equality of the abhorred Negroes; they squat, and steal, and starve, on the outskirts of this lowest of all civilized societies, and their countenances bear witness to the squalor of their condition and utter degradation of their natures."

37

The Crisis Draws
The Color Line

James M. Webb's indictment of W. E. B. DuBois' Crisis magazine as an Uncle Tom publication was not as unusual as it might seem. A. Philip Randolph's Messenger *had in 1919 called DuBois a "good nigger" and a "safe and sane" Negro. The* Messenger *that year also printed Archibald Grimké's poem, "Her Thirteen Black Soldiers," an anti-lynching effort that the* Crisis *had been too timid to publish.*

The Crisis Draws The Color Line, Charge

James M. Webb (1922)

I am one who knows that *The Crisis Magazine* is not a courageous magazine. I mean, it has drawn the color line by the dictation of a white man and this dictation was executed by the Negro business manager and approved by its Negro editorial editor.

Some time ago I had an advertisement running in *The Crisis Magazine* under the headline, "The Black Man's Part in the Bible," which is in book and picture form. The printed matter shows that Jesus, Solomon, the Queen of Sheba and other biblical ones were of Negro decent and also shows that the black man was the father of civilization. The picture portrays Jesus as a colored man. All of this matter I have received copyrights for from the U.S. Copyright Office. Among the many replies that I received from my advertisement in *The Crisis,* a certain white gentleman ordered the picture of Jesus as a colored man and the printed matter that showed that Jesus, Solomon, the Queen of Sheba and others were of Negro descent out of the book. The printed matter gives him over several hundred years of Biblical references of the Jews and Negroes amalgamation history in Africa on the River Nile and in the land of Canaan on the borders of the Mediterranean Sea.

The gentleman admits to me in a letter that he had not examined all of my Biblical references, and inasmuch as he said that he has found what he has read untrue, he came to the conclusion that the rest of the references were untrue. To attempt to show me that he was a Biblical scholar and that I was not a Biblical ethnologist, he sent me the following statement by saying that the Ethiopians are not mentioned in the Bible until after David and Solomon's time. I advised him to read the twelfth chapter of Numbers and first verse, which states that Moses married an Ethiopian woman. The gentleman wrote to *The Crisis Magazine* opposing my advertisement. "If *The Crisis* wants to make white friends it cannot do so by inserting such an advertisement as yours." The above words are some of his own statement. The business manager of *The Crisis,* Mr. Augustus Granville Dill, wrote me that the gentleman had criticised my printed matter, therefore, *The Crisis* could not carry my advertisement. As Mr. Dill believed the white man's statement instead of investigating my printed matter first, in my opinion he seemed to play the role of "Uncle Tom."

Letter to *The Crisis*

The following matter is a part of my registered letter to *The Crisis* concerning the gentleman:

"Mr. ——— shows that he is either biblical history blind or does not want to believe the truth as it is recorded in the Bible. Inasmuch as some of the white daily newspapers have received my matter of "The Black Man's Part in the Bible" and have brought forth favorable comments, I kindly ask Dr. W. E. B. DuBois as editor-in-chief of *The Crisis* to review my matter and tell the readers of *The Crisis* through its columns his opinion of the same so they will know that you reviewed my work. I hope that my letter is plain enough to *The Crisis* [and] that my matters are valuable for the money I ask for them through *The Crisis.* It is not quantity of paper I am trying to sell to the people nor novel matter, nor any of my theories; but it is pure quality matter of Biblical facts defying prejudice, ignorance and narrowness of minds and hearts. I hope to hear from you as soon as possible.

Yours very truly,
James M. Webb.

This letter was registered to the *Crisis* with a return card to me, but I failed to receive an answer from the *Crisis* from that day to this. I think I have had the patience of Job, so it is up to me to arouse the *Crisis* and let it know I am still in the land of the living and demand an answer soon.

Comments on the Book

The following comments show that my matter is recommendable and valuable, so I have nothing to fear of criticism:

"Elder James M. Webb in his book describes the black man as the father of all civilization. He takes the Bible to show that the fathers of the church and all the great leaders, even the greatest one, was black. Mr. Webb's work is able and thoughtful, whether the Anglo-Saxon believes him or not. Mr. Webb writes what he believes to be true about his race and their place in biblical history"—*Seattle Daily Post-Intelligencer*.

The following comments are from my book and lectures that Jesus was of Negro descent:

"To whom it may concern: I beg to say, after hearing Elder Webb, on the subject that the blood of the Negro coursed through the veins of Jesus and Solomon, I am frank to say I have seldom, if ever, enjoyed such an intellectual test. The position he assumes as the subject of his lecture touching the Hamitic blood and race is difficult and requires a practical knowledge of biblical and historical lore, but I am pleased to say that he not only shows himself an expert, but the master of the situation. And I commend him to the ministry and churches of the race of every denomination.

Truly,
"BISHOP H. M. TURNER."

"The evidence submitted by Elder Webb, tending to prove that the Saviour of mankind was a black man, seems to be sufficient to put those who oppose the proposition upon their proof. Now that the claim of evidence presented by Mr. Webb appears so complete it is strange that none of the delvers into the biblical records have not advanced the sensational propositions before. Not only was Christ a Negro, but it seems that Solomon, who has been held up through all the ages as the personification of wisdom, had Ethiopian blood in his veins also."— *Seattle Times*.

My advertisement was printed in six of the leading colored weekly papers and I received good results from all parts of the United States, Canada, Alaska, isles of the seas, Europe and Africa. I received numerous testimonials from these places indorsing my work. As the *Crisis* has asked the Universal Negro Improvement Association for a balance sheet of their year's business, I deem it wise to ask the N.A.A.C.P. to instruct the *Crisis* to balance up with me.

PART IX

THE LITERARY COMPETITION OF 1921

38

Selected Results

The U.N.I.A.'s 1921 literary competition predated by several years the better known contests of the mid 1920s, organized by the Crisis *and* Opportunity *magazines. Thirty-six cash prizes were awarded for poetry, short stories and essays. Results were featured in the* Negro World's *lavish Christmas number for 1921. The poetry section was restricted to poems dealing with Christmas, but the other sections revolved around themes of political importance to the organization. Judges for the contest were William H. Ferris, John Edward Bruce and Marcus Garvey. All tried, on this occasion, to strike a balance between political content and literary merit.*

Ferris' observations on his judging of the poetry selections are very instructive. Probably no single person fostered more the poetic interest of Negro World *readers. Ferris' knowledge of poetics and his deeply genuine love for the artistic endeavors of the race find ample expression here. Some of the entrants he singled out for praise were regular contributors to the* Negro World. *First place winner Charles H. Este was head of the Montreal U.N.I.A.'s literary club. A sample of his work was featured earlier in this volume.*

Eric D. Walrond, winner in the "Africa Redeemed" category, is the best known of the contest winners. He joined the editorial staff of the Negro World *around this time. His winning entry was a touching view of Africa redeemed, despite its obvious naievete.*

The Poetic Contest—
How the Winners Were Selected

Sir William H. Ferris (1921)

The first prize was awarded to Mr. Charles H. Este, of Montreal, Canada, whose poem, "The Child Is Found," impressed us as a jewel of purest ray serene. Its lightness of Spirit, simplicity of style, beauty of imagery and rhythm of verse made it a real poem. Its aerial flight of the imagination, its delicate sentiments, grace of style and music of verse made the reading of it a delight. The Christmas sentiments expressed in it constituted it a real Christmas poem.

The second prize, was awarded to June Dadd, whose poem, "Yuletide Disarmament," we read and reread with pleasure. "Yuletide Disarmament," by June Dadd, was characterized by thoughtfulness, appropriate Christmas sentiments, simplicity of style and rhythm of verse. The flow of verse carried the reader easily and naturally along. But the poem was an argument splendidly set in verse, and there was not quite enough appeal to the imagination and the emotions to entitle it to the first prize. A story told or an argument set to metre which rhymes well is poetry. But unless there is a touch of the imagination it is not poetry of the highest class. As Lucian Watkins says, to state that the sun shines is prose, but to say that it smiles is poetry. Take those lines composed either by Shakespeare or Keats, "Moving waters at their priest-like task, Of cold ablution on earth's human shores." It was years since we first read those verses in an essay by Matthew Arnold, yet there was something about those lines that arrested attention and lingered in our memory. Mark the effect of the words, "Moving" and "priest-like task," "cold ablution," etc. Now the poem of June Dadd, with its thought, sentiment and flowing verse, only needed a little more play of the imagination, a striking phrase now and then, to make it a poetic gem. As it is, it is a very readable poem. For two hours it was seriously considered for the first prize.

The third prize was awarded to Mr. Thomas Millard Henry, of Asbury Park, N.J., whose poem, "The Golden Urge," is characterized by suggestive thoughts, beautiful Christmas sentiments, felicity of phrase and rhythm of verse.

Another third prize was awarded to Miss H. Elizabeth Dowden, of Hartford, Conn., whose poem, "The Christmas Morn," is characterized by beautiful Christmas sentiments, simplicity of style, beauty of imagery and rhythm of verse. The awarding of the third was a real contest. There were two other poems which the judges liked. One judge would prefer one poem, another judge another. Finally we took charge of the poems. And thirty-six hours elapsed before we could arrive at a decision. "Sing Out the Xmas Carols," by Miss Betty Hutchins, of Cincinnati, Ohio, and "Great Things Done," by Mr. R. J. White, of Barranquilla, Colombia, were the other two poems. "Sing Out the Xmas Carols," by Miss Hutchins, was characterized by tender Christmas sentiments, brightness of spirit, simplicity of style and brilliancy of thought; but the rhythm was not perfect.

Now, we come to the poem of R. J. White, of Barranquilla Columbia, entitled "Great Things Done." This was seriously considered for a short while as worthy of the third prize, but was finally eliminated. It is full of thought and characterized by simplicity of style and rhythm of verse, but it lacks naturalness, lightness of spirit and is more of an argument in verse than an appeal to the imagination or emotion. There is no objection to a poem having an argument for its substratum. Wordsworth's "Intimations of Immortality," Gray's "Elegy," Bryant's "Thanatopsis," Tennyson's "In Memoriam" have an argument as their substratum. But Mr. White's poem only needed to soar on the wings of the imagination, only needed an aerial flight now and then to make it a powerful and telling poem. As it is, Mr. White has some possibilities as a poet.

The poem of Mrs. Katie Fenner, of Denver, Colorado, entitled "On a Christmas Morn," is one that we read with pleasure and considered at first as a worthy claimant for the third prize. It is bright in thought, buoyant in spirit, beautiful in sentiment, but not regular in rhythm. The verses are of uneven length, in one place the expression is prosaic and commonplace. There are a couple of places where the metre is defective and rhythm imperfect. The poem reveals poetic insight, imagination, passion and phrasing, possesses lightness of spirit, but lacks a perfect mastery of the technique of versification. It is poetry, but not perfect poetry. We believe that good poetry can be written in any metre or in free verse. The latter has wonderful possibilities, but requires a master's touch.

Mr. Henry's poem, "The Golden Urge," did not impress us on the first reading as favorably as "The Christmas Morn," by Miss Dowden, or the two poems which received special honorable mention. On the second reading the lines—

"When we spend all the Christmas Day
In transient trends, in circles gay,
The holly and the mistletoe
Sustain the truth we ought to know.

　　　　　*　*　*

Still in the hearts of many men
The Spirit of the Christ has been
A golden urge against the dearth
Of love and friendship on the earth.

　　　　　*　*　*

Will know how every noble aim
And liberty is nearer crowned!
Because in Jesus' life is found
Love's principle, O winds of God,
Transform our arid, sterile sod!"

arrested our attention, and then we for two hours considered this and the three above mentioned poems for third prize. After that came the reading and re-reading of the four poems for the third prize.

Had the third prize been larger we would have divided it between Miss Dowden, Mr. Henry, Mr. White and Miss Betty Hutchins. We have decided out of our personal resources to give the extra third prize. The sum is infinitesimal, but we desire to express our appreciation of the effort and the pleasure the two poems which won third prize gave us.

Africa Redeemed

December 5, 1921
Competition Editor
Negro World
56 West 135th Street
New York City, New York

Dear Sir:—

In compliance with your request, I have gone over the papers submitted to me in the competition for first, second and third prizes for the essay competition portraying "Africa Redeemed."

Among the many papers submitted, I have picked out two (2) as being meritorious. The others are lacking in literary style and proper construction. The authors ought to be more careful in their writing, especially knowing that awards for prizes can only be given on the general merit of the papers submitted.

I am unable to make an award for the third prize, because none of the papers submitted merits the place.

It is with great pleasure, therefore, that I award the first prize to paper number six (6), entitled "A Senator's Memoirs." The second prize goes to paper number four (4).

I have the honor to be,

Your obedient servant,
UNIVERSAL NEGRO IMPROVEMENT ASSOCIATION
MARCUS GARVEY
President-General

A Senator's Memoirs

(First Prize)

Eric D. Walrond (1921)

As I turn back to the period of adolescence in the history of the darker races; as I behold the strong men of the earth flying at each other's throats over the spoils of a wretched war; as I gaze upon the spectacle of nations born and bred in the cradle of chivalry sinking their claws into the treasure-chests of bedridden Africa; as I observe white men banking—laying out actual cash—on the perpetual inertia of the black race—God, how the memory of this oppresses me!—as I imagine a pageant of the crimes and blasphemies perpetrated against us for ages and ages—I shudder at the thought of the fate and future of a "backward" race.

Thanks to Jehovah, I am a free man—free to traverse the surface of the earth—free to stop and dine at any hostelry I wish—free! As I sit here and dash off these notes I cannot but think it all a massive dream. Twenty years ago, as a stranded migrant on the shores of Egypt, if I had been told that I'd be out here, on my own estate, drinking of the transcendant beauty of the Congo, a master of my people, to be honored and respected, I'd have discounted it as an overworking of the imagination. . . .

Liberty Square. This is a place that always brings me back to the age of freedom. There is a spirit of love and equality and righteousness about it that thrills me. It is a huge park, a bandstand or speakers' gallery in the center, and for three miles I saw nothing but myriad brown-faced people. From the banks of the Zambesi, from across the Nile, from South Africa, Liberia, Hayti, America—they stood, a free and redeemed people!

As Senator from the Congo, I was escorted to the gallery. To think that I, a cabinet officer, unaware of the significance of the occasion! May tenth! Ten years of African independence! Assets? Ah, tortuous memory, a stable government, an army second to none, a place among the powers of the earth—but, no, let me get off the stage of action and present the prince of men to you.

A chorus of cheers deafened us as a little man, in a white tunic, stepped forward on the principal speakers' rostrum. A life packed with dramatic climaxes, a man whose mental fibre ripened with the avalanche of time—there he stood—grim in the sunlight—there—hail him boys—Garvey!

"Citizens of Africa Redeemed, I come once more before you to give an account of ten years of my administration as President of the Republic of Africa. First, I wish it to be known that despite what the political economists had to say about us as race of shiftless parasites, we've been able to organize and operate successfully a chain of national banks throughout the continent of Africa. Also, as far as I can gather from the Minister of Commerce, the exports of Africa to foreign countries for the ten years of native rule amount to $500,000,000,000. Incidentally, the merchandise in question, which consisted of balata, cocoa, gold, diamonds, sheep skins, steel, coal, etc., was shot to all parts of the globe in the ships of the Black Star Line.

"The promulgation of the Civil Service Act and the organization of a modern system of public education throughout the land, I believe, will tend to eliminate corruption, inefficiency and graft in the governmental departments. At present, in spite of all that is being said in the enemy press, the rights of African citizens abroad are being safeguarded by a competent diplomatic corps. Only a few days ago the government of Australia was forced to abrogate its infamous exclusion laws as a result of action brought by our ambassador at Sydney.

"As regards the matter of land armament, the Republic of Africa voted at an extraordinary session of the cabinet on February 6 to appropriate £10,000,000 yearly for the maintenance of a standing army of 1,000,000 men. This is independent of naval construction, as Liberia, as you all know, is virtually a shipbuilding base, and the construction of battle cruisers is proceeding at a phenomenal rate."

Tears trickled down my enflamed cheeks as I forced my way out of the intense multitude. If the God of Hosts had come down on earth the transfiguration could not have been more complete. The Bishop of West Africa then leaped to the platform, and, as one man, the mighty arena of freemen sank down on their knees and sang hossannahs to Him.

Policy of Hon. Marcus Garvey Declared to be Only Means of Dragging Negro Out of Mire of Difficulties

(First Prize)

Neil A. Mills (1921)

In this age of advanced knowledge and improved thought we find the Negro standing on the road that leads to progress. The race, being destitute of a suitable leader, has not advanced very far along the social, political and economic ladder of life, and the reason is because the leaders of the past were men who were not daring enough to lead the race from the Egypt of a social, political and economic oppression to the Canaan of a social, political and economic progress.

The race has produced noble specimens of ministers, doctors, philosophers, sociologists and barristers—so distinguished are some of these men that the men of other races have patted them on the shoulders and have styled them the "stars" of the race. As individuals we can well be proud of them for what they have accomplished. Men of such caliber can chant a canticle of self-satisfaction for what they have made themselves. But let us remember that there is a loftier ambition than merely to stand high in the world as an intellectual giant. It is to stoop down and to uplift struggling mankind out of the mire and place him a littler higher in the scale of human progress. This principle has deeply manifested itself in the worldwide and God-approved organization, the Universal Negro Improvement Association, which organization strictly outlines and embodies the policy of Hon. Marcus Garvey.

This able, inspired and invincible leader has pledged all that is dear to him to the service of his race. He is the chief exponent in promoting race-consciousness, race-pride, and a spirit of determination that the race may emerge from its cocoon of ignorance and subserviency, and erase from the mind the sticky cloak of inertia. He has broken the cords of selfishness and has established mutual love within the race. He has taught the race to think in terms of empires, and to discard every antiquated idea and become an important and influential factor in the arena of the affairs of the world.

Some men characterize all optimistic movements regarding the political, intellectual and national development of the race as a dream, never to be realized. Well, let them feed themselves fat on their delusion while men of vision and initiative prepare the way for the spring of such a surprise on them that will knock their views into oblivion. The brains of those pessimists seen to be tied up as a dense mass in a cast-iron armor of ignorance, thus causing them to stumble before the great guns of modern reasoning. But let us bear in mind that the policy of the Hon. Marcus Garvey is no innovation in human history.

Edmund Burke in his speech on the "Reconciliation of America," declared that it is just as difficult to induce a slave to abandon his master as to get a free man to be a slave. What does that mean? It means that, the Negro has so debased his dignity and weaves more strongly around himself the tangled web of subserviency, that he depreciates the efforts of others to place him a little higher in the scale of progress.

We allow ourselves to be deceived by every mirage of friendship, and hence we become chilled by the cold deception of flattery and by making will power and initiative secondary to a desire to please those who are our oppressors. We slowly and wearily drag ourselves along, almost justifying the predictions of those who think we shall ever be a race suspended between barbarism and civilization, between pauperism and opulence, between the highest and the lowest marks on the records of progress.

In this slow and insignificant march Marcus Garvey comes along and says: "Your destiny lies in your own hands. Travel faster or else you will be overtaken by doomsday." His command met with response from four million black souls who fell in line with the organization that travels faster. And the four million Negroes did not fall in line because Marcus Garvey gave the command, but they saw something significant in the command that bade them follow.

This command also met with opposition from the elements which for centuries have been telling the people to "leave it to the Lord." Let us bear in mind that in this material world it calls for something more than the mechanical reading of Scriptural passages and the weekly delivery of pulpit orations to effect a more satisfactory result where the Negro problem is so acute.

As a race we cannot afford to be passive if we are to reach the goal of human progress. We can achieve that which is yet unachieved and can travel the path that is yet untrod if we will but follow the leadership of Marcus Garvey, the great apostle, who with his unfailing courage, determination and diplomatic manifestations has demonstrated to the world that the "rock foundation" of the Negro's ability to do great things still remains unshaken, uncrumbled, unmarred by the flight of centuries and the atrocities of slavery. Still it stands, the Rock of Ages by which he shall do, dare and accomplish that which men of other races have accomplished.

How to Unite the West Indian and American Negroes

To the Competition Editor, the *Negro World:*

Sir:—I, have carefully and critically read all of the papers submitted by contestants for the prize offered by *The Negro World* Christmas Edition for the best paper on this subject, and I have selected that written by Mr. Geo. C. Kendall, of Boston, Mass., as the best arranged, best written and thought out of the many papers I have examined. All who have written on the subject have done so with the evident purpose of answering the question:—"How to Unite the American and West Indian Negro."

In my humble judgment one of the best answers to it has been submitted by the gentleman named above, whom I have selected for first place; not only for the practical suggestions which a careful reading of his paper discloses, but for his clearness and directness of statement and intelligent grasp of the subject. Many of the other papers by contestants for these awards were not written with the care as regards neatness and correctness of the spelling of many simple words as is shown in Mr. Kendall's essay. The thought is crude and in many instances loose.

The next best of these essays was written by Mr. H. O. Pickering of this city, and is a very worthy and commendable effort and should entitle him to second place on the list of prize winners. Following Mr. Pickering comes Mr. John Hunter, also of this city, who evidently believes in brevity and conciseness of statement, since he has only used one sheet of letter paper on which to express his thoughts and has done so with fine reasoning, using much of the same logic and ideas as those advanced by Mr. Kendall.

Those deserving of honorable mention are;—Messrs. R. M. Romain, of Brooklyn, N.Y., P. L. Burrows, of Buffalo, and P. S. Richardson of this city. These gentlemen, all of them, have done wonderfully well in their efforts to answer a question which we all hope will sooner or later find its solution in the voluntary merging of all American and West Indian Negroes for the common good of all those who wear "the shadowed livery of the burnished sun."

Since we are all of one race, and have a common destiny, we should be one in thought, aim and purpose, sympathy and feeling.

Very respectfully yours,
JOHN E. BRUCE

(First Prize)

George C. Kendall (1921)

To the casual observer and to those yearning for the unification of all peoples of African ancestry into a solid race unit, it may probably appear to be something easy of accomplishment to unite the West Indian and the American Negro. In the humble opinion of the writer, however, that is no easy task. So long as these different branches of the Negro Race occupy different lands and are members of different nations, it would be just as difficult as completely to unite at the present time the British Empire and the Republic of the United States of North America. At the most the greatest that can be hoped for is greater co-operation and a better understanding.

The fact would appear to be that, though ethnologically they are the same, separation from the African Motherland for over two centuries has created for each branch of the big Afro-American Race, West Indian and American, its own problems and circumstances have inspired each with his own aspirations. Nor is it lightly to be emphasized that Great Britain, America, France, Spain and Portugal have and have had, each of them, their own national ambitions, and that contact of so long a duration as subjects of these dominant peoples, more advanced than the Negro in the scales of modern civilization could not fail to leave marks, almost indelible, in many cases upon the West Indian and the American Negro and cannot fail to influence greatly their respective future histories.

Foremost amongst all enslaved peoples of African descent in the Western

Hemisphere to be liberated, living under the benevolent aegis of Mother Britain, who, if she has not materially accelerated his progress, has never attempted seriously to hinder it, within three decades of his emancipation finding himself by British Free Trade principles the owner of all the fertile soil of the Western Indies, the once cherished sugar plantations of his former master, by this means placed in the position of a member of a plantocracy, able to give his sons and daughters the best education Great Britain can afford, the British West Indian Negro, wielding great political influence even under the seemingly autocratic Crown Colony System of Government, it must not be wondered at, regards himself as the doyen of all Negroes; and that in those islands there has grown up along the lines of the British social system a West Indian Aristocracy boasting of its few Knights and its many Honourables who would scoff at the idea of unification with less favored members of the Negro Race.

To the French Negro has been accorded the full rights of French Republic citizenship, and perhaps the black Frenchmen, less than any other Negro, has cultivated the minimum of race consciousness.

The American Negro on the whole, on the other hand, has had his own peculiar development. In his struggle to become an economic and political factor in the midst of a people who greatly outnumber him, with the painful reminder that the barriers erected by slavery can never be completely removed, swayed for nearly thirty years by a school of thought making for naked materialism for the most part, he has grown differently in many respects from the British or French West Indian Negro or the native of independent Haiti.

The growth of the Latin-American Negro, too, has been different from the development of either of the foregoing. He is apparently not so advanced as either of his brothers, and this has been due in the main to the continuous revolutionary chaos obtaining in the republics of Latin-America.

It is regrettable to record almost the same thing of the natives of the Black Republic of Haiti.

It must be left to the analytical mind of the student of psychology to tell us how to make a complete union of all these branches of the race, possessing as they do at present such a diversity of interests and of outlook. When the big differences that have arisen have been removed, and West Indian and American Negroes can each be made to yearn for the African Motherland as did his newly captured forbear, then, and only then, it would seem that unity would be within the bounds of accomplishment.

To the ordinary layman who has traveled in the West Indies, Latin America and the United States of North America, it would seem that some co-operation in matters of general importance to the race and a better understanding can easily be brought about, within a comparatively short space of time, between West Indian and American Negroes. I see in the history of the relations between the two great branches of the Anglo-Saxon race much for the enlightenment of our own people. No one should fail to appreciate the fact that often in world matters British and American statesmen have worked together for the superiority of the Anglo-Saxon. Why then, too, should not educated Negroes, oblivious to the nationalities imposed on them, work for the betterment of Negroes generally?

There is no doubt that on the whole colored West Indians, Americans and Latin-Americans are lamentably ignorant of the doings of one another since they were kidnapped from the bosom of Africa. Effort should be directed to minimizing this great degree of ignorance, to reminding us all that ours is a common ancestry, and to concentration on those things in which, despite differences of acquired nationality—acquired nationality—there is a real community of interest.

Methinks I see four means by which the bonds of estranged brotherhood between West Indian and American Negroes may be improved. The first three have for their direct object the removal of the sectional misunderstandings and ignorance of one another which exist, by bringing them more in contact with one another; the other probably makes for co-operation in matters of common interest:

  I. By colleges, universities and similar institutions.
  II. By a system of public lectures.
  III. By excursions.
  IV. By conferences and by keeping in the foreground the future of the African Motherland, and by the press.

1. By Colleges, Universities and Similar Institutions:

(a) Were I a black Cecil Rhodes, on my death I would bequeath such an amount as would give scholarships annually to West Indian and Latin-American members of my race to study in the more up-to-date colored American universities, and, vice versa, scholarships to the West Indian and to the Latin-American universities when and if such institutions exist. I would even go further and found traveling scholarships, whereby scholarly colored young men my travel, each in the field foreign to him, with a view to studying Negro social problems and making suggestions for the improvement of my people.

(b) It would seem, too, that by instituting a system of exchange-professorships, or something similar when that cannot be accomplished, much can be done. And so, too, the founding of a system of bi-annual public lectures by West Indian and American colored leaders of thought, each in a field to which he is a stranger.

Sad it is to state that very few educated colored West Indians know of Miller, Ferris and many other eminent Afro-American scholars.

True it is they may know of Washington and DuBois, but what exactly has made each of these men famous is a sealed book to the educated West Indian college man. Will it not mean much to each of these big branches of the race to know more of the race's eminent men? Who can say "No?"

It is unnecessary to dilate upon (a) and (b), for no sane man will deny that the Rhodes System of Scholarship has contributed much to the betterment of Anglo-American relations, and that Viscount Bryce and others have greatly influenced for the better American public opinion towards Great Britain, and that by their addresses they have engendered saner judgment when British and American national interests have happened to conflict.

It is inconceivable to think that something similar cannot but have the effect of creating more cordial and sympathetic relations between our own peoples.

(c) Intercollegiate Sports:

. . . Very much like his African forefather, West Indian and American Negroes are physically fine specimens of manhood and are first-class athletes. The performance of men of the British West Indies Regiment, stationed in Egypt during the great war, elicited the admiration of British commanders, many of them Oxford Blues. Surely, as in the case of inter-varsity meetings between Oxford and Cambridge and Harvard and Yale, very much good will accrue from track meetings between members of West Indian colleges and of colored American institutions. Every true member of the race would like to see Ned Gourdin measuring his strides against a Clairmonte, Carrington or Reece of Barbados; a Harris of Dominica, a Taylor or DeCoteau of Grenada, a Farrell of Trinidad, or a Stuart or Thompson of British Guiana.

(d) Affiliation of Colored American Institutions to British Seats of Learning:

Owing to their proximity and to the easier cost of studying within their walls, colored American institutions have been of great advantage to the middle class West Indian unable to go to Great Britain to obtain his profession. It is unfortunate, however, that only diplomas from British schools are recognized in the British West Indies. Cannot such arrangements be made between the foremost colored American universities and British universities whereby British West Indian graduates of the former universities may, after a short period of study in Great Britain, return to their homes in the West Indies to practice their professions? Such men will be a great medium for the improvement of West Indian and American Negro relations, as they are invariably from the peasant proprietary class, who constitute the backbone of the West Indies.

II. By a System of Public Lectures:

This has already been considered under 1.(b), Q.V.

III. By Excursions:

Though the West Indies are within comparatively easy reach of the United States, the better class colored American is completely unknown in the West Indies. Generally it may be said that perhaps the West Indian knows a little more of his colored American brother than the colored American knows of him. The West Indies are unsurpassable for bathing places, and the beauty of the different islands cannot easily be extolled. In nearly every island are to be found bathing places superior to Brighton in England and to Miami and Atlantic City in America, and the West Indian Archipelago for its scenery presents a glimpse of Paradise. These islands are visited year in and out by white English, Americans and Canadians; and it will do the colored American much good to do the same thing. It may be pleasure and business can at one and the same time be combined by giving the West Indian exhibitions of how his colored American brother has advanced musically and histrionically. About a generation ago a company of Tennessee singers visited the West Indies. They were most warmly received and applauded; their memory still lingers fondly in West Indian homes; and by a single visit they caused more sympathetic understanding between our peoples than has such a classic as *The Souls of Black Folk* or *The African Abroad.* The fact is these works are unknown in the West Indies.

IV. By Conferences and by Keeping in the Foreground the Future of the African Motherland. By the Press, etc.

Finally, I come to a question of increasingly absorbing interest, in which it would appear that there is simple room for co-operation not only between West Indian and American Negroes, but between all people of African ancestry. I refer to the subjects of the rape and spoliation of Africa and the redemption of Africa or Africa redempta.

The raping and exploitation of Africa to enrich British and Belgian commercialism, the concomitant atrocities committed thereby, the cruel subjugation of the African in his own home and the virtual reinstitution of slavery in the Belgian Congo and in British South Africa constitute a sad blot on the fair escutcheon of modern civilization. These subjects cry out for a remedy at the hands of all Christian people, and the wrong of Africa should appeal most forcibly to the West Indian and American brothers of the bleeding African. Should there not be saved for the poor African, from further white aggression, as much as possible of fertile Africa? Should there not be exposed to the world wicked legislation tending to curb his freedom and to deprive him of his all and in his own native Africa? Christianity answers all Christian peoples should assist the African, and a common ancestry dictates the duty of the West Indian and the American Negro as forcibly as it has dictated the duty of Irishmen the world over in the question of the freedom of Ireland.

I think that conferences of eminent colored men somewhat along the lines of Dr. DuBois' recent Pan-African Congress, keeping watch and ward over the action of the whites in Africa, and accusing the transgressors before the forum of the world's public opinion, will not only provide Africa with some measure of protection, but will also provide a field for co-operation for West Indian and American.

It would seem too that a great deal can be done in the field of journalism to create better co-operation and to engender a better understanding between these sections of our peoples. Both *The Crisis* and *The Negro World,* on account of their novelties, appeal to the West Indian mind, and there is no doubt that by keeping every Negro on the American Continent daily informed of the most important events affecting his race much more can be accomplished. The Associated Negro Press can well extend its operations to the West Indies, and a journal like *The Crisis,* but more international in its outlook, will be able to work wonders.

To summarize then, it is the humble opinion of the writer from an acquaintance of both the West Indies and America that, owing to the differences of conditions under which the West Indian and American Negroes have been developing, and their consequent diversity of interests, aspirations and outlooks, complete unity is too Utopian to enter the realms of serious race politics. Though complete unity may appear to be the cherished ultima thule of ardent members of the race, to me as a working man greater co-operation in race matters and a better understanding appear to be more easily within the bounds of accomplishment. And the principal means by which these very desirable objects may be brought about I have briefly attempted to indicate in this short essay.

(Second Prize)

Hamilton O. Pickering (1921)

This is indeed a problem of great moment, the solution of which is pregnant with inconceivable blessings and unlimited possibilities to the parties involved. The chief cause of the hostile attitude of the people toward each other is due, to my way of thinking, to the unforgivefulness of the former, caused through the lack of a broader education of the latter, together with their blind acceptance of the untruths told upon the party of the first part by the yellow press. Again, there is a growing consciousness among the American Negroes of their assumed superiority over the West Indian Negroes, which they no doubt love to express in no unknown terms whenever and wherever a dispute arises among them. By right they should be superior in learning, literature, music, art and mental and scientific achievements, since Fate or Providence has placed them (irrespective of the atrocities inflicted upon them) in contact with the greatest and most progressive civilization yet known to mankind. But in spite of the almost unlimited free educational facilities at their disposal, we find their supposed inferiors their leaders: further, when we look for the achievements from this presumed superior part of our race resultant or commensurate with their assumed attitude plus their educational advantages over the West Indian Negroes, we find more assumption than fact, more theories than practicalities. Therefore, I assume the only method by which these groups can be amalgamated is: first, by the founding of a Universal African School, whose executive staff should embrace these two nationalities especially; second, this board of directors should be chosen from the rank and file of the U.N.I.A., sponsored and, if necessary, educated by said organization and financially assisted and instructed in the system of compilation of the various textbooks from which our posterity must be taught if we desire true freedom; third, the history taught in this Universal African School should cover and include all the important activities of our people in the western world prior to and since our emancipation plus those of our mother country; fourth, in order to achieve our desire I would suggest that a staff or corps of international African teachers or educators be secured or formed, the American element of which should be exchanged [with] the West Indies; and those . . . of the West Indies should be dispersed among our people throughout the Union, with the provision that after the problem has been solved the exchange of teachers be curtailed. These suggestions, I hold, will bring groups together, enabling them to study each other in their respective homes, thereby enabling them to perceive the true situations, environments and atmosphere surrounding our people, which will bring about the change or unification desired.

(Third Prize)

John Hunter (1921)

The idea of cementing the Negro peoples of the West Indies and those of America is a noble one and deserves serious attention, although complex in its nature. Yet the task is not an impossible one; but it will require tact and carefully mapped out course of action, planned by men and women who are acquainted with the peculiarities of both peoples. That there is a misunderstanding one cannot deny . . . , and the American Negro, in a way, is responsible for its inception. When his brother of the West Indian Islands came to live among him, he was made the object of ridicule and mimicry on account of his peculiarities, which the West Indian brother looked upon as humiliating, especially as he soon discovered that his American brother was not accorded a better treatment from the Caucasian than he; nor was he superior intellectually, physically or otherwise. This unfriendliness has been the foundation of an estrangement that has kept the two peoples from true friendship and real amalgamation; but, as I said, the task is not an impossible one, although it is a difficult one. The means, I believe, that will help to overcome this estrangement are the following:

(1) Realization of both West Indian and American Negroes in America, in acknowledgement of the fact that they are "black," and therefore their interests are common, and that the other races consider them as such and care "nothing" about their birthplace.

(2) Periodical visits by Americans to the various West Indian islands to learn the ways and habits of the West Indian at home. This will create a feeling of sympathy, and thus cement the bonds of friendship.

(3) Exchange of teachers, preachers and lecturers, etc., portraying Negro greatness and Negro progress. One of the reasons why the English have such influence over the West Indians is a lack of outside knowledge from members of their own race, save that which the Caucasians give for their own purposes.

(4) Commercial intercourse—the importing and exporting of materials put up by black people here and in the West Indies.

(5) Cessation of mimicry on the part of both people. No people can live together in peace when one has to remind the other of its inefficiencies. There must be a feeling of love, sympathy, and of a racial ambition to meet the modern exigencies of a great people. Foster these by sending men and women of both countries among the people of America and the West Indies and we will be surprised to see the result.

Aims And Objects Of The Universal Negro Improvement Association

Competition Editor
Negro World
56 West 135th St.,
New York City, N.Y.

My Dear Sir:—You were good enough to submit to me the papers for the Essay Competition on the "Aims and Objects" of the Universal Negro Improvement Association, and it is for me to report that several of the papers were well written and revealed a great deal of knowledge on the part of the writers of the higher aims of the Universal Negro Improvement Association.

There being only three (3) prizes, I would recommend that the other papers marked and recommended by me be used, if possible, so as to give to the public the interpretation of the work of the organization by the authors.

I have awarded the first prize to the paper number one (1), the second prize to paper number three (3) and the third prize to paper number six (6).

I have the honor to be,
Your obedient servant,
UNIVERSAL NEGRO IMPROVEMENT ASSOCIATION,
MARCUS GARVEY,
President-General.
December 5, 1921

(First Prize)

Herman A. McKenzie (1921)

The U.N.I.A. was organized about four and a half-years ago in New York City by the Hon. Marcus Garvey, with a membership of thirteen. Within that time it has increased to four million—an increase which is phenomenal and almost inconceivable. At its birth predictions were made that its usefulness as an organization would be shortlived. Nevertheless, four and a half years have shown marked interest and dynamic enthusiasm in this entirely new organization.

At this period in the world's history, when dominant races still continue to oppress the weaker, an organization such as the U.N.I.A. becomes absolutely essential and indispensable to the Negro's future welfare. Now, then, the question is asked: What are the aims and objects of the U.N.I.A. and has it a definite program for the Negro? This question can be answered affirmatively.

Centuries ago Negroes were stolen from Africa, their motherland, and scattered throughout the New World as slaves. Sixty years ago they were freed in the United States and eighty years ago in the West Indies, Central and South America. Since freedom they have been the economic burden bearers of the white races. Their political, social, industrial and economic powers are limited and restrained. The white races taught them to disregard the African and pictured Africa as a land of cannibals and roaming wild beasts. All this was done to camouflage the real worth of the people and their land and country. Negroes living in the New World would naturally have little interest in a country and its people under such discouraging conditions.

The U.N.I.A. intends to destroy such detrimental propaganda. It seeks to unite the four hundred million Negroes of the world into one great fraternity, having one definite purpose, the redemption of Africa; one destiny, the creation of democratic and strong governments, and one eternal God, the God of Ethiopia. The U.N.I.A. wants to make black men and women independent and self-supporting. It intends to build factories and industrial plants to give the Negro economic freedom. The U.N.I.A. is going to improve the intellectual output of the Negro by founding universities, colleges and schools. It is going to encourage the artistic instinct of the Negro, by the creation of art schools. It is going to enhance the Negro's scientific genius, by founding scientific schools. It is going to produce better literary men, by encouraging the Negro to write more about the race and its problems. It is going to encourage the Negro to be interested in politics, by the creation of governments.

Organized power is the Negro's only salvation. There is no other organization in the world that is better prepared for the work or task of African redemption than the U.N.I.A. If the Negro wants to be a free man—free from every vestige of white domination, free to think, to act and to do for himself as God created him so to do—then he must join hands and heart in the redemption of Africa.

Contributors

DUSE MOHAMED ALI (1866-1945) was an African of Egyptian-Sudanese parentage. He was partly educated in England and travelled widely as an actor. In 1912 he founded, in London, the *Africa Times and Orient Review,* the leading Pan-African and Pan-Oriental magazine of the time. The magazine, never liked by the British authorities, was suspended in August, 1914, shortly after the outbreak of the first World War. It reappeared in 1917 and 1918 and was replaced in 1920 by the *Africa and Orient Review.* Ali employed Marcus Garvey on the *Africa Times and Orient Review* in 1913. In 1922 Garvey was able to return the favor, employing Ali as foreign affairs specialist for the *Negro World.* Some highranking U.N.I.A. members and sympathizers, among them John Edward Bruce and William H. Ferris, had corresponded with Ali for many years. In fact, it was indirectly through Ali that Garvey first established contact with these men. Ali later emigrated to Nigeria, where he edited the *Nigerian Comet.* He sold this paper eventually to the Nigerian nationalist, Nnamdi Azikiwe. Ali died in Nigeria and had one of the largest funerals there up to that time. His study of Egyptian politics, *In the Land of the Pharoahs,* was published in London in 1911.

CHARLES S. BETTIS was one of the many unknowns who contributed poetry to the *Negro World.* No information is available as to his identity.

LEONARD I. BRATHWAITE was a Garveyite and a resident of Harlem. His poems appeared frequently in the *Negro World.* He also submitted the occasional, apparently unsolicited prose article.

JOHN EDWARD BRUCE (1856-1924) was born a slave in Maryland. He managed to obtain a public school education in Connecticut and Washington, D.C. after the end of slavery. He spent many decades as a reporter and served as correspondent for many newspapers, including publications in South Africa and Jamaica. He was the United States agent for Dusé Mohamed Ali's (q.v.) *Africa Times and Orient Review.* His pen name of "Bruce Grit" was a familiar one to readers of the Black press. He also spent many years as a Republican Party activist. Bruce was one of Afro-America's important bibliophiles. In 1911 he founded, with Arthur Schomburg (q.v.) the Negro Society for Historical Research at Yonkers, New York. This was Afro-America's second historical society. Bruce corresponded with an incredible array of leaders from throughout the African world. After some initial hesitation, he threw in his lot with Marcus Garvey and the U.N.I.A. He was associate editor both of the *Negro World* and its companion *Daily Negro Times*. Bruce was knighted by the U.N.I.A. At his death in 1924 the U.N.I.A. honored him with an impressive state funeral. He authored many books and pamphlets, among them *Short biographical Sketches of Eminent Negro Men and Women in Europe and the United States* (1910) and *The Awakening of Hezekiah Jones: A Story Dealing With Some of The Problems Affecting the Political Rewards Due the Negro* (1916).

J. R. RALPH CASIMIR has lived in Dominica, West Indies for all of his approximately ninety years. In the early 1920s he was head of the Dominica U.N.I.A. His poems and articles appeared regularly in the *Negro World,* sometimes under the pen name of "Civis Africanus" (Latin for "Citizen of Africa"). Casimir was also active in the Dominica U.N.I.A.'s literary club. He wrote and sold books and was a bookbinder as well. Among the many books of poetry he has authored and edited are the following: *Poesy: An Anthology of Dominica Verse* (in four volumes—Volume 4, 1948); *The Negro Speaks* (1969); *Farewell (And Other Poems), 1971;* and *Black Man, Listen! And Other Poems* (1978). Casimir's interest in Pan-Africanism neither began nor ended with the Garvey Movement. He corresponded with the Gold Coast (Ghana) nationalist Casely Hayford and with Carter G. Woodson, founder of the *Journal of Negro History.* In the 1930s he distributed the *Negro Worker,* edited by the Trinidad-born Pan-Africanist, George Padmore. He later fell out with this publication over its anti-Garvey attitude. Mr. Casimir still (1990) lives in Roseau and maintains his Pan-African interests.

CARITA OWENS COLLINS' poem, "This Must Not Be!" was among the most militant appearing in the *Negro World.* The Lusk Committee of the New York State legislature singled it out for condemnation in its 1919 report into revolutionary radicalism.

CHARLES W. CRANFORD lived in Clarksburg, West Virginia.

ETHEL TREW DUNLAP was the most prolific and perhaps the best loved of the *Negro World* poets. Her earlier *Negro World* poems were written in Chicago, the later ones in Watts, Los Angeles. Her themes reflected such Garveyite ideals as race pride, African redemption, and the rehabilitation of

Black history. She also wrote about her personal dilemma as a light-skinned champion of the African race.

CHARLES H. ESTE was head of the literary club of the Montreal U.N.I.A. and one of the *Negro World's* most frequent contributors. He won the first prize for poetry in the U.N.I.A.'s 1921 literary competition.

WILLIAM H. FERRIS (1874-1941) was born in New Haven, Connecticut. He was a graduate of Yale (class of 1895) and Harvard (M.A. in journalism, 1900). From 1897 to 1899 he was a student at the Harvard Divinity School. Before joining Garvey he had worked, at varying times, with William Monroe Trotter and the *Boston Guardian,* W. E. B. DuBois and the Niagara Movement and John Edward Bruce (q.v.) and the Negro Society for Historical Research. Shortly after graduating from Harvard he worked with the Republican campaign committee of Massachusetts and Connecticut. In 1914 Ferris published an article in Dusé Mohamed Ali's (q.v.) *Africa Times and Orient Review* in which he praised Garvey's earlier article. As literary editor of the *Negro World,* Ferris probably contributed more than anyone else to the nurturing of poetic talent within the paper's readership. He published a two-volume work, *The African Abroad,* in 1913. As of 1922 he was working on a projected volume which he hoped to call *The African in Western Lands.*

ARNOLD J. FORD (ca. 1876-1935) was born in Barbados and worked as a musician in the British Royal Navy before settling in the United States. He was a talented linguist, poet and musician and composed many U.N.I.A. songs. He co-authored the organization's "Universal Ethiopian Anthem." Ford's official functions included direction of the U.N.I.A. Band and Orchestra, the Band of the African Legion and the Liberty Hall Choir (also known as the Universal Choir). Ford was also a prominent member of Harlem's Black Jews. He emigrated to Ethiopia in 1930 and died there. His *Universal Ethiopian Hymnal* was published in 1920.

T. THOMAS FORTUNE (1856-1928) was popularly known as the "dean" of Afro-American journalists. His several decades of experience included such papers as the *New York Globe* and the *New York Age.* For many years he had been a confidant of Booker T. Washington. He had a long history, too, of activism in the Republican Party. Fortune assumed editorship of the *Negro World* in 1923, after a stint as editor of the U.N.I.A.'s *Daily Negro Times.* He dictated his last *Negro World* editorials from his deathbed. His published books included *Black and White: Land, Labor and Politics in the South* (1884) and *the Negro in Politics* (1885).

AMY JACQUES GARVEY (1896-1973) married Marcus Garvey in 1922 after serving for three years as his private secretary and secretary to the U.N.I.A.'s Negro Factories Corporation. Mrs. Garvey played a very active role within the U.N.I.A. She was a very effective public speaker and an energetic author and editor. After her husband's death she struggled for years to keep his name alive. She lived long enough to see the resurgence of interest in Garveyism which gathered momentum in the 1960s and 1970s. She edited the seminal two-volume work, *The Philosophy and Opinions of Marcus Garvey, or, Africa for the Africans* (1923 and 1925), as well as two volumes of Garvey's poetry. Her many other books, articles and pamphlets included a biography of her husband, *Garvey and Garveyism* (1963). Mrs. Garvey served for a while as an associate editor of the *Negro World* and edited the paper's women's page.

MARCUS GARVEY (1887-1940) was a printer and journalist by profession. Between 1910 and 1914 he travelled widely through Central and South America, Europe and the Caribbean. He founded the Universal Negro Improvement Association in his native Jamaica in 1914. In 1916 he moved to Harlem, New York. Using Harlem as a base he toured the United States until 1917. On his return to Harlem he re-established the U.N.I.A. and moved its headquarters from Kingston, Jamaica. The organization's growth was phenomenal. The *Negro World* appeared in 1918 and other ventures followed in quick succession. These included the Negro Factories Corporation and the Black Star Line Steamship Corporation. Throughout the whole month of August, 1920, the U.N.I.A. celebrated its First International Convention of the Negro Peoples of the World in New York. Twenty-five thousand African people from all over the world attended the opening ceremonies. Membership in the organization quickly spread to over forty countries. Garvey's success attracted a disparate group of enemies, many of them opposed to his Black nationalist philosophy. He was imprisoned by the United States government in 1925 for alleged mail fraud and deported to Jamaica in 1927. There he founded the People's Political Party and became active in local politics. He was hounded by the local British authorities and eventually relocated to London in 1935. He died there in 1940. Garvey published several newspapers and magazines during his life, in Jamaica, Costa Rica, Panama, the United States and England. The *Negro World* (1918-1933) was by far the most successful. The *Black Man* magazine (1933-1939) was his last. Several volumes of his speeches, essays and poems were edited by Amy Jacques Garvey (q.v.). The two-volume *Philosophy and Opinions of Marcus Garvey, or Africa for the Africans* (1923 and 1925) is the most important. Other speeches and essays also appeared in pamphlet form.

"HAGAR" was the pseudonym for a correspondent writing from New York. Her use of the name "Hagar" is not without significance. The Black woman during slavery was often identified with the Hagar of Biblical legend, who, though made into an outcast by the people of this world, nevertheless attracted the sympathy of her Maker.

HUBERT H. HARRISON (1883-1927) emigrated to New York from St. Croix, Danish West Indies, in 1900. He was largely a self-taught man yet came in time to be widely hailed as one of Harlem's foremost intellectuals. His knowledge was encyclopaedic and legendary. He lectured on everything from literature to politics to chiropractic. His lectures were delivered in a variety of forums—on street corners, in Harlem halls and in white schools and universities downtown. In 1917 Harrison founded the Liberty League of Negro Americans. It was at a Liberty League function that Marcus Garvey received his most important early opportunity to charm a large Harlem audience. Harrison joined the *Negro World* as an associate editor in January, 1920. He claimed credit for pioneering, in this paper, the first regular book review section in an Afro-American publication. Prior to joining the *Negro World* he had edited *The Voice.* Harrison died unexpectedly in 1927 after a minor operation. He authored *The Negro and the Nation* (1917) and *When Africa Awakes* (1920).

RICHARD A. HENRY was a contributor from St. Croix, United States Virgin Islands.

JOHN HUNTER, a 1921 literary competition prize winner, was from New York.

ZORA NEALE HURSTON (190?-1960) attended Howard University and Barnard College. She published several poetry and prose pieces in the *Negro World* in 1922. She appears to have been living in New York at the time, at least temporarily. From the *Negro World* she moved on to publish in *Opportunity* magazine, obtained white sponsors and did well, at least for a time. She did field work in anthropology in the southern United States and the Caribbean. Her published works included novels, such as *Jonah's Gourd Vine* (1934) and *Their Eyes Were Watching God* (1937) and works on folklore, including *Mules and Men* (1935) and *Tell My Horse* (1938). Her autobiography, *Dust Tracks on a Road,* appeared in 1942.

WILLIAM ISLES was director of the Black Star Line Band. In 1921 he published a musical tribute to Garvey entitled "Our Leader—March Song."

GEORGE C. KENDALL, 1921 literary competition prize winner, was a resident of Boston.

HODGE KIRNON of New York was a regular contributor to the *Negro World* and a Garveyite.

MARION S. LAKEY of Muskogee, Oklahoma, was a regular contributor of poetry to the *Negro World*. He authored a book which Eric D. Walrond (q.v.) promised to review in 1922. The review apparently was never published.

D. T. LAWSON was a contributor from Paraiso, United States Canal Zone, Panama.

ALAIN LOCKE (1886-1954) was for years professor of philosophy at Howard University. He studied at Oxford University as a Rhodes Scholar and obtained his Ph.D. from Harvard in 1918. His 1925 anthology on *The New Negro* confirmed him as a major authority on the literary movement of the period. He was a member of John Edward Bruce's (q.v.) Negro Society for Historical Research.

ERNEST E. MAIR, originally of St. Ann parish, Jamaica, was a frequent contributor of poetry and an occasional contributor of prose to the *Negro World*.

ARNOLD HAMILTON MALONEY, originally from Trinidad, was assistant and sometime acting chaplain-general of the U.N.I.A. before becoming a professor of psychology at Wilberforce University in 1922. He spoke regularly at the U.N.I.A.'s Liberty Hall in 1922, sometimes on a weekly basis. He was also a very prolific contributor of articles to the *Negro World*. His *Essentials of Race Leadership* (1924) was a collection of essays, some of which had first appeared in the *Negro World*. Maloney authored several other books, including *Adequate Norm* (1922).

T. ALBERT MARRYSHOW (1885-1958) was a dominant figure in Grenadian and West Indian politics for over thirty years. He was also a major figure in journalism, principally via the *West Indian* newspaper which he founded in 1913. The *West Indian* carried articles favorable to Marcus Garvey in the 1920s. Marryshow was a leader in the struggle for a West Indian federation and a Pan-Africanist.

ESTELLA MATTHEWS was lady president of the Philadelphia U.N.I.A.

HERMAN A. McKENZIE was a first prize winner in the U.N.I.A.'s 1921 literary competition.

V. L. McPHERSON's review of "Tallaboo" seems to have been a one shot affair. He was not a regular *Negro World* contributor.

NEIL A. MILLS, a first prize winner in the 1921 literary contest, was a student at Lincoln University. It is not clear which of the Lincoln Universities (Pennsylvania or Missouri) he attended.

H. G. MUDGAL was an East Indian Hindu who came to Harlem via Trinidad. Late in 1922 he took over the *Negro World's* foreign affairs column from Dusé Mohamed Ali. His editorship of the column, however, lasted only a few months. Ten years later, in 1932, he reappeared as editor of the paper. In this latter period he travelled around New York debating rival organizations (especially communists) on the correctness of Garvey's program. In 1932 Mudgal authored a spirited defence of Garvey entitled *Marcus Garvey—Is He the True Redeemer of the Negro?* Mudgal's later activities are obscure, but there is evidence that he may have returned to India and joined the Indian National Congress of Mahatma Gandhi. Several of Mudgal's poems appeared in the *Negro World.*

H. DAVID MURRAY was a resident of Chicago.

H. A. NURSE lived at 237 1/2 Isabel Street, Winnipeg, Canada.

MARY WHITE OVINGTON occupied an anomalous position as a white book reviewer for the *Negro World* and chairman of the board of the rival NAACP. She had a long history as a social worker involved in Afro-American causes. Her books included *Half a Man: the Status of the Negro in New York* (1911) and *The Walls Came Tumbling Down* (1947).

GEORGE WELLS PARKER (d. ca. 1931) was a student at Creighton University in Omaha, Nebraska. He was well known in nationalist circles in Chicago and elsewhere. He was a founder of the Hamitic League of the World and published, under its auspices, *Children of the Sun* (1918). Parker was an admirer of Marcus Garvey. J. A. Rogers (q.v.) acknowledged his debt to Parker's work.

G. M. PATTERSON—no information available.

ROSALIE PHYFER lived in New York City and contributed occasional poems to the *Negro World*.

HAMILTON O. PICKERING, a prize winner in the 1921 literary contest, lived in New York City.

ROBERT LINCOLN POSTON (1890-1924) was one of the U.N.I.A.'s most promising young leaders until his untimely death. He was a native of Hopkinsville, Kentucky and one of a family of distinguished journalists and writers. He came to the headquarters of the U.N.I.A. in 1921 after a career of newspaper publishing in Kentucky and Detroit. He had attended Walden University in Nashville and Howard University and served in the armed forces of the United States during World War I. Poston was assistant secretary-general of the U.N.I.A. in 1921 and secretary-general in 1922. He published many poems and articles of literary criticism in the *Negro World*. He sometimes wrote editorials for the paper. (His brother, Ulysses, was an associate editor). The two Poston brothers were among the co-directors of "Tallaboo," a play put on by the U.N.I.A. Dramatic Club in 1922. Poston died at sea in 1924, on his way back from Liberia, where he had led a U.N.I.A. delegation. He left a widow, Augusta Savage (q.v.). He received a state funeral from the U.N.I.A., the most elaborate staged by the organization, at least up to that time. He was posthumously elevated to the rank of "prince," the U.N.I.A.'s highest honor.

ANDREA RAZAFKERIEFO contributed occasional poems to the *Negro World*. He was also known as Andy Razafkeriefo or Andy Razaf. Razaf's family emigrated from Madagascar. He was an important song writer and collaborated with the celebrated jazz musician, Fats Waller.

J. A. ROGERS (1880-1966) has been one of Afro-America's most popular historians for over sixty years. Professional historians have been slow in giving him his due, even when they have leaned heavily on his work. Born in Jamaica, he lived in Chicago before moving to Harlem after the publication of his first important work, *From Superman to Man* (1917). In between writing books and pamphlets, Rogers supported himself by working as a freelance journalist. His columns appeared in several Black publications. He wrote regularly for the *Negro World* and lectured to U.N.I.A. locals. He had known Garvey from their youth in Jamaica. Established publishers could not appreciate Rogers' work and so he self-published all his books. It was only after his death that one of his works, the two volume *World's Great Men of Color* (first published in 1947) was reissued by a major company. Rogers travelled widely in his quest for little-known information of Black history.

Among his many works were *Sex and Race* (three volumes, 1944), *Nature Knows No Color Line* (1952) and *100 Amazing Facts About the Negro* (n.d.).

AUGUSTA SAVAGE (1900-1962) was a multi-talented member of the 1920s Harlem literary and cultural milieu. She is best known as a sculptor, but her poetry also appeared regularly in the *Negro World.* She was very much a part of the Garvey Movement in the early 1920s. She married the organization's secretary-general, Robert L. Poston (q.v.). Her busts of Marcus Garvey were advertised in the *Negro World.* The African influence evident in her sculpture doubtless owes something to her U.N.I.A. involvement.

ARTHUR A. SCHOMBURG (1874-1938) was the best known of a group of dedicated, pioneer Black bibliophiles who laid a lasting foundation for the subsequent pursuit of Black Studies. His private library had been legendary long before it was purchased for the 135th Street library in Harlem in 1926. Schomburg was born in San Juan, Puerto Rico. His mother came originally from St. Croix in the then Danish West Indies. Like Marcus Garvey (q.v.), Schomburg trained as a printer. He emigrated to New York in 1891, where he was active in the Puerto Rican and Cuban nationalist movements. He read law for five years and contributed to several newspapers under the nom de plume "Guarionex." In 1911 he co-founded the Negro Society for Historical Research with John Edward Bruce (q.v.). In the 1920s he was president of the American Negro Academy to which W. H. Ferris (q.v.), A. H. Maloney (q.v.), Bruce and other *Negro World* regulars belonged. Schomburg published frequently in the *Negro World.* He authored many books, pamphlets and articles, among them *Racial Integrity: A Plea for the Establishment of a Chair of Negro History in Our Schools and Colleges* (1913), *Phyllis Wheatley* (1916) and *A Check List of American Negro Poetry* (1916). The *Negro World* commented on his whereabouts in 1922 as follows—"Mr. A. A. Schomburg, the peripatetic book fiend, is in Boston rumaging among the old book stores. He took with him two pairs of glasses and a large Gladstone bag."

KOBINA SEKYI was a London trained lawyer. Back home in the Gold Coast (Ghana) he became an influential nationalist and Pan-Africanist and later a mentor of Ghanaian President Kwame Nkrumah. Sekyi was a good friend of Dusé Mohamed Ali (q.v.). It was through Ali that he submitted his first poems to the *Negro World.* Sekyi was one of the staunchest defenders of Marcus Garvey among the West African intelligentsia. He published *The Parting of the Ways* in 1925.

DE VERE STUART lived in Brooklyn, New York.

LESTER TAYLOR contributed several poems to the *Negro World* and was an active participant in the literary life of Harlem. He co-directed the U.N.I.A. Dramatic Club's presentation of "Tallaboo" in 1922.

NORTON A. THOMAS was an associate editor of the *Negro World.*

ERIC D. WALROND (1898-1966) was born in British Guiana (Guyana) and grew up in Barbados and the Canal Zone, Panama. He emigrated to New York in 1918. Walrond had extensive experience as a journalist, working on the *Star and Herald* (Panama) and the *Brooklyn and Long Island Informer.* Walrond joined the *Negro World* in 1921, almost simultaneously with winning a first prize in the paper's literary competition. He rose quickly from assistant to associate editor and remained with the paper until 1923. His espousal of the "anti-propaganda" school of literary thought caused him to drift gradually away from Garveyism. Walrond's stories and articles appeared in several white publications, even during his stay at the *Negro World.* From 1925 to 1927 he served as business manager for *Opportunity* magazine. Walrond left New York for Europe in 1928. In the late 1930s he became reconciled with Garvey and once again contributed regularly to a Garveyite publication, this time the *Black Man* magazine. Both men were living in England at the time. Walrond is best remembered for his collection of short stories, *Tropic Death* (1926).

WILLIAM WARE was head of the Cincinnati U.N.I.A.

LUCIAN B. WATKINS (1879-1921) was a widely respected poet. His verse appeared in many newspapers, magazines and anthologies. He served overseas during the First World War and held the rank of sergeant. Watkins was a regular contributor to the *Negro World's* "Poetry for the People" section. "Loved and Lost," his last poem, was submitted to the *Negro World* a few days before he died. It actually appeared on February 5, 1921, four days after his death. Watkins authored *Voices of Solitude* (1907).

JAMES M. WEBB was a nationalist historian. Like J. A. Rogers (q.v.) he was in the tradition of 19th century Black scholars who used the Bible and classical sources to show the importance of the African race in antiquity. Webb was author of *The Black Man, the Father of Civilization, Proven by Biblical History* (1910).

Bibliographical Note

The question of the Garvey Movement's links to the Harlem Renaissance has been examined closely on only a few rare occasions. John Henrik Clarke's pioneering article on "The Impact of Marcus Garvey on the Harlem Renaissance" was published in his edited volume, *Marcus Garvey and the Vision of Africa* (New York: Random House, 1974), after having appeared as a journal article.

The present author first introduced his argument for Garvey's major impact on the Harlem Renaissance in his *Race First: the Ideological and Organizational Struggles of Marcus Garvey and the Universal Negro Improvement Association* (Dover, MA: The Majority Press, 1986, first pub. 1976). He then expanded his argument into a full length work in *Literary Garveyism: Garvey, Black Arts and the Harlem Renaissance* (Dover, MA: The Majority Press, 1983). He simultaneously compiled and edited *The Poetical Works of Marcus Garvey* (Dover, MA: The Majority Press, 1983).

The present volume is based almost entirely on the Garvey Movement's *Negro World* newspaper, a seemingly inexhaustible source of information on most aspects of the movement.

Index

Books from the Majority Press

THE NEW MARCUS GARVEY LIBRARY

Literary Garveyism: Garvey, Black Arts and the Harlem Renaissance. Tony Martin. $19.95 (cloth), $9.95 (paper).

The Poetical Works of Marcus Garvey. Tony Martin, Ed. $17.95 (cloth), $9.95 (paper).

Marcus Garvey, Hero: A First Biography. Tony Martin. $19.95 (cloth), $8.95 (paper).

The Pan-African Connection. Tony Martin. $22.95 (cloth), $10.95 (paper).

Message to the People: The Course of African Philosophy. Marcus Garvey. Ed. by Tony Martin. $22.95 (cloth), $9.95 (paper).

Race First: The Ideological and Organizational Struggles of Marcus Garvey and the Universal Negro Improvement Association. Tony Martin. $10.95 (paper).

The Philosophy and Opinions of Marcus Garvey. Amy Jacques Garvey, Ed. $12.95 (paper).

Amy Ashwood Garvey: Pan-Africanist, Feminist and Wife No. 1. Tony Martin. Forthcoming 1994.

African Fundamentalism: A Literary and Cultural Anthology of Garvey's Harlem Renaissance. Tony Martin, Ed. $14.95 (paper).

THE BLACK WORLD

Brazil: Mixture or Massacre? Essays in the Genocide of a Black People. Abdias do Nascimento. $12.95 (paper).

Studies in the African Diaspora: A Memorial to James R. Hooker (1929-1976). John P. Henderson and Harry A. Reed, Eds. $39.95 (cloth).

In Nobody's Backyard: The Grenada Revolution in its Own Words. Vol. I, the Revolution at Home. Tony Martin, Ed. $22.95 (cloth). **Vol. II, Facing the World.** Tony Martin, Ed. $22.95 (cloth).

Guinea's Other Suns: The African Dynamic in Trinidad Culture. Maureen Warner-Lewis. $9.95 (paper).

Carlos Cooks: And Black Nationalism from Garvey to Malcolm. Robert, Nyota and Grandassa Harris, Eds. $9.95 (paper).

From Kingston to Kenya: The Making of a Pan-Africanist Lawyer. Dudley Thompson, with Margaret Cezair Thompson. $10.95 (paper).

Order from The Majority Press, P.O. Box 538, Dover, MA 02030, U.S.A. Mass. residents add 5% sales tax.